SHE W

Detective Lane Yo... heard Patrol Sergear... the line. A woman hac... ing parlor on a dairy f... on the southeastern s... victim was thirty-one-year-old Frankie Cochran. She was still alive, but just barely, having been struck in the head numerous times with a hammer.

The suspect, thirty-six-year-old David Gerard, had attacked his ex-girlfriend Frankie Cochran as she worked there, milking cows. Gerard had beat her savagely with the claw hammer on the head and left her for dead. Beat her so hard, in fact, that it had caved in a portion of her skull. Frankie had lain on the cold, wet concrete floor of the milking shed for two hours before the dairy owner found her lying there. He immediately called 911 and Deputy Fouts arrived to find Frankie lying in her own blood, frozen water and cow excrement. Incredibly, it was the combination of icy water and cow excrement that had kept her from bleeding to death. These unlikely elements had acted as a kind of compress on her severe wounds. Even more incredibly, after two hours of being immobile, and near death, Frankie had opened her eyes and informed Deputy Fouts, "David Gerard did this to me!"

Describing the crime scene later on, Lane Youmans said, "There was a rage—an explosion of violence. I had seen this before, at another crime scene, at another time. I stood there silently in the cold, and the crap, and the crying cows, and stared down at the ramp leading into the milking parlor. Suddenly it hit me—an epiphany, just like you see in the movies. David Gerard. David Gerard! I knew that name. I knew it from another very violent scene, where four people had died!"

BLOOD FRENZY

ROBERT SCOTT

PINNACLE BOOKS
Kensington Publishing Corp.
http://www.kensingtonbooks.com

Some names have been changed to protect the privacy of individuals connected to this story.

PINNACLE BOOKS are published by

Kensington Publishing Corp.
119 West 40th Street
New York, NY 10018

All Kensington Titles, Imprints, and Distributed Lines are available at special quantity discounts for bulk purchases for sales promotions, premiums, fund-raising, and educational or institutional use. Special book excerpts or customized printings can also be created to fit specific needs. For details, write or phone the office of the Kensington special sales manager: Kensington Publishing Corp., 119 West 40th Street, New York, NY 10018, attn: Special Sales Departmen, Phone: 1-800-221-2647.

Pinnacle and the P logo Reg. U.S. Pat. & TM Off.

ISBN-13: 978-0-7860-2036-2
ISBN-10: 0-7860-2036-9

First Printing: November 2010

10 9 8 7 6 5 4 3 2 1

Printed in the United States of America

Acknowledgments

I'd like to thank Rick Scott, Matt Organ, Gary Parfitt and Brian McDonnell for their help on this book. And I'd especially like to thank Lane Youmans and Frankie Cochran, without whose help this project would have been impossible. Thanks also go to my editors at Kensington, Mike Shohl, Richard Ember, and Michaela Hamilton.

You have robbed me of my life as I knew it. A life sentence is what you deserve, for that is the inhumane and vicious sentence that you have inflicted on me.

—Frankie Cochran to David Gerard

In all the murders I've investigated, there were only two that stuck out for their level of violence. They were the murders of the two women on the Weyco Haul Road. The image of the two women stayed with me, lying on the gravel road, faces covered with their own blood.

—Detective Lane Youmans

Mr. Gerard is like a serial suspect. Is Gerard responsible for every unsolved crime he's a suspect in? Probably not. But I can't put it past him.

—County Prosecutor Steward Menefee

He alone is dead who has been forgotten.

—Anonymous

1

HAMMER BLOWS

Grays Harbor County, Washington

On March 17, 1999, Grays Harbor County Sheriff's Office (GHSO) detective Lane Youmans was at home watching television. By 1999, Lane had been with GHSO for twenty-two years. Starting as a deputy patrolling the county's roads, he eventually worked his way up to the detective division within GHSO and had seen just about everything in his time at GHSO, from petty crimes to violent murder. In a county of nineteen hundred square miles, Lane's job took him from the suburbs of the city of Aberdeen to the wilds deep within the forest. Some of the back roads were little more than dirt trails winding down through blackberry thickets, alders and Sitka spruces. In this area it was little wonder why Washington had the nickname of the Evergreen State.

By 1999, Aberdeen was mainly famous for one of its former citizens, Kurt Cobain. Cobain had gone on to international fame in the band Nirvana, with his iconic lyrics and tormented persona. Kurt had both loved and hated the area, and it was as much a part of who he was as the fog and forests of Grays Harbor. Cobain would travel upon the world stage, from New York to London to Tokyo, but there was always a bit of Aberdeen that stayed within him, from his days down along the Wishkah River.

The evening of March 17 was winding down and Lane was thinking of going to bed, when the telephone suddenly rang. He picked up the receiver and heard Patrol Sergeant Keith Fouts's voice on the other end of the line. Fouts said that a woman had been savagely assaulted at a milking parlor on a dairy farm in the small town of Oakville, on the southeastern side of Grays Harbor County. The victim was thirty-one-year-old Frankie Cochran. Frankie was still alive, but just barely, having been struck in the head numerous times with a hammer. She was in the process of being airlifted to Harborview Medical Center in Seattle in hopes that she could be saved. Harborview was a Level 1 trauma center and had the best hospital in the region for someone suffering from a massive head injury.

Even though the prognosis did not look good for the young woman, Sergeant Fouts told Lane that Frankie had been able to identify her attacker before slipping into a semicomatose state. Units were now out looking for the individual who, she said, had beat her with the hammer. Then Fouts asked Lane to come out to the crime scene and process it.

Lane put on his cotton jumpsuit, shoulder holster, department baseball cap, and kissed his wife good-bye. He knew that he was in for a long night of crime scene processing. Climbing into his vehicle, Lane started driving east from his home in Hoquiam toward the crime scene, about twenty-five miles away. He didn't go very far, however, before he received a message that a suspect had been detained in downtown Aberdeen. The suspect was a man named David Gerard, and he had just been arrested at a 7-Eleven mini-mart on B Street. It was the same David Gerard who Frankie Cochran had indicated was the person who had attacked her.

Lane drove to the 7-Eleven and spotted a burly young man sitting in the backseat of Sergeant Fouts's patrol car. A tow truck was called to the scene to hook up Gerard's vehicle, which was in the 7-Eleven parking lot, and then haul it to a police compound. Once it was there, it could be thoroughly searched later. Lane knew from experience that it was a good idea to impound a suspect's vehicle early on in the process to determine if it had been at a crime scene or not. In this case the vehicle was a four-door red-colored Ford Escort.

When Lane got out of his vehicle at the 7-Eleven, Sergeant Fouts told him that the suspect, thirty-six-year-old David Gerard, had apparently attacked his ex-girlfriend Frankie Cochran with a claw hammer as she worked milking cows. Allegedly, Gerard had beat her savagely with the claw hammer on the head and left her for dead. Beat her so hard, in fact, that it had caved in a portion of her skull. Frankie had lain on the cold, wet concrete floor of the milking shed for two hours before dairy owner Eugene Clark found her lying there. Clark immediately called 911, and Fouts went out to the dairy to find Frankie lying in her own blood, frozen water and cow excrement. Incredibly, it was the combination of icy water and cow excrement that had kept her from bleeding to death. These unlikely elements had acted as a kind of compress on her severe wounds. Even more incredibly, after two hours of being immobile, and near death, Frankie had opened her eyes and informed Deputy Fouts, "David Gerard did this to me!"

An all points bulletin (APB) had been put out for the arrest of David Gerard at that juncture, and within a short time frame, an Aberdeen police officer spotted Gerard's vehicle in Aberdeen. Gerard was driving around aimlessly on the backstreets of north Aberdeen until he pulled into a 7-Eleven store, where he was immediately arrested.

As Sergeant Fouts transported Gerard to the GHSO main office in Montesano, Lane stayed at the 7-Eleven store and photographed the exterior of the Ford Escort. When the tow truck arrived, Lane followed it and the Ford Escort to the Aberdeen auto yard on the south side of town. He waited until the operator unhitched the vehicle, and once the Escort was parked at the lot, Lane placed official DO NOT TOUCH stickers on the doors and windshield. Lane also contacted Detective Matt Organ and Detective Ed McGowan, of the GHSO, since they were just then heading to the sheriff's office building to question David Gerard. Both Organ and McGowan were good detectives with a lot of years of experience in law enforcement. They'd both seen their share of murder and mayhem in Grays Harbor County.

After securing the Ford Escort at the auto yard, Lane drove to the sheriff's office in Montesano as well. Detectives Organ and McGowan were already in the process of interviewing David Gerard, and Detective Organ stepped outside of the interview room for a moment, telling Lane that Gerard denied assaulting Frankie Cochran with a hammer. In fact, Gerard was now saying that he'd spent the day driving around the Loop, which was the nickname for Highway 101, which made a large loop around the Olympic Peninsula. Lane knew that driving the entire

Loop could take up to six hours, a good alibi for Gerard if it held up.

Detective Organ briefed Lane about all the details he was able to get out of Gerard so far, and then Lane took off for the crime scene in Oakville, which was being protected by Deputy Dan Wells. While on the way to Oakville, Lane suddenly remembered having heard on the evening news that Highway 101 had been blocked by a landslide, north of the town of Shelton, for the previous two weeks. David Gerard had to be lying about driving the entire Loop if it was still blocked. It would have been impossible to have done so with that landslide lying across the road. There were absolutely no roads that crossed the peninsula through Olympic National Park from one side to the other. It might have been possible to take a side road around the slide area, but Gerard insisted that he had never left Highway 101 the whole time.

Lane hurriedly picked up his cell phone and called Matt Organ about this important detail and asked Organ to contact the state highway patrol to confirm that Highway 101 had been blocked when Gerard claimed to have driven the Loop. Lane recalled later, "I thought, if it was blocked, that blew Gerard's alibi clear out of the water!" Then Lane's next thought was "It didn't look good for the victim. This could soon be turning from an assault investigation into a murder investigation."

Lane reached Clark's Dairy at around 11:00 P.M. and Deputy Wells was still protecting the crime scene. The sky was cloudy, and the temperature was in the 40s. Lane put on his rubber boots, grabbed his camera and shoved several extra rolls of film into his jacket pocket. He also grabbed a handful of rubber gloves and put them into a pocket on the back of his jumpsuit.

Deputy Wells escorted Lane to the milking parlor,

where the assault had occurred. There were no cows in the milking parlor now, but Lane could hear them mooing in a holding pen nearby. Lane later noted, "Most of the seventy cows had not been milked, and they were not happy."

On one side of the parlor was a sliding wooden door, and past the door was a concrete ramp leading down into a holding pen, which was now empty. On the floor Lane spotted a large streak of blood running down the manure-covered ramp. Some blood was spattered on a wall of the milking parlor a few inches above the floor, and at the base of the ramp were several blood-soaked towels. There were also a pair of rubber boots partially covered with manure sitting upright, side by side.

Amongst the blood and cow manure, about midway down the ramp, Lane spotted something glittering in the beam of his flashlight. He picked it up to examine the object, and noted that it was an earring in the shape of a heart, which appeared to be gold in color. On one side of the ramp there was a handrail, and on the other side he found a clear vinyl apron that had blood smeared on it. There were also medical wrappers and debris scattered on the floor near the apron, tossed there by medical personnel who had arrived on scene to try and save Frankie's life.

Lane photographed the scene from various angles, trying to avoid stepping in important areas, and also trying to keep from sliding in the slippery manure. He then stepped back into a holding pen, cow manure up to the ankles of his rubber boots, to look over the whole scene. The night air was cold enough that he could see his breath, and the cows were mooing louder and louder, obviously distressed at not having been milked.

The one overall thing that Lane noticed from the scene

was that there had been a great deal of violence connected to this ex-couple. As he said later, "There was a rage—an explosion of violence. I had seen this before, at another crime scene, at another time. I stood there silently in the cold, and the crap, and the crying cows, and stared down at the ramp leading into the milking parlor. Suddenly it hit me—an epiphany, just like you see in the movies. David Gerard. David Gerard! I knew that name. I knew it from another very violent scene where four people had died!"

2

BETWEEN LIFE
AND DEATH

Whether David Gerard was linked to other crimes, at the moment the paramount thing for Lane Youmans and the other detectives was to process the Frankie Cochran crime scene. After thoroughly photographing the milking parlor and collecting evidence, Lane let Eugene Clark back in to milk the cows. Lane then loaded evidence into his green Jeep Cherokee, took off his rubber boots and turned on the heater to warm up after such a long cold spell in the milking shed.

Lane headed back to the sheriff's office in Montesano, where he placed the evidence bags, which contained milking boots, apron, bloody towels, earring and blood samples, in the old jail exercise room so that the blood and manure could dry. After that was done, he contacted Detective Matt Organ. By this point Lane discovered that Organ had arrested Gerard for first-degree assault, which was the same category as attempted murder in

Washington State. Lane asked Organ what Gerard had said when confronted with the fact that the Loop had been closed by a landslide for the past two weeks. Organ chuckled and replied, "He said, 'Well, that's the way I went.'" Organ then added that Gerard offered as an alibi that he had called a friend named Polly Miller from the town of Forks, midway along the Loop. Of course, it was an impossibility that he had driven the entire Loop because of the landslide.

The detectives contacted Polly Miller and she told them, "It was so weird. Out of the blue, David Gerard called me and announced that he was in Forks. It didn't make any sense. He was always driving to different places, but he had never called me like that before!"

Lane and the others assumed that Gerard had telephoned Miller after assaulting Frankie Cochran, trying to set up an alibi. But even calling from Forks did not explain how he could have completed the whole Loop. He had to be lying.

The next step for the detectives was to check Frankie's condition at the hospital, and things did not look good in that regard. Frankie had been airlifted 110 miles to Harborview Medical Center in an attempt to save her life. When Lane called Harborview, he found out that Frankie was in the head trauma unit and was booked in under an alias. This had been done, as in many domestic violence situations, in case the "loved one" decided to drop in and finish what he had started. Harborview was a huge facility, sprawling out over an entire city block, with fourteen floors. Because of the alias, someone would literally have to go from floor to floor, trying to find the person they were looking for if they didn't know the alias the person was listed under.

Lane phoned Harborview and identified himself as a

Grays Harbor County detective to the intake nurse. Only after the intake nurse was convinced that Lane was, in fact, a GHSO detective, he was given Frankie's assumed name and where in the hospital she was located.

Lane Youmans and GHSO sergeant Dave Pimentel, who was in charge of GHSO's Investigation Division, drove to Seattle and parked in the law enforcement parking lot at Harborview. Lane grabbed his camera and notebook, and they headed for the head trauma unit. Once there, they presented their credentials to the nurse, and Lane asked one of the nurses about Frankie's condition. The nurse told him that Frankie was in very serious condition after having undergone surgery. The repeated hammer blows to the right side of her skull had broken loose a fist-sized piece of skull. During surgery the doctors removed that piece of skull and saved it for later replacement. They then covered the hole with Frankie's own scalp and stapled it closed.

The doctors also repaired Frankie's right forearm and put a metal brace on her fractured jaw. A half-inch stab wound on the right side of her neck was stitched up as well. Sergeant Pimentel continued talking to the nurses about Frankie's condition, while Lane went into Frankie's room. She was in and out of consciousness, her head and jaw heavily bandaged, as well as her arm. Lane photographed Frankie lying in her hospital bed, and he lifted up the bedsheet to check for other bruises and injuries. Lane said later, "I suddenly felt uncomfortable doing this. I was used to photographing dead bodies, and looking under sheets or clothing for wounds. This had always been no big deal—just part of the job. But here I was, dealing with a live victim, and I felt that I was somehow violating her privacy. I had photographed hundreds of live victims before as well, but I had always asked permission first. Frankie was a borderline case. Not dead, but not much alive."

As Lane was photographing her, Frankie woke up. Her eyes were partially open, and her right eye was blood-red. Sergeant Pimentel came into the room, and Lane leaned close to Frankie, asking, "Who did this to you?" Frankie replied, "David." Lane then asked, "What is his last name?" Frankie said, "Gerard."

Lane asked Frankie what David Gerard had hit her with, and she replied, "A hammer." All of this reinforced what Frankie had told Sergeant Fouts earlier. Both Lane and Pimentel wanted this on the record, just in case Frankie didn't make it. And from the looks of her and the doctors' reports, it wasn't a sure thing that she was going to survive.

It was obvious to Lane that Frankie was in a lot of pain, and heavily medicated. He decided they had put her through enough already, and they'd gotten a firsthand wit-ness statement about her attacker and the weapon he had used. As Lane noted later, "It was really touch and go for her. If things turned sour later, we could speak for her, to be her voice and testify in court when David Gerard went to trial. As things stood, she might not only never make it to trial, she might not be alive."

Lane Youmans knew that in Washington State, David Gerard could be brought to trial within sixty days, unless the defense lawyer asked for more time. Because of that, the prosecution would have to be ready, just in case, and everything that Lane and the other detectives gathered now would be vitally important. They would have to get medical records describing Frankie's injuries, search Gerard's vehicle and apartment in Aberdeen, find the hammer he had used to attack Frankie and the clothes he had been wearing when he attacked her.

When Gerard had been picked up, he was wearing clean, bloodstain-free clothing, so he must have dumped his bloodied clothing elsewhere. They also had to find out about Gerard's background and his relationship to Frankie Cochran. Had there been previous verbal threats by him against her? Or physical violence as well?

The detectives obtained search warrants for Gerard's car and apartment. Sergeant Rod Johnson, Detective Gary Parfitt and Detective Ed McGowan searched his apartment, while Lane and Detective Doug Smythe examined the vehicle. The interior of the vehicle was somewhat dirty, and the passenger seat and backseat were cluttered with clothing and other items. A pair of women's leather slippers were found on the floor on the front passenger side. A woman's watch and makeup were found in the glove compartment.

Lane noticed several possible small blood spots located on the center console of the vehicle and in the middle of the dashboard. Beneath the driver's seat was a partially empty jar of Vaseline. In the trunk Lane discovered a black plastic bag containing men's clothing. One of the pairs of jeans in the bag had possible bloodstains on the pants legs. The stain was already set, as if the jeans had been washed. In the trunk Lane also found a bottle of bleach and an enlarged photo of a woman, who was not Frankie. There were two young boys with the woman in the photograph. Lane wasn't sure how this woman and the boys were connected to all of this, but he saved the photo, anyway. And there was something about the photograph that stuck in his mind.

The clothing in the back area of the car consisted of men's plaid shirts and sweatpants. Since they were dark in color, it was hard to tell by mere observation if there were bloodstains on them or not. None of the clothing smelled of manure, and there was no hammer anywhere in the vehicle. Lane seized the various items of clothing, then swabbed the possible bloodstains on the center console and dashboard. He also collected the women's items found in the car, since they might have belonged to Frankie. Lane wasn't sure how the enlarged photograph of the woman and two boys fit into all of this, but there was something about it that rang a bell in the back of his head. Something bad had happened to those individuals. But what was it that had occurred?

Lane filled out a search warrant with the items he had seized and left a copy of it on the dashboard of the car. Then he took some more photographs of the car from many different angles. Lane didn't mind taking lots of photos. He knew that even just one photo might lead to a key piece of evidence or be a solid documentation of some aspect of the case.

Lane took the evidence from Gerard's Ford Escort to the sheriff's office in Montesano; by then, Sergeant Johnson and Detective Gary Parfitt had completed their search of Gerard's apartment and had come up empty. No hammer or bloody clothing was found there. All the detectives knew that Gerard had had about two and a half hours after attacking Frankie Cochran to drive away, wash up and change his clothing, disposing of any bloodstained items. And with a large county full of creeks, ponds and rivers, there were any number of places Gerard could have jettisoned the incriminating items. The detectives also surmised that Gerard had tried implementing an alibi when he phoned Polly Miller from Forks. But Gerard hadn't known about the landslide near Shelton, so his alibi had been foiled.

Lane Youmans and Detective Smythe went back to Clark's Dairy, because Lane wanted to take more photographs of the crime scene in the daylight. Lane also wanted Smythe to take a look at the bloodstains on the wall of the milking parlor. Since Smythe had been to "blood spatter school," he was the GHSO's expert when it came to reading and documenting bloodstain patterns. Smythe knew about how blood patterns differed depending on what caused the injuries, the force of the blow and angles at which the wound had been inflicted. Blood patterns and blood pools told their own stories, even when a victim was no longer there to explain what had occurred.

About the same time Detectives Dave Pimentel and Tony Catlow arrived at the dairy and began searching the brush alongside a road leading to the dairy. They were looking for the hammer used in the attack and any other kind of incriminating evidence. Even though they searched for hours, they located nothing of interest.

In the milking shed Detective Smythe discovered a number of medium-velocity blood spots around the doorway, leading to the milking parlor, that were consistent with hammer blows to a human head. His expert opinion confirmed what Lane had already surmised about the crime scene. Indications pointed to where the victim had stood and where the attacker had performed his assault.

After they left Clark's Dairy, the detectives began looking into the relationship between David Gerard and Frankie Cochran. David and Frankie had shared an apartment in Aberdeen, but recently they had a falling-out. They had both worked at Clark's Dairy, she as a milker and he as a handyman. A week before the hammer assault, the detectives learned, Frankie and David had both arrived to work at the dairy in Gerard's Ford Escort. While they were sitting in the car, parked by the milking parlor before the workday had begun, they had gotten into an argument. David, who was paranoid and very jealous about Frankie, accused her of having an affair with Eugene Clark. Frankie told him that was ridiculous, and she was tired of his accusations and irrational jealousy. She then told him they were through.

Without any warning, David grabbed Frankie and pulled her out the driver's-side door of the car. He grabbed her so violently and unexpectedly that her slippers fell off onto the passenger-side floor mat. As soon as she was pulled out the door, Frankie knew he was going to hit her. She struck first. She was holding a travel mug full of hot coffee, and before David was able to land a punch, she threw the coffee in his face and upper body. Then she stiffened, waiting for the blow to fall.

In total surprise to Frankie, David didn't swing at her or say anything. Instead, he slowly and methodically walked to a nearby toolshed and reemerged from it, holding a claw hammer. Frankie said later, "He had a wild look in his eyes, like he was demented."

David held the hammer up over his head and slowly walked toward her. When he was only a few feet from her, Frankie stood her ground and spat out, "Go ahead, if you're man enough!"

Against all expectations Gerard stopped in his tracks, lowered the hammer to his side and quietly walked back into the toolshed. He put the hammer back on a nail on the wall, walked by Frankie without a word, got into his car and left. Eugene Clark, who had witnessed the whole thing from a distance, called 911 and reported the incident.

Incredibly, David Gerard was by then making a 911 call of his own. He drove to Oakville and phoned the sheriff's office, reporting that he'd just been assaulted by his girlfriend, Frankie Cochran. A deputy responded to this call and met David Gerard at a convenience store in the area. He showed the deputy the coffee burn marks on his chest and his lip, which was still bleeding. The blood had run down onto his shirt and pants. Lane noted later, "It was obvious to the deputy that Gerard was trying to make himself look more like a victim, since he had made no attempt to wipe blood from his chin. And it appeared that he had chewed on the inside of his lip to make it bleed." Nonetheless, the deputy took photographs of Gerard's "injuries."

Meanwhile, another deputy contacted Frankie Cochran, who was still crying about the incident. The deputy took photographs of the coffee stains on her blouse and where coffee had sloshed when she threw the mug's contents onto Gerard. Once all the facts were in, it was David Gerard who was arrested in violation of the Washington State domestic violence act, and not Frankie. Gerard was booked into the county jail, and he appeared before a district court judge the next day. After that process was completed, Judge Thomas Copeland issued a No-Contact Order (NOCON) upon Gerard, which meant he could not be in the same vicinity as Frankie Cochran. Then Judge Copeland set a trial date, and Gerard promised to appear.

After David Gerard was released from jail, he was contacted by Eugene Clark and told that he was fired. Seething with resentment for not only losing his girlfriend, but his job as well, Gerard was in an angry and violent mood that next week. Frankie moved out of the apartment, which she had shared with Gerard, to a relative's residence twenty miles away, in the town of Elma. Even though she was now away from Gerard, she had the uneasy feeling that he was stalking her. Worried and on the alert, she had her uncle drive her to work for her protection.

On the day she was assaulted, Frankie was asked by Eugene Clark if she could work a double shift. His cows needed to be milked twice daily, and the milker who generally worked the evening shift couldn't make it that day. Frankie normally only worked the morning shift, and she quit the morning milking on March 17 at about 1:00 P.M. Frankie, however, said that she could work that evening as well, and a friend of her uncle's, named Tom Scott, drove her back to Clark's Dairy for the evening shift.

On the way there, Scott stopped his vehicle at the Del Cris convenience store in the town of Elma. After purchasing a few items, Scott drove Frankie to Clark's Dairy and let her off there for the evening milking shift. Then Scott left.

What was interesting to Lane and the other detectives was that a surveillance camera at the Del Cris market showed David Gerard entering the store at approximately 5:45 P.M., right around the same time that Tom Scott and Frankie Cochran were there. Gerard was wearing a white T-shirt and a pair of dark sweatpants. The clothes he was wearing then were different from the ones he was wearing when arrested at the 7-Eleven store in Aberdeen a few hours later, after the attack. Gerard purchased a soda at the store and then left. The detectives surmised that he went from there to Clark's Dairy to try and kill Frankie with the hammer.

One of the interesting sidelights of all of this was that David Gerard phoned Frankie's uncle at around 7:30 P.M., allegedly looking for Frankie. By that time he had probably already assaulted Frankie with the hammer and was trying to set up an alibi that he didn't know where she was. Just like his "driving the Loop" alibi, which had been scuttled by the landslide, this alibi was ruined by the fact that Gerard had been caught on videotape at the Del Cris market. He didn't have to phone Frankie's uncle to know where she was. He had just seen her at the market.

As Lane went through the collected evidence, he was looking for items of particular interest that he could send on to the state lab. It was already obvious that the clothes that Gerard had worn to the milking parlor, where he assaulted Frankie, had been thrown away, perhaps never to be found. Lane went through a red nylon wallet Gerard had carried in his pants pocket and it was stuffed with paperwork. Amongst all the papers Lane found a small photo of Frankie and her three children. These were children by two previous marriages.

Lane also found a small photo of a woman named Patty Rodriguez and her two sons. Next to it was a small newspaper article, which Lane carefully unfolded and read. It was about Patty Rodriguez's funeral service in 1995. This set off immediate alarm bells in Lane's head. He had already seized an enlarged photograph from the trunk of Gerards' car, and that photo depicted Patty Rodriguez and her two boys. These individuals had all died in a house fire in 1995, and Lane knew all about the case, having been part of an investigation on it at the time. It had been ruled an accidental fire, but even then, he'd had his doubts. The one interesting thing occurring to Lane now was that David Gerard had been Patty's live-in boyfriend in 1995. In fact, she had just broken up with him before she, her sons and her mother had all died in that fire. And Lane and Detective Parfitt had questioned David Gerard in relation to that 1995 fire. Although Gerard had acted

strangely after the fire, Lane and Parfitt had chalked that
up to grief on Gerard's part at the time.

   Lane realized that in order to have the blood samples
already seized from Gerard's vehicle analyzed, he had to
get blood samples from David Gerard and Frankie as
well. Frankie by now had been moved to Providence Centralia Hospital, closer to Grays Harbor County. Lane went
to see her there, and the nurse drew a sample of Frankie's
blood and put it into a tube. Once again, Lane spoke with
Frankie about the assault. Not only was she still alive, but
some of her memory had returned as well. Frankie told
Lane about moving fourteen cows into the milking parlor
on the day she was assaulted, and she was getting them
hooked up to the milking machine. Suddenly the sliding
door opened, she turned around and just caught a glimpse
of David Gerard standing behind her with a hammer held
over his head. Gerard didn't say a word. He brought the
hammer down toward her head with a savage blow, and
Frankie managed to raise her arm upward. The hammer
blow shattered her forearm. Before she could react again,
Gerard swung the hammer and hit her on the right side of
the head. Frankie collapsed to the floor, and recalled
being struck in the head at least three more times. Then,
as if to finish the job, Gerard either pulled out a knife and
stabbed her in the neck with it, or used the claws on the
hammer to stab her neck. Assuming she was now dead or
soon would be, Gerard left the milking parlor without
saying a word.
   From that point on, Frankie slipped in and out of consciousness. She did so for nearly two hours. One thing
she recalled was telling herself she was not going to die
on that filthy, bloody milking floor. Her memory was,

of course, fragmented, and she was receiving a lot of morphine in the hospital. Frankie needed it. She had excruciating pain from head to foot, and at times it felt as if she were being stretched on the rack. The morphine had its side effects, however. Frankie was haunted by frightening morphine-enhanced dreams—dreams in which she was still in grave danger.

Frankie told Lane of having several nightmares of David Gerard coming through her hospital room window to finish the job. In the dreams he would sneak in, unseen by the staff, and once again have a hammer in his hand. This time he was intent on finishing the job he had begun in the milking parlor. Lane reassured her that Gerard was in jail now and he wasn't getting out. Lane Youmans also said that he would do everything possible to put David Gerard away for a long, long time.

3

A STIFF SENTENCE

Lane Youmans obtained a search warrant to seize a blood sample from David Gerard. This was signed by Judge Stephen Brown, and with the order in hand, Lane had Gerard brought to the nurses' station at the county jail. Gerard's attorney had already been notified about this, and Lane assured the attorney that he would not ask Gerard any questions while drawing the blood. Lane phoned the Montesano Fire Department (MFD) and had a medic come to the jail for the blood draw. Lane introduced himself to Gerard and the medic, and had the medic draw two blood tubes of Gerard's blood. The medic tied a rubber strap around Gerard's upper arm and stuck him with a needle. Gerard winced, and Lane thought, *Now that's something! He's afraid of a needle, but he can try and beat his girlfriend to death with a hammer! He's afraid to look at even a little bit of his own blood. But it didn't bother him a bit to spatter Frankie's blood all over the walls and floor of the milking parlor.*

After the medic had filled the two tubes with Gerard's

blood, he handed them to Lane, who wrote Gerard's name on each and the date as well. Then Lane placed each tube into a separate envelope, marking one as *64-A* and the other as *64-B*. After that, the envelopes were placed into a refrigerator in the evidence room. Gerard was given a copy of the search warrant and was returned to his cell.

Lane often went over to Centralia to check on Frankie. He learned from the medical personnel there that she was never expected to walk again. Lane asked if Frankie had any feeling in her legs, and was informed that she did, but still the prognosis was not encouraging. Nonetheless, Lane told the male nurse if Frankie had some feeling in her legs, she shouldn't be written off as having to spend the rest of her life in a wheelchair. Lane later noted, "What none of us knew at the time was how much of a fighter Frankie was. She was determined not to let David win."

Fighter or not, it took all of Frankie's strength and determination to fight through her pain and the incredible damage that had been done. Each day was a torment, not only physically, but mentally as well. And it was never a straight shot on the road to recovery. Every small gain was often counteracted by a sliding back toward disability. Each small step forward was measured in inches, not yards. She had a hard time getting meds that would ease her pain. One medication after another was tried, but all seemed to have very little effect or, on the flip side, put her into a stupor. One agonizing day followed another in a seemingly endless array of tests, treatments and pills.

Lane was also there to gather more background information about the relationship between Frankie and David. Lane knew that the assault case would one day go to trial, and he wanted as much down on paper as possible against Gerard. In one report Lane stated, "I interviewed Frankie

Cochran at her residence in Centralia. Frankie told me that she and David Gerard had been together for about a year and had met at the Red Barn Restaurant in Grand Mound. They moved in together, initially at a sister-in-law's residence, and then a short time later to a mobile home park in Mossyrock. Frankie described Gerard as being very possessive and she had to be with him twenty-four hours a day when he wasn't working. He kept asking her to marry him, and even bought her a ring.

"Frankie said that Gerard drank rum and Cokes and would get belligerent with her when he drank. She described him as a big liar. When he got diabetes, he told the doctor that he gave himself insulin shots. She said it was a lie. She was the one who gave him the shots. Every time someone phoned their residence, he would want to know who was calling. He was very jealous. While Gerard was not necessarily physically abusive, she stated he was sexually abusive, demanding sex from her twice a day, every day. Whenever she didn't want to have sex, he accused her of cheating on him. He told her that she loved her cats more than him. Frankie said that eventually she felt like a whore who was only there to satisfy him.

"I asked Frankie about other girlfriends that Gerard had mentioned. She recalled a woman named Tracy, who had two of Gerard's kids. Gerard hated her for taking the two kids away."

(Lane never saw any documents that David Gerard ever had children. He wondered if this was just one more of Gerard's "big lies" that Frankie had spoken about.)

"Frankie told me that Gerard never did drugs. He never went to church, was not into pornography, books or movies. He liked to hunt, but he never had a hunting license, and worried that he would get caught."

* * *

The charges against David Gerard were in two categories. Count I was an "attempt to commit murder in the first degree." It included that "David Gerard did on March 17, 1999, with premeditation, attempted to cause the death of Frankie Cochran by assaulting her with a weapon or instrument, likely to produce death." Count II was assault in the first degree. This stated that David Gerard at minimum attempted to inflict great bodily harm upon Frankie Cochran. At that time Gerard was noted to be 220 pounds and was five feet eleven inches tall. His hair was blond and his eyes were blue.

Gerard seemed intent on pleading not guilty and fighting the matter out, all the way through a jury trial. He seemed to be just as stubborn in this as he had been on insisting that he had driven the entire Loop of the day that Frankie Cochran had been assaulted with a hammer. Lane noted, "Gerard would dig in his heels and defend his position, no matter how ridiculous it looked to others. He wasn't very bright, but he was persistent." And all indications were that Gerard was going to duke this out in court, as various documents went into the court system from his lawyer.

The months went by as Lane and the other detectives gathered more and more information on David Gerard. Then Lane spoke with Gerard's defense attorney again. He told the lawyer, "How do you think it's going to look for your client when Frankie is wheeled into a courtroom with her head bandaged, and she raises a cast-covered arm to point at the man who did this to her?" This image must have been driven home, because several weeks later, Lane was informed that David Gerard was going to plead guilty to attempted murder.

On April 30, 1999, all parties sat down with Judge Mark McCauley and discussed the matter. David Gerard filled out an official form that he was freely and voluntarily going into the agreement, and that no one had coerced him to do so. He also agreed that no one had made any promises to him about sentencing at this point. On the form Gerard wrote: *On March 17, 1999, in Grays Harbor County, Washington, with premeditated intent, I took a substantial step toward the commission of the crime of murder in the first degree by striking Frankie Cochran in the head with a hammer.* Since Gerard often said he had trouble writing, he may have been walked through this particular wording by the others present. The document was signed by David Gerard, County Prosecutor Steward Menefee, defense attorney Brett Ballew and Judge McCauley. The next step before sentencing was going to be much more legally time-consuming and detailed.

Both the defense and prosecution sent briefs to Judge McCauley before the actual sentencing date. County Prosecutor Menefee sent the judge a list of people he intended to call as witnesses in that phase. The list included thirty names and covered key people in law enforcement, such as Detectives Lane Youmans and Dave Pimentel. It also included citizens, such as Polly Miller and Eugene Clark, and crime techs from the Washington State Laboratory, and doctors from Harborview Medical Center.

By presenting mitigating circumstances, Gerard's defense attorney was, of course, trying to minimize the years David would serve in prison. In one document the defense attorney wrote to Judge McCauley that David only finished eighth grade and never got his GED. The document claimed that Gerard had a very difficult time reading and comprehending material. Ballew listed

Gerard's employment record as being a farmhand and farmyard truck driver.

Then the document noted that the defense had spent time with Gerard in his jail cell and had shown him police reports about what he had done to Frankie Cochran. The defense attorney wrote, *Whenever I read to Mr. Gerard the portions of reports which referred to injuries sustained by Frankie Cochran, Mr. Gerard wept and sobbed. I believe this to be showing sincere remorse.*

It was added that after viewing the police reports, David Gerard decided to plead guilty. In the words of the defense, Gerard did so because *he did not want to put Ms. Cochran through the ordeal of a jury trial.* In his bid for leniency it was asked that Judge McCauley impose a standard range sentence, plus twenty-four months that included the deadly weapon enhancement.

Steward Menefee, for his part, was having none of this leniency business. The day after the defense sent this document to Judge McCauley, Menefee sent a document of his own. The document began with a retelling of the incident of March 13, 1999, when Gerard had physically pulled Frankie Cochran out of his car and she had thrown a cup of coffee on him. After she had done that, Gerard, of course, had gone to a toolshed and grabbed a hammer, threatening to beat her in the head with it. That is exactly what occurred at Clark's Dairy on March 17.

Menefee also noted that Gerard's alibi of driving around the Loop didn't hold any water because of the road closure on Highway 101. And Menefee added that Gerard was caught on videotape at the Del Cris Grocery & Deli in Elma, at the exact time he was supposedly driving around the Loop. Menefee stressed all the physical and emotional damage David Gerard had inflicted upon Frankie Cochran. Menefee noted that even at this point in time Frankie's condition was judged to be "fragile." If the swelling in her brain got worse, she might not survive another surgery. Addressing Gerard's supposed feelings of remorse, Menefee wrote, *The brutal nature of the crime, in combination with the seriousness of the attack, warrants that David Gerard should receive the harshest possible sentence allowed by the law.*

Along with the documents sent to Judge McCauley by the defense and prosecution, there were also letters sent to him from Frankie Cochran's family members. These letters were hopeful that Judge McCauley would give Gerard a stiff sentence for the brutal, and nearly fatal, attack upon Frankie. One letter was from the Physical Medicine and Rehabilitation Program of Centralia, Washington. The letter stated: *Ms. Cochran is severely brain injured from a beating she received on March 17, 1999. She will have severe permanent impairment in her ability to think and function physically.* It was signed by Dr. Greg Carter.

Another letter came in from Debbie Winkler, Frankie's aunt. She said she had been visiting Tucson, Arizona, when she learned about the assault upon her niece. Winkler took a flight to Seattle the next day. Winkler said that she suffered from depression, and now she carried a double load, trying to be with Frankie every day, and keeping her spirits up.

Winkler wrote, *Frankie says quite often, that she can't keep going on like this. She has pain every second of the day. She fears that David Gerard will send a friend to finish her off. She is having a hard time in dealing with how she looks and with all of the injuries. With me trying to constantly help her, I have been draining myself.*

Winkler said that between the time Gerard had pulled Frankie out of the car, a week before, and the hammer attack, he had stalked Frankie. Gerard had even come around Winkler's residence, where Frankie was staying that week. During that period of time, Winkler said, her neighbor had been scared to death by Gerard's activities. The neighbor had seen him go to Winkler's door, and Gerard had pounded so hard on it, the neighbor thought he would break it down.

Winkler hoped that Judge McCauley would give David Gerard the severest sentence possible for his attempt to kill Frankie, as she termed it. She wrote, *In doing what he did, he took away her livelihood and made her an invalid with psychological problems for the rest of her life.*

Frankie's grandparents agreed with that assessment. They wrote the judge that David Gerard had *totally destroyed Frankie's life. It is a miracle that Frankie is still alive with the injuries that she received. As a matter of fact, we understand that she could still die, since her condition is so fragile.* The grandparents listed all of Frankie's injuries and the therapy she continued to receive. Then they wrote, *Please, Judge. Give this girl a break and put that man away for good.*

The letter from Frankie's parents was just as adamant in their hopes that Judge McCauley would give Gerard the most stringent sentence possible. They started out by writing, *We did not realize the impact of this incident until writing this letter. All the strength that we thought we were portraying was nothing but a false front. Just being there was not facing the long term consequences of the terrible act that David Gerard inflicted on our daughter.*

Frankie's parents stated that for years to come she would have "demons" to contend with, and at present she was very confused. As she stared off into space, they often wondered where her mind was. Frankie's parents, Gary and MaryLou, began listing the long set of burdens that Frankie was enduring then, and things she would have to endure in the future. These included short-term memory loss, long-term memory loss, constant fear of being attacked again, frustrating confusion about what had occurred and terrible nightmares.

The list went on to detail about a spinal fluid leak that was causing dangerous levels of fluid to enter her brain. The blows from the hammer had not only crushed her skull, but had sent dangerous pieces of bone into her brain, which caused problems. There was a constant concern about infections to her brain.

Anytime Frankie moved from her bed, she had to wear a football-type helmet. It was not only a nuisance, but it gave her shots of pain. The prospect that she would at some point have to have the bone fragment reinserted into her skull by surgery made Frankie terribly frightened. They also noted that when Gerard stabbed her in the neck, it caused damage to the arteries in the brain.

Dealing with Frankie's paralysis, her parents noted that her entire left side was paralyzed. This impaired the muscles in her face to function properly, and it would eventually lead to a sagging aspect in that part of her face. They said Frankie had always been prideful of her looks and appearance, and it would be one more blow to her psychological condition. There were doubts that Frankie would ever be able to use her left arm again.

Frankie's right hand, which she had tried to use to protect her head, was still broken and not healing well. This would require more surgery. The left quadrant of both of her eyes had suffered damage, and they would never be the same as before the attack. Her eye sockets and eyebrow area had suffered extensive damage. Although those injuries were repaired, her parents noted: *Someday she will have to look at herself in a mirror again. That day will be very tragic for her.*

There were still problems in her neck area where she had been stabbed by Gerard. These problems required more surgery in the future. Frankie's lungs had been compromised, and she had to be constantly monitored in this area, to prevent serious problems from the fluid building up there.

And there was the matter of pain. It was a constant, and it promised to be a factor for the rest of her life. The idleness of her being in bed most of the time was going to cause problems for her muscles in the future as well. And her bladder did not properly function. Frankie was having to use a Foley catheter. In the future a tube might have to be inserted into her bladder.

In closing, asking for a severe sentence, Gary and Mary-Lou wrote, *Frankie will forever be a prisoner to a wheelchair, and her freedom will be restricted to a piece of metal and wheels. Her physical handicap is extensive, but her emotional state will have to be dealt with constantly.*

Perhaps the most graphic and impassioned letter of all came from Frankie herself. Since she could not write the letter, because of her injuries, the letter had to be dictated to her mother, who wrote it instead. It began by asking David Gerard: *Why?* Why had he done this terrible thing to her? She said that any reason she tried to come up with, she could not find any justification in that reasoning. So then she began telling him how she felt.

Frankie explained that pain and confusion were only the beginning. She said that a pastor who regularly came to visit her told her that she had to get over her hatred of David. That it was consuming her. And then she stated,

God is the only one who knows how long it will take to heal my heart and mind.

That being said, her feelings toward David were extremely hateful: *You have robbed me of my life as I knew it. Even simple things, such as taking a walk on the beach, or taking my children on an outing are forever out of reach. Both my children and my family have suffered greatly because of your thoughtless deed.*

She was particularly angry at how the assault had affected her children. Keith, who was ten, had never come to see her after the attack because it was so traumatic to witness her condition. Billy, who was thirteen, *cries at the drop of a hat, and walks around, very confused about life.* Frankie declared that Amber, at fifteen, should have been thinking about what kind of car she was going to get, school dances and all the things that teenage girls were interested in. Yet, not unlike Billy, seeing counselors and psychiatrists were now a constant part of her life.

Frankie listed her parents, aunts, uncles and grandparents as people who suffered because of his act. They worried about her constantly and wondered how they were going to take care of her in the years to come. She said she could no longer walk, and David didn't deserve to. She was constantly in pain—as he deserved to be. Her mind didn't function the way it used to, and she wished his mind were equally inhibited.

Frankie related, *I should end the letter with, '"May God have mercy on your soul." But I won't, as I really don't feel that you deserve any. A life sentence is what I think you deserve, for that is the inhumane and vicious sentence that you inflicted on me with every blow of the hammer.*

* * *

On July 19, David Gerard appeared before superior court judge Mark McCauley for sentencing, and Judge McCauley handed down a very stringent thirty-seven-year sentence. As Lane noted, "Everyone was surprised. I couldn't wait to tell Frankie." This thirty-seven-year sentence was as harsh as it could be. Most court observers and detectives thought that Gerard would receive fifteen to twenty years at most. But Judge McCauley obviously took into account the brutality of the attack and how it had changed Frankie Cochran's life forever. She was never going to be free of pain, to some degree. More than just *live,* she was going to have to *endure.*

Judge McCauley did not detail at length why he had handed down such a harsh sentence, except to say, "As a result of the defendant's assault of the victim, the victim has endured and continues to endure severe pain and suffering, partial and possibly permanent paralysis, probable long-term disability and multiple future surgical procedures to attempt to repair the damage done by the defendant's assault. For that reason the court's findings justify a sentence which exceeds the standard range sentence of two hundred forty-nine months." In essence, David Gerard was getting 444 months of prison time.

In addition to having to serve thirty-seven years in prison, Gerard was ordered to pay $500 for a victim's assessment fee, $100 for a criminal filing fee, $400 for a court-appointed attorney and $100 for a crime lab fee. Gerard was also never to contact Frankie Cochran, her family or friends for the "rest of his natural life."

Lane Youmans had other ideas in mind, as well, after the sentence was handed down. Now that David Gerard wasn't going anywhere for a long, long time, Lane began to work on his theory that Gerard was not only responsible for the attempted murder of Frankie Cochran, but the deaths of Patty Rodriguez, her mother and Patty's two sons in a house fire. And Lane also began to wonder if Gerard was guilty of a brutal murder of a woman named Elaine "Brooke" McCollum on the nearby Weyco Haul Road in 1991, and the murder of Carol Leighton in 1996 on that same logging road.

4

A DARK
AND LONELY ROAD

On February 6, 1991, Lane Youmans got up as usual, and as he shaved, he made a mental note of what his plans were for the day. These plans included cases related to burglaries, thefts and bad checks. If those didn't fill up all his time, he could take another look at an unsolved Jane Doe homicide from 1988. Mushroom pickers out in the woods near the town of Elma had stumbled upon a human skull, and it turned out to be a homicide. And then if those weren't enough, he was going to have to testify in another murder case at court in the near future. As the various plans became focused in his mind, the telephone suddenly rang, and Lane went to answer it.

It was a phone call from the GHSO, and it blew all of Lane's plans clear out of the water. The body of a young woman had just been discovered on the Weyco Haul Road, short for the Weyerhauser Lumber/Paper Mill Company haul road that was only a few miles south of

Aberdeen. Lane knew that the Weyco Haul Road was a gravel road built by the timber company near the Blue Slough Road, outside of the town of Cosmopolis, so that their logging truck drivers didn't have to drive their loaded rigs up the steep and winding highway over Cosmopolis Hill.

The first person to spot a body lying off to the side of the Weyco Haul Road was a Hispanic man on his way to a job while he was in his pickup truck. This man drove to Cosmopolis, and in broken English told a Cosmopolis police officer about the body. But the man's English was so poor, the Cosmopolis officer had a hard time understanding what he was trying to say. To remedy that situation, the officer decided to follow the Hispanic man to try and figure out what he was talking about. It was obvious that he was very excited and upset about something.

When the Cosmopolis officer got to the location of the body, it was quite apparent why the Hispanic man had been so upset and agitated. To help the officer, a GHSO deputy who spoke Spanish was called to the scene to help interpret. This GHSO officer interviewed the Hispanic man and took a statement.

After the phone call from GHSO, Lane began assembling his homicide kit, and added enough food and water to last him three days in case he had to stay there that long. Lane related later, "I have been to crime scenes in remote areas of Grays Harbor County, and I never want to leave a scene until all the processing is done. I try to equip my van with everything I would need, but every scene presents unique problems. One of the main things was to make sure I had enough food and water to last me for a few days."

Lane looked outside his window to check the weather conditions, and guessed that he was lucky this time. It would be cold, but it didn't look like rain. There wouldn't be any need for tarps, shelters or additional equipment. That done, he jumped into his van and drove the eight miles from his home to the crime scene.

Once he arrived and got out of the van, the weather was indeed cold, but there was no snow on the ground. Lane made contact with officers and other detectives at the east end of the Weyco Haul Road and learned that the body of a woman was found lying on the south side of the road, about a mile from State Highway 107. Lane went down toward the body and could tell that she was white and appeared to be in her late twenties. She lay on her back, with her head pointing west toward Cosmopolis and Aberdeen.

It was apparent that the young woman had been run over several times by a pickup truck or large car, and distinctive tire tracks were present in the mud near her body. She had sustained massive injuries, including a broken right leg, and her scalp had been torn loose, or avulsed, by the spinning tires. She was wearing a short black jacket, red shirt, bra, panties, socks and one shoe. Tire tracks and scrapes from the vehicle and road surface were present on every part of her body.

It appeared that she had been struck and dragged a short distance before coming to rest alongside the shoulder of the road. The vehicle then drove over her, backed up over her, and then moved forward once again over her body before proceeding west. In other words, it appeared that by the second time the vehicle moved forward, it had to be an intentional act and not just an accident. In the mud around the body was a lot of blood, clumps of hair, an upper denture, a single tooth and the woman's wristwatch. On the road to the east of the body was a woman's hat, one of her shoes, a pair of black sweatpants, which were turned inside out, and a purse. Lane checked the purse and found an identification inside for Elaine M. McCollum, thirty-three years old, of Aberdeen. Lane looked at the woman's body beside the road and determined that the dead young woman was indeed Elaine McCollum.

Lane checked Elaine's body for approximate time of death. He knew that temperature and weather were factors in that determination, and could alter stiffening of the body, known as rigor mortis. There was also pooling of blood on the lowest portions of the body, known as livor mortis. Lane checked Elaine's fingers, wrists, elbows and other joints, and found them to be somewhat flexible. He knew that rigor began about two hours after death, and a body became completely stiff for approximately the next twelve hours. From this knowledge, it appeared to Lane that Elaine McCollum had been dead for about eight hours by the time he examined her. Which would have made her death occur sometime around midnight.

The purse contained $300 in cash, which tended to rule out robbery as a motive for her death. Lane photographed the scene from every angle; then he stood back and just gazed at the scene in its totality. As he recalled later, "I stood there in the cold morning air and took in every detail. The tire tracks in the gravel indicated that the suspect had chased the victim west down the road, knocking her down near the center of the road. But it hadn't been at a high rate of speed, since her lower legs were not broken by the vehicle bumper. The clothing was spread out on the roadway in almost a straight line. The victim had probably not run off the road because it was dark at that time of night and there was a steep drop-off on one side, and a steep hillside on the other side of the road."

Lane examined the sweatpants, which had been turned

inside out, and noticed that there was no dirt or mud on the outside of them. He doubted very much that the vehicle had struck Elaine with such force that it had knocked her sweatpants off upon first impact. Another thing that Lane saw made him take notice. Elaine's panties were partially torn and the waistband was rolled inward. Lane noted, "This could have been caused by the spinning tire or by Elaine hurriedly pulling her panties up." The state of the panties indicated that she'd had sex there in the woods and then had pulled up her panties afterward. Whether it was consensual sex or not, he couldn't determine at that point.

Lane worked on and around the crime scene as Elaine McCollum's body lay near the gravel road. He liked working from the outside perimeter inward toward a body as he collected evidence. After several hours Lane had to turn the scene over to another detective, because he was subpoenaed to appear in court that day and testify in a murder trial at superior court. It was the case of a man who had been shot and his body left in an isolated area of the county. And if that wasn't enough, there was another murder case going forward about a man who had killed his girlfriend and dumped her body into the Pacific Ocean.

While Lane Youmans was in court, Detectives Gary Parfitt and Doug Smythe scoured the Elaine McCollum crime scene for additional evidence. They put together a crime scene sketch and evidence log, documenting the items that had been collected. Sketches were necessary, because unlike photos, they gave a sense of perspective and depth. Photos were often good at depicting very definite items or scenes, but they did not give a sense of the crime scene in its totality.

The detectives also made plaster casts of the tire tread marks in the road next to Elaine's body. These tire tread casts were generally made by spraying the area with a fixative to create a moulage. Then a portable frame was placed around the track. Using a bucket and stirring stick, the officers mixed plaster with water to the necessary consistency. Then the plaster was carefully poured into the frame, making sure to even out the texture. Often the plaster was reinforced with twigs, straw, craft sticks or anything else that was available. And then it was left to dry, anywhere from fifteen minutes to two hours, depending upon atmospheric conditions. Casting tire tracks was as much an art as a science.

After he testified in court, Lane returned and reviewed the list that the other detectives had made, which included the clothing, hair samples, teeth and tire tread casts. A unit from the Washington State Patrol (WSP) was also there when Lane returned. They were a squad of accident investigation detectives and they brought along a device called a Total Station. It could electronically mark the location of various points of a scene, which could later be reconstructed as an exact scale map of the crime area. In conjunction with crime photos and physical measurements, the Total Station gave a very accurate reading about vehicles involved in accidents or crime scenes. As the name implied, the Total Station was helpful in gathering all relevant information in one central location.

It was dark by the time all the evidence had been collected, and finally Elaine McCollum's hands and feet were placed in paper bags so that no trace evidence would fall off them. Then her body was placed into a plastic bag and turned over to Fern Hill Mortuary.

* * *

   The next morning Lane Youmans attended the autopsy
of Elaine McCollum at the Fern Hill Mortuary in Aberdeen. The autopsy was performed by Dr. Sally Fitterer,
who worked for the King County Medical Examiner's
Office in Seattle, but she had a contract with the state to
do autopsies for Grays Harbor County as well. As Lane
noted, "Dr. Fitterer was young and rather petite, not what
one would expect a forensic pathologist to look like. But
she was very good at what she did. It did look a little odd,
since she was performing postmortem exams when she
was eight months pregnant, but she didn't let that slow
her down."
   The dimensions of the prep room at the Fern Hill Mortuary was about ten feet by twenty feet, and a quarter of
that was taken up by a cooler in which bodies were
stored. As in all homicides in Grays Harbor County,
there were, besides the medical doctor performing the
autopsy, other individuals who crowded into the small
space, including detectives and administrators. All of
those people jammed together in the tiny room made for
a very tight squeeze, and Lane recalled, "It made things
interesting for me to take photos, take custody of the
clothing and other items of evidence removed from the
body. Then I had to make sure everything was bagged
and documented and take care of all the other little tasks
that needed to be done."
   In this very cramped atmosphere, Dr. Fitterer began the
autopsy of Elaine McCollum by first conducting a complete external examination of the deceased's body. Lane
snapped photographs of the body while it was clothed
and also as items of clothing were removed. Dr. Fitterer
removed each item of clothing and marked them with a

unique number on a plastic tag. She then documented in her notes what the item was, and handed the article to Lane. He placed it in a separate paper bag and marked what the item was on the outside of the bag.

When every item of clothing was removed, Dr. Fitterer continued with the external examination, and Lane noted all the damage done to Elaine McCollum. She had large scrape marks running in different directions all over her body. From experience Lane surmised these had been caused when she had been dragged on the road by a vehicle. Dr. Fitterer began her internal examination, removing and documenting each organ. After completing this, Fitterer determined that Elaine McCollum's cause of death was due to trauma to the liver caused by the weight of the vehicle as it drove over her.

Dr. Fitterer also completed a rape kit, which consisted of fingernail scrapings, oral, anal and vaginal swabs, along with Elaine's panties. Fitterer took blood and urine samples from the body, and all of this evidence was turned over to Lane, who catalogued them before he submitted them into evidence. Lane put the rape kit into a refrigerator to preserve any biological material. The urine sample was sent to the Washington State Toxicology Laboratory in Seattle, and those results would later show that Elaine had no signs of drugs in her system, but she did have a .12 blood alcohol level, which was higher than the limit on a DUI test in Washington State.

Detective Ed McGowan contacted Elaine McCollum's parents, who lived in Aberdeen, and he learned that she lived with a heroin addict named David Simmons, of that same city. In fact, Simmons had reported Elaine missing to the Aberdeen Police Department (APD) on the morning after she hadn't returned home the previous night. It was not like Elaine to be out all night long without telling him where she was. According to Simmons, he had spent the previous night trying to kick his heroin habit, and Elaine had gone to the local taverns in downtown Aberdeen. At those taverns everyone knew her as Brooke, a name she called herself there. Brooke was a character on Elaine's favorite soap opera, *All My Children.*

Detective McGowan learned that six years previously, Elaine had moved home into her parents' house after a bad relationship. At that point she'd had some sort of mental breakdown and had become a virtual recluse in their home. Elaine stayed in her room almost all the time, not even going out to dine anywhere around town. Old friends didn't come by, no one called her—other than siblings—and she all but withdrew from the world.

Then after time passed, Elaine slowly came out of her shell and started going to the local taverns, not only to drink but to socialize. In fact, the taverns became Elaine's social meeting place in town. It was at one of the taverns that she met David Simmons, and after a short period of time, they fell in love. The tavern scene may not have been the best in the world for Elaine, and being in love with a drug addict was difficult, but at least they had each other. And after so many years of seclusion, Elaine seemed happy again.

David Simmons wasn't a bad guy at heart, but his heroin addiction did strain the relationship, as did Elaine's emotional problems. Despite all that, they decided to move in together at a small residence in Aberdeen. Detective McGowan noted, "Elaine spent most evenings in the downtown taverns of Aberdeen, where she was friends with all the regulars and never caused any problems." In fact, most of the people around there liked Elaine, and she seemed to always be upbeat and happy in such surroundings. After her years of self-imposed confinement, downtown Aberdeen was her escape from a life behind four walls.

Detective McGowan learned that on the evening of February 5, 1991, Elaine visited several taverns in downtown Aberdeen and was looking for a friend of hers named Todd Bigelow. That made all the GHSO detectives' "radar" perk up. Bigelow was a well-known character around Aberdeen, known for his alcoholism and combative nature when he was drunk. And detectives at the time knew that Todd was also the son of a man who owned one of Aberdeen's largest car dealerships. Law enforcement authorities had plenty of run-ins with Todd over the years, but these had generally been of a drunk and disorderly nature and driving-under-the-influence (DUI) incidents, not murder.

Detective McGowan was able to track Todd Bigelow down, and according to Bigelow, he and Elaine had spoken briefly outside a tavern in Aberdeen on the night of the murder. Then Bigelow said he had gone drinking at several taverns around town. Later he had supposedly passed out at a friend's house. Drinking to excess and passing out somewhere was not new to Bigelow.

Detective McGowan also learned through a woman named Karen Luther that Elaine had been seen that evening at a restaurant called the Smoke Shop (sometimes referred to as the Smoke Shop Restaurant or Smoke Shop Café). Luther also said that Elaine had been wearing a floppy red hat, which she often wore while downtown, and she'd been looking for someone. Elaine apparently didn't tell Karen Luther who that someone was.

Luther and Elaine spoke briefly on the sidewalk outside the Smoke Shop and then a pickup truck and white sedan pulled up near them. Elaine told Luther that she was going to a party somewhere, and said, "There's my ride." At that point Luther walked into the Smoke Shop and didn't see which vehicle Elaine got into, but she sensed that it was either the white sedan or pickup truck that were on the street nearby.

The detectives scoured all the taverns of downtown Aberdeen and learned that no one had seen Elaine after 10:00 P.M. on February 5. The detectives also learned that many people at the taverns thought that Todd Bigelow had killed Elaine. Lane Youmans noted later, "They said Bigelow was a drunk and capable of running someone over. He was the son of Jack Bigelow, who owned Bigelow Chevrolet in Aberdeen. The family was influential, living in a big house on Bigelow Drive on the hill above Aberdeen. Todd was one of those kids who didn't have to work, and when he got into trouble, it seemed like daddy would take care of things for him. I told other detectives, 'If people were voting, Todd Bigelow would be going to prison for murder.' But what we needed was evidence, and until we had more, Todd was just a person of interest."

In fact, what the detectives did next was spend a lot of time trying to prove that Todd Bigelow *had not* killed Elaine McCollum. They checked out his white Cadillac and all the rumors about him, but no hard facts placed Bigelow at the murder scene on the Weyco Haul Road. And the Cadillac had no front end or undercarriage damage. Many detectives believed a valid theory was that Todd might have run Elaine over in a drunken stupor. However, the lack of damage on the Cadillac tended to rule that out. And Bigelow could never quite be placed at the crime scene at the time in question. One thing that made him more of a suspect, than not, was the fact that the detectives learned through friends of Elaine's that she had been trying to find Todd Bigelow just before she disappeared from the streets of Aberdeen on February 5, 1991. It had been more than just a request on her part. She had been very insistent about it. Just why she wanted to meet up with him again was not readily apparent.

The common theme of these stories concerned Elaine having heard that Todd had gone to a tavern in Montesano from Aberdeen. For whatever reason, she wanted to meet him there. Not having a ride, she actively began searching for one to Montesano. It was quite possible that Elaine climbed into a white sedan or pickup truck in front of the Smoke Shop in Aberdeen around the time that Karen Luther had spoken to her on the street. What wasn't known was whether she had ever made it to Montesano, and was on her way back to Aberdeen when murdered, or she had never made it there at all.

5

VICTIMOLOGY

To try and get into the background and mind-set of Elaine McCollum, Lane Youmans wrote up what he termed a "victimology report." Lane stated in it: *Elaine "Brooke" McCollum lived in Aberdeen with her boyfriend, David Simmons. Mr. Simmons was a heroin addict and was not employed. Brooke McCollum was also not employed but was seeking employment. McCollum has been described as a very caring person who was trying to get her boyfriend off of heroin. Her parents lived in Aberdeen, and she kept in close contact with them. She also had a brother who lived in the Seattle area and she often sent him taped audio letters. She had no children or pets and was a relatively organized person. She kept a clean house, her purse was organized to include envelopes containing various sums of cash and the envelopes were labeled with the names of various places where she owed money.*

McCollum had a driver's license but did not have a vehicle, nor did David Simmons. McCollum would frequently

*hitchhike if she had to go farther than the downtown
Aberdeen area, which was about three blocks from her
residence. McCollum has been described as a "bar
person," and would spend most of her time with friends
in the local bars. On the evening of February 5, 1991,
McCollum walked downtown and went to several of the
local bars while her boyfriend, Dave Simmons, stayed
home. While McCollum was in the downtown area, she
met up with Todd Bigelow and another male. They went
to several taverns while riding in Mr. Bigelow's car. At
one point McCollum apparently got separated from
Todd Bigelow. She and the other male, Fred Jarmin,
split up and she attempted to find Mr. Bigelow, but was
unsuccessful. Mr. Bigelow went to a friend's house
where he passed out in the evening hours. His car has
been examined and he has been questioned, but he has
a solid alibi for that night.*

*McCollum was last seen leaving the Smoke Shop Café
and Lounge at 10:30 PM. She walked out to the curb
where a white sedan and brown pickup truck pulled up to
the curb. The witness believed that McCollum got into
one of the vehicles, but did not know which one. McCollum's body was found the next morning around 6 AM,
lying on the Weyco Haul Road. Her purse containing
money was still with her. Her pants were off and turned
inside out and she had been run over by a vehicle approximately three times. Just east of the body site, there were
indications that McCollum had been running westbound
down the road toward Aberdeen and the vehicle was pursuing her.*

*There is no indication that Elaine McCollum was a
prostitute, nor any indication that she was unfaithful to
her boyfriend. The last person to see Elaine McCollum
alive was a person of questionable credibility, a woman*

*named Karen. Karen stated that McCollum had just
scored some dope for her boyfriend and then got into a
vehicle. Although David Simmons said that in the past,
McCollum had done this, he stated that she would not
have done that on the evening before she was murdered.
She knew he was trying to go cold turkey off of heroin. It
is unknown why Elaine Brooke McCollum would willingly get into a person's car in the downtown Aberdeen
area unless it was someone she knew. She did not need a
ride to go home, since she was only a few blocks from
there when last seen.*

The detectives also began checking out a lot of rumors
that someone in the Grays Harbor's Hispanic community
had killed Elaine. It was no secret that many people in the
area's drug culture did not like the Hispanics in the area,
and blamed them for every unsolved crime that came
down the pike. Lane Youmans noted, "There were lots of
stories about gangs of Mexican males raping women,
killing people because of drug debts and things like that.
While we were aware of some incidents involving young
Mexican men, underage girls and alcohol, I knew a lot of
the rumors were just talk. Besides, Elaine McCollum's
murder didn't feel like a group thing. Plus, when you
have a group of any race involved in a crime like this,
chances are good that one of them would have taken the
money in her purse. And chances are good that at least
one person would talk to others about the crime, but so
far, no one was talking.

The obituary for Elaine McCollum in the Aberdeen
Daily World was as short as her life had been. It spoke

of her being born in Aberdeen and graduating from Aberdeen High School. It spoke of her love for animals and listed a few of her family members and David Simmons. She had spent nearly her entire life in Grays Harbor County and rarely traveled out of the county. Her entire life span had run thirty-three years.

Before her nervous breakdown in her early twenties, Elaine had gone to high school in the area. She hadn't been in any student clubs or organizations in her freshman and junior years, but by her senior year that had changed. She seemed to blossom that year and was in the Leaderette club. This club assisted in plays put on at the school, concerts and basketball games. Elaine was also in the Spanish club and the pep club. In a photograph showing her in the Leaderettes, Elaine is smiling and appears to be enjoying herself. It may have been one of the happiest times in her short life.

There was very little news in the *Daily World* about the murder, except for an article about how the Washington State Patrol had used a high-tech device to help in the investigation. The newspaper wrote about how the experts from the state patrol in Seattle went out to the Weyco Haul Road with their Total Station Measuring System, and the article told about how the operators could produce a precise diagram of the crime scene in a fraction of the time compared to older methods. The device was so new, it had barely been used for a year at other crime and accident scenes. For its day it was very high-tech.

The newspaper went on to report that GHSO detectives were still scouring the crime scene area for bits of evidence. Lane Youmans was quoted as saying that a vehicle may have been used in the murder, but he would not elaborate on this. (By this point Lane knew that it had been a vehicle that had killed Elaine, but he decided not to release any more information about that at the present time.) And then there was one other important sentence in the article. The article related: *Slowing the department down is a homicide trial in Grays Harbor Superior Court this week. Several sheriff's investigators are testifying, which left the office with a smaller contingent of investigators.* Lane had been one of those investigators called away from the Elaine McCollum crime scene to testify at court.

The homicide that was drawing away so many GHSO investigators concerned a Cambodian immigrant named Kly Bun Meas, who had allegedly killed another Cambodian immigrant. In fact, Meas had allegedly taken a pendant from the dead man, which his girlfriend saw, and Meas supposedly confessed to her, "Look, I killed this man." While the victim, Uan Teng, had been fishing near Elma, he had been shot twice in the head. Teng apparently had had money stolen from him and the gold pendant. A few days later, Meas gave his girlfriend and friends some large amounts of cash. They all wondered where he had suddenly gotten the money. Meas worked sometimes at odd jobs and fighting forest fires, but more often than not, he was unemployed and had little cash on hand.

Lane Youmans and the other detectives had spoken to various people concerning the murder, and one of them was Gabriel Espinoza. He had seen a blue pickup truck pass him by twice while he was at his house on the day of the crime. Espinoza lived less than a mile from the murder scene, and Meas drove a blue pickup truck. Even Meas's neighbor said that he had loaned Meas a rifle a few days before the murder.

In his closing arguments County Prosecutor Steward

Menefee told the jurors, "The one thing that ties this case up was literally a stone around the defendant's neck, that pendant. Because any way you cut it, that pendant makes the case." In the end it was a pretty open-and-shut case, and the jury found Kly Meas guilty of first-degree murder.

All of this had one detrimental effect, however, as the newspaper article had noted. It took key investigators away from the Elaine McCollum crime scene, early in its inception, which is often a critical time in the collection of evidence and information.

By February 11, 1991, there was an article in the *Daily World* headlined: DETECTIVES SEEK HELP IN TRACING LAST HOURS OF MURDERED WOMAN. Lane was quoted as saying that the public's input in piecing together the last hours that Elaine had spent in Aberdeen could help the investigation. Among the questions were both how and why Elaine had either been walking on or been transported to the Weyco Haul Road in the middle of the night. A few people reported a woman hitchhiking in the south Aberdeen and Cosmopolis areas on the night in question, but whether the woman matched the description of Elaine McCollum couldn't be determined. Lane stated that it was known that Elaine had been at the Time Out Tavern early in the evening on February 5. The Time Out Tavern, along with the Smoke Shop, was one of Elaine's main hangouts in town. It was also a place that Todd Bigelow knew well.

Going back to forensic fluids that might help implicate or eliminate suspects, the detectives obtained blood samples from David Simmons, Todd Bigelow and Fred Jarmin, a friend of Elaine's who had been with her during her final hours on February 5 while she had been looking for Todd Bigelow.

Lane Youmans could have sent the blood samples to the Washington State Patrol Crime Lab in Seattle, but at that time, all that lab was doing was ABO blood typing. This was very early in the new forensic science of DNA testing, and the only national lab doing vital forensic work at the time was the FBI Laboratory in Quantico, Virginia. In 1991, there was a huge backlog of DNA requests from law enforcement around the nation. Nonetheless, Lane determined the best results might occur if he did send the blood samples to the FBI Laboratory, and he did so, knowing there would be a long wait until the results came back.

Detectives Doug Smythe and Bill Stocks, meanwhile, checked out David Simmons's alibi. They discovered that he didn't have a vehicle, so any vehicles he did have access to were put on a rack and their undercarriage examined for evidence related to the murder. No evidence from those vehicles indicated that they had been at the murder scene.

The relationship between David and Elaine was looked into, and although it may not have been the best in the world, it was apparent that they did care for each other. There was one very outrageous remark on David's part, however, at one point. Elaine had told a counselor at Evergreen Counseling Center that David had once said to her, "If I find you're cheating on me, I'll cut you from clit to forehead." Despite this remark, though, there were never any indications of domestic violence between David and Elaine. He might have uttered those words when he was high.

All indications also pointed to David Simmons having been home on the evening when Elaine went missing, and that he was indeed trying to go cold turkey from heroin. He took the phone off the hook and went to bed. His story, more or less, held up.

Even though Lane tried to set up a polygraph exam of David Simmons, it was never done. Around that time Detectives Smythe and Stocks were busy checking out the Hispanic gang angle, which went nowhere. Perhaps they thought there were some good leads there, but the time spent on that did have consequences. Lane wanted them to go and photograph David Simmons and Elaine McCollum's residence. By the time the detectives got around to doing so, David had cleaned out the residence and moved to another location. Lane heaved a large sigh. He had taken twelve hundred photos of the crime scene on the Weyco Haul Road, autopsy and other evidence, but there would never be relevant photos of the Simmons/McCollum residence. As Lane Youmans said later, "What's done was done, and you live with it and move on. I can't think of a murder case I've worked on, that there was something I would have liked to have done over."

Lane went to Sheriff Dennis Morrisette to contact the county commissioners and request a $2,000 reward for information on the murder of Elaine McCollum, which was approved. GHSO also posted notices in the region's newspaper, the *Daily World,* with some more information about the case, and asking the residents for help.

The *Daily World* ran a few more stories about the murder on the Weyco Haul Road and the reward as well. Despite these steps, though, the only tips that came in were about Hispanic gang members and the Todd Bigelow angle. Lane recalled, "No one got drunk and bragged about it. No one snitched on someone else to get out of a jam. There were no useful tips. Soon the tips dried up and the case went cold. The only evidence we had that belonged to the suspect were the plaster molds of the tire tracks."

The tires were identified from the molds as being Les Schwab Classic Premium tires, which had only been on the market since October 1990. About sixty thousand of these had been sold in western Washington State, and there were 213 people who had purchased the Classic Premium tires at the Aberdeen Les Schwab store.

Lane assigned Detective Stocks and Detective Smythe to make a list of customers who had bought those tires in Aberdeen, and check the people out as far as criminal records went. The list was broken down alphabetically, by city and tire size. Detective Stocks also obtained a list of vehicles from the University of Michigan, based on tire size and wheel base. Due to the fact that the tire tracks were left on a gravel road, exact measurement wasn't possible. But the detectives were able to narrow down the possible vehicles that could have left the tire tread marks on the Weyco Haul Road to fifty types. This was based upon certain vehicles able to use Les Schwab Classic Premium tires.

Detective Smythe and Detective Stocks prioritized the list of customers' vehicles based on the list from the University of Michigan. They contacted a number of customers on the list, and were able to exclude them one by one. Even though the name David Gerard, of Montesano, came up, it was not the same David Gerard connected to Frankie Cochran in later years. In fact, it was another individual who had nothing to do with Frankie's attempted murder or the murders of women on the Weyco Haul Road.

The David Gerard who was connected to Frankie was not checked out at the time. This may have been because all he had listed was a post office box (POB) with no notation of his actual physical address. In fact, over the years this David Gerard had a habit of only using POBs as a mailing address. It made it hard to keep track of his whereabouts at any particular time. This was exacerbated by the fact that he moved around so often. He would move around from place to place almost on a yearly basis. In the last ten years this Gerard had lived at ten different locations.

When the DNA results concerning Elaine McCollum finally came back from the FBI Laboratory, their report indicated that David Simmons was one contributor to semen found on the vaginal swab. This was not a huge surprise, since Simmons was Elaine's live-in boyfriend at the time. There was a second unidentified contributor of semen as well. Just who this person was did not show up in any database.

As the case progressed, David Simmons was ruled out as Elaine McCollum's killer. Some individual was still out there who had ruthlessly run over Elaine McCollum, backed up over her as she lay on the road, then drove over her again to make sure she was dead.

If the Uan Teng murder trial wasn't enough to retard further progress on the Elaine McCollum case, Lane Youmans and the other GHSO detectives had another murder trial on their hands that soon took up a lot of their time as well. This related to a woman named Robin Rose, who had moved up to Washington State from Arcata, California. She had fallen in love with a man named David Coleman in Grays Harbor County. One day in 1990, Coleman contacted GHSO and said that Robin was missing. Deputy John Olsen went to Coleman's residence and took a report. According to Coleman, Robin had gotten up, kissed him good-bye and said that she was going out to shop. He stated that he drove across the Olympic Peninsula, took the ferry and visited friends in Tacoma. From Tacoma, Coleman said, he called her twice, but he only got the answering machine. Coleman said that when he returned that evening, Robin's Ford Explorer was in the driveway and her keys for the Explorer were on a hook in the kitchen. Coleman stated that he looked around and saw that her sleeping bag, a .22 rifle and all of her pain medications were missing.

Deputy Olsen had Coleman write out a statement, which he did. But then Coleman crumpled up the page he had just written and threw it into a wastepaper basket. Olsen thought this was odd. In fact, Olsen thought it was so odd, that when Coleman wasn't looking, Olsen snatched the crumpled-up piece of paper from the wastepaper basket and put it into his pocket. Coleman wrote another statement and gave it to Olsen. When Deputy Olsen left, he compared the two statements, and there were several differences between the two.

A missing persons report was made and Lane Youmans was sent to investigate and contact David Coleman. Lane said later, "I spent several days sitting with Coleman, drinking coffee with him and talking about Robin. I didn't take notes, as I didn't want to arouse his suspicion. I wanted to befriend him and gain his confidence. As soon as I would leave, I would park down the road and furiously write down all he had told me.

"David said that he suspected California marijuana dealers, who Robin had dealt with in the past, had come up to Hoquiam and kidnapped Robin, and possibly killed her. He said he became scared they might return and he was now sleeping on the couch, armed with a shotgun.

"During one of the visits, I asked if I could search the

residence and he said okay. He didn't seem to be upset or concerned about this. David's mother had come up from California to stay with him. She had cleaned the kitchen and had found a spent twenty-two casing. I did a cursory search, but nothing really looked suspicious. In their bedroom Robin had lined all of her shoes along one wall. Several of the shoes had been kicked or moved, while the rest were neatly lined up. In the dirty clothes hamper I found a pair of sweatpants with fresh mud on the knees.

"I photographed the residence and then the vehicles. In the rear of Robin's Ford Explorer, there was a new water heater in a cardboard container. The heater was along the driver's side and clean. David's Oldsmobile wasn't nearly as clean. On the dashboard of his car, I found a receipt for the ferry ride he said he took to Tacoma. After several days we arranged for our search-and-rescue group to search the woods surrounding the residence. While we were involved with the search, a father and son stopped our vehicle near a cliff overlooking the Pacific Ocean at Kalaloch. They had seen a sleeping bag on the slope below the road. The search team investigated and found a woman's body inside.

"The Clallam County Sheriff's Office was called, and an autopsy confirmed that it was the body of Robin Rose. She had been shot twice in the head with a twenty-two-caliber weapon. We served a search warrant on Robin's residence and both vehicles. Luminol was sprayed in the bedroom, and blood showed up that had been wiped. We found the same thing in Robin's Ford Explorer. There was an outline of blood where the water heater had been sitting.

"A service sticker on the driver's door of the Ford Explorer indicated that it had an oil change at a Jiffy Lube in Seattle. The employees recalled that David Coleman had the vehicle serviced and he had vacuumed it out, but he didn't want them to help. I found that Robin had purchased the twenty-two rifle at a sporting goods store in Arcata. The owner of that store knew Robin, and knew she had gone to a friend's residence at one time to test-fire the rifle. I went to that location and spent hours searching behind the residence where the owner indicated that Robin had fired her weapon. I found seven .22 casings that were later matched to the one Coleman's mother found. The rifle was never found, nor were Robin's purse or fanny pack. David Coleman was arrested for her murder.

"We think that Robin was getting tired of Coleman. She had received eighty-six thousand dollars in a settlement after being injured at a mill where she worked near Arcata. She probably got tired of him living off of her money. She may have tried to end the relationship, got into a fight in the yard, and her sweatpants got muddy there. It appeared that she had been sitting on the edge of her bed, changing her sweatpants, when Coleman grabbed the rifle and shot her twice. He then put her body in her sleeping bag, loaded it in the Explorer, and drove up to Kalaloch. He attempted to throw the sleeping bag with Robin's body into the Pacific Ocean, but it got hung up halfway down the cliff. Either he didn't see that, or he was afraid to go down there and possibly be seen by someone as he pushed it into the ocean. He then probably drove to Tacoma, caught the ferry and visited some friends, to try and set up an alibi. He also went to the Jiffy Lube in Seattle and tried to clean up the Ford Explorer. He called the answering machine twice, but never left a message, knowing that Robin would never hear it.

"David Coleman was tried and convicted for the murder of Robin Rose. As he was being led from the courtroom after sentencing, he turned and threatened to get me when he got out. He never got the chance, however. He was diagnosed with cancer and died in prison."

All of the detective work on the Robin Rose case and the trial interrupted whatever efforts could still be made on Elaine McCollum's case. As Lane Youmans noted later, "After a year or so, the steam began to run out of the Elaine McCollum investigation. Other murders occurred, other crimes took precedence, and the Elaine McCollum murder was pushed to the back burner. Detective Stocks was promoted to patrol sergeant and Detective Smythe returned to the drug task force. In 1993, I was assigned to the drug task force for a year and a half. By the time I returned to my regular investigation duties, the three-ring binder containing the McCollum homicide investigation was sitting on a bookshelf in the undersheriff's office. I took Elaine McCollum's driver's license and taped it to the wall by my desk. The case was inactive, but not forgotten."

Not helping matters in any further progress in Elaine McCollum's murder was a new grisly murder case only months after Elaine's. Once again there was a blood frenzy involved, and all the detectives, including Lane, who had spent so many hours on Elaine's case, were soon collecting evidence at a blood-soaked crime scene. Even though this new murder was eventually deemed not to be connected to the murder of Elaine McCollum, it helped Lane and the other detectives hone their forensic skills and ability to gather evidence.

As it turned out, they were going to need every bit of those skills concerning McCollum. It wouldn't be long before another murder on the very same Weyco Haul

Road occurred. And that murder was going to have a direct link to McCollum's murder. The detectives were going to need every bit of experience they could get in solving that murder, since the County Prosecutor wanted much more than just circumstantial evidence in bringing it to trial. Before all was said and done, the detectives, including Lane, would gather hundreds of bits of evidence and amass thousands of pages of documents. It would be a long, tiring, very tough road. And that road ran right through a new murder case that popped up near the Grays Harbor resort community of Ocean Shores.

6

VIRGINIA

Whatever time and energy GHSO detectives could spend on Elaine McCollum's case came to a screeching halt on August 26, 1991. On that day the detectives had another brutal murder on their hands in the county. It all began when Detective Gary Parfitt, who had collected evidence at the McCollum murder scene, went out to Ocean Shores, a new and expanding resort community on the Pacific Ocean. Parfitt sat down with a teenager named Becky, who had an incredible story to tell. A friend of hers named Derek, who had recently dropped by the gift shop that Becky's parents owned, showed her some Polaroid photos he'd just taken with some friends of his. In the photos were depictions of Derek, Cyndi and Donna. The photos had been taken at Virginia "Ginny" Barsic's apartment in nearby Hogan's Corner.

Then, almost as an afterthought, Derek told Becky, "You know the lady that lives at the apartment in Hogan's Corner?"

Becky said she knew the lady was named Ginny.

Derek added, "We killed her." And then he indicated that the others in the Polaroid shots had helped in killing the woman, or at least had viewed the woman's body after she was dead.

Becky told Detective Parfitt, "I kind of grinned, and said, 'I don't believe you.' But he replied, 'You don't believe me? We were there, and Ginny started freaking out, and the next thing I know, she was dead.'"

Not knowing if this was true or not, Parfitt called for backup before heading to Virginia Barsic's apartment in Hogan's Corner. Soon his backup was coming from Montesano, and it included Detectives Bill Stocks, Doug Smythe, S. C. Larson and Lane Youmans.

Stocks was the first detective on the scene, and since he saw no police activity around Ginny Barsic's apartment, he decided to drive five more minutes into Ocean Shores. While Detective Parfitt was still there, Stocks spoke with Becky and also believed that she might be telling the truth. The young woman was composed, straightforward and didn't seem to be making this up.

By the time Detective Stocks reached Ginny's apartment, Detective Larson was just driving up as well. The two detectives started walking toward the building, which contained an upstairs and downstairs apartment, and as they did so, they noticed reddish brown drag marks on the cement sidewalk and on the grass. The detectives peered through the windows of the downstairs apartment and saw more reddish brown marks on the floor of the kitchen. From his vantage point Stocks could see a piece of paper on the kitchen table. On the paper was written *Fuck you!*

Fairly certain they were looking at a crime scene, and possibly a murder scene, Stocks went to a nearby phone booth (cell phones were a new item around that time), and Larson followed some more reddish brown drag marks over the grass and toward a lot behind the local VFW hall. As Stocks spoke into the phone to chief criminal investigator Mike Whelan, Larson continued following the reddish brown marks to an area covered with a small amount of dirt. It was apparent right away that this was the ending spot for the reddish brown marks.

Sticking out of a mound of freshly dug dirt was a female's arm, part of a leg and her face. The woman had curly brown hair and she'd been savagely beaten around the face. One of her eyes had been pierced by a sharp instrument. From the description he already had, Detective Larson was pretty sure this was Virginia Barsic.

It started to rain hard, and Larson placed a tarp over the body of the woman. Detective Stocks advised Detective Smythe, who was on his way to the scene, "Get on your grubbies, Doug. It's raining and it's a muddy mess around here."

Lane Youmans arrived shortly after the others and was soon put in charge of the scene. He recalled later, "When I arrived and did my initial assessment, it was getting dark and the clouds were rolling in. I decided that we would leave Virginia where she was until morning, and we covered up the dirt pile and all of the footprints and drag marks with plastic. The footsteps were perfect, and I planned on casting many of them the next morning. I stayed in my vehicle parked in the driveway to protect the scene. My county vehicle was a dark blue Ford Aerostar, nicknamed the war wagon, because I kept everything in there to process any type of crime scene. I also kept a sleeping bag and enough food and water to last me five days."

Meanwhile, Stocks and Parfitt went to Ocean Shores and began picking up more stories about how Ginny Barsic had invited some local teenagers over to her apartment because she was lonely. Her husband was a fisherman out in the Pacific, and he was gone for months at a time. The stories revolved around how six teenagers had gone to Ginny's place and started drinking alcohol. After a while things got out of hand, and Ginny asked them to leave. Instead, Ray Baca, one of the teenagers, decided to kill her, mainly to see what it was actually like to kill a person. Just exactly what he had done would come to light soon enough once the detectives began collecting all the evidence. And the most important portions of that would come from Ray Baca himself.

Ginny Barsic and the footprints might have been covered up with plastic tarps, but not even Lane, who had been to plenty of crime scenes over the years, expected what happened next. He remembered, "As night came on, the skies opened up. It rained so hard that I was hardly able to sleep with the rain pounding on the roof of the war wagon, directly over my head. When dawn broke, I went to the field to check the footprints. It had rained so hard that all of the impressions were flattened out and now useless. I'd seen rain before on crime scenes, but nothing like this. To say I wasn't happy doesn't begin to describe how I felt. But I was about to get lucky. The idiots who had done this murder had hardly cleaned up at all in the house where it occurred."

In the morning hours of August 27, the detectives entered the apartment and took photographs of blood in the kitchen and hallway. They also took swabs of blood for evidence. In the hallway there were several holes punched into the Sheetrock of the walls, and spatters of blood surrounded the holes. There were what appeared to be knife stabs in the bathroom walls, with blood surrounding the stab marks. There were even several bloody shoe prints on the floors of the hallway and kitchen area. All of this pointed to a very violent murder within Virginia Barsic's residence.

Lane Youmans recalled of the crime scene in the apartment: "I had total control over this crime scene. In the past there would be defense attorneys who asked during a trial, 'Who was in charge of the crime scene?' He would get answers such as 'the sheriff, Detective so-and-so, Sergeant so-and-so.' It might be three or four different people who had been in charge at one time or another, during one crime scene investigation. That wasn't going to happen this time.

"When I first went in, I just stood at the entryway and stared at the scene. I didn't do any crime scene tech work at all. I spent about ten to fifteen minutes taking in all I could, putting a game plan together. Then I walked to every pertinent location and took photographs of everything before anything was touched. I dusted the hallway and got shoe prints all up and down the hallway. This was fortunate, since the footprints outside had been ruined by the downpour.

"There was blood everywhere. There had been some attempts at cleaning up the scene, but it was poorly done. A person had even taken a shower afterward in the apartment to try and wash blood off their body. An individual had stuffed his bloody underwear in the toilet tank. It was a very shoddy attempt at a cover-up."

In late morning Detectives Stocks and Smythe walked over one more time to where Virginia Barsic's body lay.

As they did so, the coroner, a medical examiner (ME) tech and a vehicle from Coleman's Mortuary arrived. The coroner and detectives all observed multiple stab wounds to Ginny's neck region, breasts and torso. These wounds obviously corresponded to all the blood found in her apartment. Finally Ginny's body was placed into a body bag and was taken away to a mortuary.

Because of all the stories coming out of Ocean Shores, especially the one from Becky, a statewide alert went out for the six teenagers suspected of murdering Virginia Barsic. These six teenagers were to some degree responsible, and none of them were criminal masterminds. The oldest, Marilyn, had just turned twenty, and the youngest two, Cyndi and Donna, were only fourteen. Instead of heading out of state as soon as possible, most of them hung around the immediate area after the murder. Ray even cooked up a crazy scheme to go back to Hogan's Corner, unearth Ginny's body, drag it into her apartment, then burn the whole place down. This scheme never got off the ground. In fact, Ray, Cyndi and Donna were wandering around the streets of Aberdeen after the murder. They were walking down Wishkah Street when an Aberdeen police officer happened to drive by. This officer had a description of the teenagers connected to the Hogan's Corner murder, and this trio looked like some of them.

The officer pulled over at 11:05 A.M. on August 2 and questioned the trio. Ray and Cyndi tried giving fake names, but Donna gave her real name. The officer asked them to come down to the Aberdeen police headquarters and all three complied without making a fuss. Soon they were being questioned and pointing fingers at each other as to what had happened in Ginny's apartment.

Even though Derek and Marilyn made it a little farther

away to Olympia, it wasn't long before they were picked
up as well.

Ray was unexpectedly cooperative with the police,
even though he was the most involved in the murder. He
willingly went with detectives back to Ginny's apartment
and began telling them and showing them how things had
gone down. Right in front of Detectives Lane Youmans
and Doug Smythe, Ray said that there had been an argument with Ginny, and she'd locked herself in her bathroom. Ray said he was able to talk her out into the
hallway and reached out toward her as if he were going to
give her a hug. She went to hug him, and he grabbed her
and threw her on her back on the hallway floor. Ray was
handed a pillow by Derek and started trying to suffocate
Ginny. But this wasn't working, so Ray jabbed two of
his fingers into Ginny's right eye socket clear down to the
second knuckle. Then he gave her a choke hold he had
learned in karate lessons.

Thinking she was dead, Ray began to walk away. Derek
spoke up and said, "Hey, she's still moving." Ray went
back and did two or three karate twists on her neck, in
essence to break her neck. But that didn't work, either.
So Ray grabbed a screwdriver and jabbed it into Virginia's
eye clear down to the handle of the screwdriver.

By all reasoning, Ginny should have been dead at that
point. But she wasn't. In a frenzy Ray went to the kitchen,
grabbed a butcher knife and began stabbing Ginny in the
face, the chest and in her back. He stabbed her so many
times that he, the floor and the wall were spattered in
blood. Finally, after an absolute butchery, Virginia Barsic
was dead.

Ray and Derek grabbed ahold of her body and dragged
it out of the apartment, across the sidewalk and lawn, to
a dirt mound behind the VFW building. They covered

the body with some dirt, but it was a sloppy job at best, because it was so dark outside at the time. All during his recitation Ray seemed almost proud of what he had done. He showed no signs of remorse.

After all six teenagers were in custody, it was never a matter of proving they had been at Virginia Barsic's apartment when she was murdered; rather, it was of determining the amount of responsibility for each individual. Ray, Derek, John and Marilyn were held in the GHSO Jail, while the two fourteen-year-old girls were held in the Juvenile Detention Center. Both Ray and Derek were eventually charged with first-degree murder, while the others got lesser charges of accessory to murder.

An obituary in the Aberdeen *Daily World* stated that Virginia had been born in Bremerton, Washington, in April 1941, raised in Ketchi-kan, Alaska, and met and married Gregory Barsic in San Diego in 1987. Virginia had won several poetry awards, including the Golden Poet Award.

For the next several weeks the *Daily World* ran stories about Virginia Barsic, Ray Baca and the others involved. The region was shocked by the brutality and senselessness of the crime.

When the trial for the chief instigator, Ray Baca, occurred at the Grays Harbor County Courthouse in Montesano, David Foscue was the judge, Baca's defense attorney was Jim Heard, and Steward Menefee was the main prosecutor. In years to come, Menefee would play a very important role in David Gerard's life.

When put on the stand, all the teenagers gave the same general story line that Ray Baca had told investigators about how the murder had occurred. The most chilling testimony of all came from Ray Baca, who seemed almost detached from what he was telling. He spoke of trying to smother Virginia with a pillow, trying to break her neck, gouging her eyes with his fingers, stabbing her with a screwdriver and finally finishing her off with a knife. Part of the testimony left the court observers gasping. Ray Baca spoke of drinking some of Virginia Barsic's blood and painting a design on his chest with her blood.

> *Q: Why did you drink the blood?*
> *A: First kill. For strength. For protection. I painted a tree and the earth on my chest.*
> *Q: Why did you need protection?*
> *A: Because I didn't want her to get up again. I told her, "You're dead. I killed you." But she would sit up again. I was trying to get her to stop moving. With the knife I finally got her to stop moving.*

For his heinous crime Ray Baca was found guilty of first-degree murder. Lane noted one important fact about his own participation in the trial. He said later, "In the past there would be more than one officer who had been in charge of a murder scene. Not this time. When the defense attorney asked me on the stand who was in charge of the Barsic crime scene, I simply answered, 'I was. It was my responsibility to make the decisions concerning what was done.' I knew that in closing arguments he was going to try and point out to the jury that no one was actually in charge of the crime scene. That, of course, didn't work for him, and it kind of took the wind out of his sails. He didn't even mention it in closing."

* * *

As things would prove later, this aspect of one law enforcement officer in charge of a murder scene would help paint David Gerard into a corner. His defense attorney on two different cases could not come back and say that either no one, or too many officers, had been in charge of a crime scene.

In the long run, none of what happened to Virginia Barsic would lead back to the murder of Elaine McCollum on the Weyco Haul Road. In fact, it would have two diametrically opposed consequences—one good and one bad. The bad consequence was that it took away all the resources that might have looked into the McCollum murder for a greater length of time in 1991. On the flip side the Barsic crime scene helped the GHSO detectives hone their skills. And they were going to need all of those for the McCollum murder, and one more that had not yet occurred. Steward Menefee always wanted as much evidence as possible before he went to trial. And the detectives were going to need every bit, no matter how small, when it came to anything concerning David Gerard.

The Virginia Barsic murder may not have led to the Elaine McCollum murder, but just around the bend was another set of murders that would lead directly back to McCollum's death. What made these murders so hard to link back to McCollum was that they occurred in a very different manner. MO and location would not be the common denominator. What would be was a link to one man: David Allen Gerard.

7

UP IN FLAMES

February 15, 1995

A logging trucker was driving his rig down East Hoquiam Road around 4:45 A.M. on February 15, 1995, when he glanced over to the side of the road and was stunned. Smoke and flames were erupting from a house beside the road, and the driver grabbed a .22 pistol he had in the cab of his vehicle, stepped outside and fired several shots into the air to alert anyone inside the house and neighbors as well.

Ernie Shumate, who lived with his family right next door to the burning house, was having a restless night, with bad dreams. Things that occurred within his dreams, and noise from outside the house, blended into unreality. The gunshots were real, however, and Ernie sprang out of bed to witness his neighbor's home filled with flames and smoke. Ernie knew that sixty-six-year-old Patricia McDonnell lived there, and so did Patricia's thirty-four year old daughter Patty Rodriguez and Patty's two sons,

Matthew, eight, and Joshua, six. There was also some guy named David who lived in the house part-time. He was Patty's boyfriend. Or at least sometimes boyfriend. David seemed to be a lot more attached to her than she was to him.

Ernie threw on some clothes, rushed next door and saw that the fire was too intense near the front of the house for him to enter. So he moved to a side entrance, a sliding glass door, and managed to get it open. Poking his head inside, Ernie yelled for the residents to wake up and escape, but he heard no reply. Not even the two dogs in the house made any noise, and Ernie heard no smoke alarms going off. Ernie was soon pushed back by the smoke and flames.

Rick Doyle, who lived across the street from the Mc-Donnell residence, also rushed to the house. Just like Ernie Shumate, Doyle was pushed back by the intense heat and flames. He had to stand helplessly outside the house and watch it burn.

Ernie Shumate later told a *Daily World* reporter, "We knew they were in there, and we knew there wasn't anything we could do. Most of the house was already on fire."

Volunteer firefighters from Wishkah Fire District 10 arrived on the scene within fourteen minutes of Ernie calling it in. By the time they arrived, the house was fully engulfed in flames. It took seventeen firefighters to battle the blaze, and by the time they finally had the fire beaten down, all the occupants were found to be dead inside the house. It was one of the worst fires in Grays Harbor history.

Both print and television news station reporters were soon on the scene, and Ernie Shumate told them that at around 1:00 A.M., he had picked up his children from a dance and had noticed that lights were still on in the McDonnell residence next door. McDonnell had recently injured her knee and was sleeping on a reclining chair in the front room. Shumate said that the boys often slept on the living-room floor near a woodstove. In fact, firefighters found the boys' bodies on the floor, and McDonnell's body twenty feet away from the recliner, as if she might have made an attempt at escape and been overcome by flames or smoke. Patty Rodriguez's body was found sprawled across a bed in a back bedroom.

After a preliminary observation of the scene, Fire Chief Bill Knannline said there was no indication that the fire was anything besides accidental. He surmised the fire might have smoldered for quite a while near the woodstove before engulfing the whole house. The woodstove appeared to be the point of origin.

Friends of the victims began to surround the house in stunned silence after the fire. All that remained were smoldering ruins and two vehicles in the driveway. In fact, the fire had been so hot, it had scorched those vehicles. A friend of McDonnell's, Marsha Peterson, was returning from Seattle when she heard on her car radio about a fire near Hoquiam. No name was given about who owned the house, but Peterson had one name run through her head as she listened to the news report: *Pat.*

When Peterson got to the scene, she joined the others in silence, staring at the burned house. Peterson later told a reporter that she had asked McDonnell to go on the trip to Seattle with her, but the woman had remained home instead to take care of her grandsons. It had cost her, her life.

Peterson told the reporter that some logs that were visible in the front yard were for McDonnell, who was going to make a new flower bed with them. Now that flower bed would never be constructed. The whole scene was surreal to Peterson. It seemed impossible that all her friends inside were dead.

Rick Doyle, who had tried saving the victims, as Ernie Shumate had, said, "It was tough. A helpless feeling." As he held his two daughters, one who was in the same kindergarten class as Joshua Rodriguez, Doyle talked to reporters about how suddenly a tragedy could occur. Doyle comforted his daughters, knowing that the loss of their friends, the boys next door, was going to hit them especially hard.

Clay Micheau, a family friend who had actually lived in the house for a while, said that the burned house contained smoke alarms, and they had worked only weeks previously when they went off while Patricia McDonnell was cooking. Clay had actually been there at the time. The *Daily World* reported, *It's not known if the smoke detectors now did not work, or simply failed to wake the family.*

Patricia McDonnell had lived in that house most of her life, and had raised two boys and two girls there, one of them being Patty. Patricia knew almost everyone in the neighborhood, and when her husband was alive, they had hosted barbecues and square dances: Everyone in the neighborhood liked the McDonnells for their open nature and friendly ways. They had seen Patricia often working in the garden in front of the house.

Patty Rodriguez, meanwhile, had been recently divorced and living in Arizona with her two boys, until they all returned to the area, only four months previously. When Patty's ex-husband, Sergio Rodriguez, of Aberdeen, was contacted about the tragedy, he was understandably distraught. In a telephone interview with a reporter, Sergio could barely speak, he was so overwhelmed. "What can I say?" he declared. "There are no words to say." And then he added, "Patty and her mom were wonderful people. We always got along, even after the divorce." Sergio had been glad when Patty and the boys had moved back to the area, after living in Arizona. Sergio had stayed in the Grays Harbor area while Patty and the boys had been away, and he especially missed the boys.

The last time he had seen his boys was only a few days previously. Sergio had visited the home on East Hoquiam Road and said of Patty and the boys, "It was fine, then. They were fine."

Early Saturday morning a neighbor of the McDonnell residence had phoned Sergio and told him about the fire. That person hopefully asked if the boys had been spending the night with Sergio. They, of course, had not done so. When Sergio rushed to the scene, he was in time to see the firefighters still battling the blaze. But all hopes that those who were inside had survived was gone.

Perhaps the most ironic circumstance in this tragedy was that Patricia McDonnell's son, Patty's brother Brian McDonnell, was a volunteer firefighter in the area. He spoke of his sister Patty as a loving mother, and Joshua as a spitting image of her. Growing up, he and Patty had been great friends, and Brian spoke about how she always stood her ground and stuck up for herself. She was outgoing, funny and a quick learner.

Brian declared, "The house was one where the kids were usually roller-skating up and down the hallway. There were dogs barking, and I was those boys' rough-and-tumble uncle. They were typical boys, full of energy."

* * *

What made the fire in the McDonnell home seem so accidental in nature, even to Brian, was that on the same day, fires claimed a total of sixteen children and five adults nationwide. Beside the four on Hoquiam Road, one adult and six children had died in a fire in Burbank, Illinois. Even with smoke alarms blaring, they had not survived the blaze. That same day in Moorhead, Minnesota, a woman and her six children perished in a house fire. And in Columbus, Ohio, three family members—an adult and two kids—died in a blaze. All these fires made the fire in the McDonnell household seem like no more than a tragic and deadly accident. An accident that could occur in any home that had a woodstove or faulty heater.

And if that wasn't enough, a few days later in Grays Harbor County, another fire nearly took the life of a woman and her sixteen-year-old son, near Aberdeen. Karen Tuffery and her son, Brandon, clad only in pajamas, escaped from their mobile home. As they stood outside in the cold air, the mobile home quickly burned to the ground. The mobile home had not been hooked up to electricity, and a woodstove acted as a heater, while kerosene lanterns were used for lighting.

It had been a near escape for Karen and Brandon. Karen had awakened to glimpse a strange red glow on the ceiling of her bedroom. She opened the bedroom door to see fire and smoke down the hallway near Brandon's room. Karen ran outside to Brandon's window and screamed for him to wake up. He awakened, and tried escaping through the hallway, but the smoke and fire were too intense. So he grabbed a chair in his room, smashed the bedroom window and tumbled out that way. Both Karen and Brandon considered how lucky they were, in comparison to what had happened at the McDonnell household. Their near escape reinforced the scenario that

Patricia McDonnell, Patty Rodriguez and her two sons had perished in a tragic accident.

Out of routine procedure, GHSO detective Gary Parfitt began investigating the house fire, and Lane Youmans attended the autopsies of Patty Rodriguez, Patricia McDonnell, Joshua and Matthew Rodriguez. In some ways Detective Parfitt's route to becoming a GHSO detective was just as colorful as that of Lane Youmans's. Parfitt had been in the U.S. Marine Corps and was stationed all over the world. After the Marine Corps he decided to join GHSO. There was just one big obstacle to overcome. He was forty-eight years old and going into the police academy with some guys twenty-five years younger than he was. Nonetheless, Parfitt started working out at a local park and climbing over walls there, which he knew would be his toughest challenge. It all paid off. Parfitt came in fourth in his class that graduated from the academy.

When Detective Parfitt looked at the fire situation, Mrs. McDonnell and the boys had been badly burned from the fire. The boys had been found on the floor of the living room near the woodstove, where Detective Parfitt believed the fire had originated. Patricia McDonnell was found on the floor of the dining room next to the living room, several feet away from a sliding glass door. She had possibly been trying to escape, but was overcome by the fire. Patty Rodriguez was discovered in bed in a back bedroom, the farthest room from the living room, which was the supposed point of origin of the fire. There were some signs of burning on her body, but the body was intact.

Dr. Daniel Selove performed the autopsies and determined that Patty had died from smoke inhalation. She

had also sustained a fracture on the right side of her skull
from what was believed to have been falling debris, possibly from the ceiling. Patricia McDonnell and the boys
had no soot in their throats, which normally occurs when
someone inhales smoke from a fire. Dr. Selove believed
the lack of soot could have occurred from a blast of superheated air, which might have killed them. He also
found that Mrs. McDonnell had a bad heart, which might
have been a factor in her death. Perhaps she had been
overcome by a heart attack while trying to reach safety.

What was intriguing from Detective Parfitt's point of
view was that Patty Rodriguez had supposedly broken up
with her boyfriend the night before she and the others
died in the fire. Her boyfriend's name was David Gerard.

Detective Parfitt asked Lane to contact Gerard and
arrange for him to come to the sheriff's office for an interview. Lane phoned Gerard at his friend Polly Miller's
house and spoke with him. (The same Polly Miller who
later wondered why David Gerard had called her in
1999 just to say that he was in the town of Forks, when,
in actuality, he had just beaten Frankie Cochran with a
hammer.)

Lane identified himself and told Gerard that the sheriff's office was investigating a house fire on East Hoquiam Road. Lane asked Gerard if he would come down
to the sheriff's office in Montesano, since he and other
detectives were talking with family and friends of the
deceased. Lane said later, "I was stunned when he answered, 'No, I don't want to.' I asked him why not, and all
he would say was because he didn't want to. He would
not explain further."

Talking with Gerard was like talking to a recalcitrant
child who did not want to do something an adult asked

him to do. The child's one and only response would be "No, I don't want to!"

After his conversation with Gerard, Lane Youmans hung up the phone and told Detective Parfitt what had just occurred. It was such an odd response from Gerard that they both hopped into Parfitt's vehicle and drove four miles to the Miller residence on Wynoochee Valley Road.

Once they arrived there, the two detectives went up and knocked on the door. David Gerard answered the door and stepped outside to talk with them. It was late in the evening and the trio stood outside in the cool air, talking. Gerard expanded upon his earlier refusal to come down to the sheriff's office by saying he didn't like cops. The detectives explained that they were talking to a lot of people, and not picking on him, just because he was Patty's ex-boyfriend. One thing they really wanted to know was when was the last time Gerard had seen the victims alive, especially Patty. The detectives added that Gerard wasn't under arrest, and that he could follow them to the sheriff's office, where everyone might be more comfortable. He could leave that office at any time.

Hearing that said, Gerard seemed to change his mood, and he agreed to meet the detectives back at the office in Montesano. Once the detectives got there, Gerard arrived a short time later, and they all went into a break room in the complex. They sat down, and Lane took notes as Detective Parfitt began the interview. Asked about the evening prior to the fire, Gerard said that he and Patty Rodriguez had been at Muddy Waters, a cocktail lounge in south Aberdeen with two of Patty's friends. It was at that location, Gerard said, that he and Patty had a "little spat." Gerard added that he soon left and went to the Pioneer Cocktail Lounge, about fifteen miles away in Montesano, with a person named Steve Stoken and someone Gerard only knew by the name of Mike. Gerard said that he never knew Mike's last name.

All three drank for a while there, and then they went to the Tyee Lounge in Olympia, according to Gerard, which was thirty miles farther down the road. After drinking at the lounge for a while, they all went to the Red Barn Restaurant in Grand Mound, where they ate breakfast around 2:00 A.M. After breakfast they drove back to the Muddy Waters Lounge, where one man drove Gerard's truck back to his brother's place at the Kimberly Apartments in Hoquiam. Gerard said that he was in no shape to drive the truck, and that's why the other guy had done it. Gerard said he couldn't recall if Steve or Mike had driven him home.

Gerard added that he had slept for a few hours after a night of drinking, took a shower, then headed to the Millers' house outside of Montesano. It was there, Gerard said, that he first learned about the house fire at the Rodriguez/McDonnell residence. The Millers were absolutely shocked when Gerard showed up at their door. They had heard about the fire on the morning news and had assumed that Gerard had perished in the fire as well. It was like a ghost suddenly appearing at their door.

Both detectives noted that Gerard seemed calm as he spoke about where he had been and what he had been doing on the night of February 14 and early morning of February 15. Neither detective was confrontational, since Detective Parfitt had already examined the burned house and surmised that the fire had been accidental in nature. Parfitt agreed with the others that it had probably been caused by a faulty woodstove used for heating. Detective Parfitt asked Gerard about the woodstove, and Gerard said the family had been having problems with it. Gerard described the stove as being so clogged with creosote that you could hit it with your hand and hear the sound of soot breaking free and falling down the pipe.

Detective Parfitt asked Gerard if there had been smoke detectors in the house, and where they were located. Gerard replied that there were two, one by the doorway between the living room and dining room, and the second at the end of the hallway by Patty's room. He added that several days before the fire, Mrs. McDonnell asked him to purchase new batteries for the smoke detectors. Gerard added that he didn't know if she had ever installed them. As Gerard spoke about the smoke detectors, he became more emotional.

Toward the end of the interview, Lane gave Gerard his business card and told him if he thought of anything else to give him a call. Gerard's response to this was so unusual that even years later Lane recalled in exact detail what had occurred.

Lane Youmans said, "At that point Gerard grew silent, sat in his chair, legs spread apart, leaning somewhat forward, staring at the floor. His forearms were resting on his knees, and he was holding my business card between his thumb and forefinger in the center of the card, slowing turning the card by pushing the corners of it downward with his left index finger. He stopped talking, so we stopped talking and just watched him. The three of us sat quietly in the break room, Gerard staring at the floor in an almost catatonic state, while Detective Parfitt and I sat there studying him. After around five minutes I asked Gerard if there was something he wanted to tell us. He didn't look up, just stared at the floor and then slowly replied, 'No.'"

The interview was over. Gerard silently rose and walked out the door without saying another word. After Gerard was gone, the detectives discussed his strange behavior. They finally concluded it was due to grief or feelings of guilt for not having put the batteries in the smoke detectors himself. After all, Parfitt was good at his job, and by all indications it looked as if the fire had been accidental. Parfitt had taken some photos of the scene, and those pointed to "accidental status" as well. But Gerard's behavior had been so bizarre at the end of the interview that the detectives began looking more closely into the house fire. Both of them got a "hinky" feeling about David Gerard.

Since Patty Rodriguez had suffered some kind of head injury, either before or after death, the detectives returned to the remnants of her bedroom to try and find out why. Lane Youmans shot some photos of her room and the attic area directly above her bed. They then searched the area around Patty's bed and found a piece of burned two-by-six lumber that was about eighteen inches in length. The ceiling had burned through, and it appeared that the piece of lumber had fallen from the ceiling and had struck her on the head. She might have risen from bed and was either hit in the head by that lumber, or it occurred a short time later as she was trying to escape. Her legs were over the side of the bed, with her feet almost touching the floor. Patty was on her back, and her hands were up by her head. Her arms had been bent at the elbows—as if in the process of moving, she became incapacitated by smoke and fell back on the bed. It could have been at that point that the board from the ceiling fell down and hit Patty in the head.

The detectives went through the remnants of the house and looked at every aspect of it. They noted that the roof area over Patty's room was partially collapsed, and the roof was completely gone over the front room and kitchen area. For the first time Lane took notes about the woodstove, which now jutted out of the rubble of the front room. The boys had been sleeping in the front room near the stove and may have been the first to succumb to its smoke, or overcome by a blast of superheated air, as Dr. Selove conjectured.

Lane went and spoke with Dr. Selove again about the injury to Patty's head. Dr. Selove described it as having been caused by either someone swinging a heavy object, which hit her in the head, or being struck by a falling piece of lumber, end first. Of course, that seemed the most logical explanation to Lane at the time. It was only later, after Frankie Cochran had been hit in the side of the head by a hammer swung by David Gerard, that other deadly scenarios would occur to him.

Brian McDonnell also began to have his doubts about what had occurred to his mother, his sister and her two boys. It was mainly from David Gerard's strange behavior after the fire, but also the way he was with Patty before the fire. Brian said that Gerard was very jealous if she even spoke to another man. It didn't matter if she'd known the man for years, and they were just friends.

Brian said, "There was a get-together one time at my mom's house, and everybody was joking and having a good time. But Gerard just kind of sat in the background, glowering about something. He wasn't participating. He seemed to be angry about something. I didn't particularly like him even then."

* * *

Detective Parfitt continued to work on the case for a while longer to try and tie up loose ends. He was able to identify who Steve Stoken was, but Parfitt was unable to locate Stoken. As for "Mike," whom Gerard had mentioned, Parfitt was not able to identify that person at all. After a while, the Rodriguez/McDonnell fire was put on the back burner and the case files stuffed into a cardboard box and placed on a shelf near Detective Parfitt's desk.

Lane Youmans, however, was still uneasy about the whole episode. Even though everything pointed to an accidental fire, caused by a faulty woodstove and the lack of batteries in the smoke alarms, there was something just not right about the whole thing. *Especially* David Gerard's unorthodox behavior while being interviewed. Lane said later, "Detective Parfitt was the department expert when it came to fire investigation. He was the expert because he had some training. We had access to fire investigation expert Richard Carman, who was one of the best fire investigators around. But he charged several thousand dollars when he investigated a fire. He had been used on several fire scenes by the department, but not this one. I always felt that a fire where four people died should have been thoroughly investigated, and to hell with the cost. I knew death scenes, and could read them and reconstruct what happened. Unfortunately, I didn't know fire scenes. I hadn't had the training about what to recognize, what to look for. It all just looked like burned wood to me.

"I could find the obvious signs of arson, like pour patterns where a flammable liquid was poured on the floor and ignited. But it takes an expert to read the subtle changes in the charring on wood. Detective Parfitt had gone on the scene while the firefighters were still there, and concluded that the origin of the fire was the woodstove, while everything around it had been reduced to ashes. The theory was the stove was the cause, and Gerard supported that theory with his information about the creosote. More should have been done, but hindsight is always perfect. No photographs were taken of the inside of the stove pipes, or the interior of the woodstove, or even the smoke detectors. The red flags either weren't there, or we just didn't see them."

There may have been no red flags concerning David Gerard at the moment, but there would be plenty as time moved inexorably on toward his assault on Frankie Cochran. And there would emerge a photographic clue right in plain sight, which was not obvious unless you knew where to look. The photo had been shot by a news photographer outside Patty Rodriguez's house. It was only much later that Lane would look at that photo and say, "Wow!"

Unfortunately, in the meantime, before that happened, another woman would be murdered under mysterious circumstances a year after the Rodriguez/McDonnell fire. And this woman's body would turn up on the Weyco Haul Road, not far from where Elaine McCollum's body had been found. Not unlike Elaine, this woman, too, would suffer horrendous injuries before dying. She would be butchered in what could be termed a blood frenzy.

8

BLOOD FRENZY ON THE WEYCO HAUL ROAD

Lane Youmans awoke on the morning of August 3, 1996, and got ready for work at the Montesano sheriff's headquarters as usual. His morning routine was suddenly broken by a phone call he received. Another woman's body had just been found on the Weyco Haul Road. Lane said later, "I shuddered and thought, 'Oh shit! Not again!'"

The woman's body had initially been spotted by a Weyerhauser employee heading to work. Before any deputies could shut off the Weyco Haul Road, someone spotted two men in a truck slowly driving down the road. When officers found these men, they were questioned and said that they had been looking for deer. Their story was checked out, and eventually they were eliminated as suspects.

Lane dressed quickly and hurried to the scene, where

he found a cluster of officers already gathered a half mile
from the west end of the road. They were all standing near
a woman's body. Lane walked up toward the body, which
was on the south side of the gravel road, with her head
pointing to the west. She was a white female, lying on her
back and fully clothed. Her face and chest were saturated
with blood. Lane began jotting down notes of what he
saw at the scene:

*The temperature is in the low 50s; the sky is partially
cloudy. The sky to the west is lit up from the lights of
Cosmopolis and Aberdeen. There are machinery sounds
coming from the Weyerhauser sawmill, and no other
sounds are detected.*

*The body is next to a hillside that is approximately 45
degrees in angle. On the south side, there is high grass,
several trees and then a steep embankment down to Blue
Slough Road. It is possible that the victim tried leaving
the scene. The suspect got out of a vehicle and tried to
find her on foot, leaving his shoe prints along the north
side of the road. He got back in the vehicle and acceler-
ated quickly, spinning out his tire.*

*Only one of the victim's shoes is dirty and there is no
grass found on them, indicating she did not try to run into
the woods. The dirt on the one shoe is from when a knife
attack occurred and she fell to the ground. At that point,
the victim was possibly struck on the right side of her
head with a blunt object, possibly knocking her senseless
or unconscious. The suspect then used a knife when she
was on the ground, and she may have been in a sitting position. There are no defensive wounds on her hands, but
there is blood on both of them, indicating that when the
attacker used the knife on her throat, she was alive and
conscious. She grabbed her throat, getting blood on her
hands, and she may have rubbed her hands on her pant*

legs, leaving a blood stain there. That stain has voids in it, indicating the jeans were wrinkled, possibly when she was in a sitting position.

The victim then lay face down and was bleeding profusely from the throat injury. The suspect began stabbing her on various spots on her back. There are a group of stab wounds around her shoulders, several on her lower back and buttocks. It would have been difficult to see her if she was lying alongside the road, and the suspect's headlights were probably on, illuminating the scene.

She was rolled over and dragged approximately two feet west, and was lying on her back when the suspect began stabbing her in the face, chest and vaginal area. These wounds are mostly post mortem, and were possibly done to make sure the victim was dead. The victim had a purse slung across her body so that the purse was under her left arm. The suspect took the knife and cut the two straps next to the purse, leaving two cut marks in the soil to an approximate depth of ³⁄₈ of an inch.

There is no indication of a vehicle accelerating rapidly from this area. It appears the suspect drove normally from the location after obtaining the purse. There were a number of Kleenex-type tissues on the road just west of the body and a partial piece of Maalox wrapper, indicating the possibility that the suspect opened the purse and looked through it, pulling these items out in the process.

It didn't take a long time to process this scene, since there were few physical items attached to it. Lane collected all the relevant items on the road, placed the victim in a body bag, then turned her over to a vehicle that would take her to Coleman's Mortuary.

* * *

Lane Youmans said later, "We worked the scene until two P.M., and by then, it was hot and I was tired. There was little evidence to collect, and I felt that we had collected everything worthwhile. I planned on driving west to Aberdeen to get something to eat, but something told me that I should drive east to the end of the Weyco Haul Road just to see if there was anything else to collect."

The detectives had the Weyco Haul Road sealed off during the early-morning hours, but Weyerhauser wanted the road reopened as soon as possible for their logging trucks. For that reason Lane decided his lunch could wait. About two-tenths of a mile from the murder scene, over a rise in the road, Lane saw several items lying in the roadway. He stopped his vehicle and checked them out, discovering the items were a used condom, a condom wrapper and seven paper napkins. The condom still contained liquid semen and none of the items had gravel or dust on them.

Just as he had done at scene one, Lane began taking notations about scene two. He wrote: *At this location the suspect's vehicle parked in a location where the road dips down so that it would not be immediately visible to vehicles traveling east on the haul road, but anyone in the vehicle could see the headlights shining over their top. They could also detect vehicles approaching from the east as the headlights would shine off the trees. It appears as though the vehicle began to pull off to the south side of the haul road, and then proceeded a short distance where it was turned around, and driven back to the same location and stopped in the middle of the road.*

A condom wrapper, condom and napkins at that spot indicates that the suspect and victim had sex there. They most likely had sex in the vehicle and then the suspect dropped the condom, condom wrapper and used napkins

*out the driver's side window. Just west of that location,
there is one mark in the middle of the road where a tire
spun out which is west of the condom. This indicates the
possibility that the vehicle is a front wheel drive vehicle.*

*The width of that mark is approximately seven inches, al-
though there is no discernible tire track. The tire track
found along the south side of the road is about 5¼ inches
wide. On some branches by a downed tree next to the tire
track, there was some used motor oil on the branch, indicating that when the vehicle drove over the branch, the oil
pan came in contact with the limb which is about eight
inches off the ground. It's very possibly an older car, a
smaller sedan with narrow tires approximately 13" or 14".*

*There are approximately nine shoe prints found along
the north side of the Weyco Haul Road just east of the
condom. The shoe prints are 33" apart and consist pri-
marily of the sole and toe portions of the shoe. The shoe
print consists of bars that are about 1½ inches in length
and triangles are present. The shoe prints appear to be
heading west. Directly south of the condom there is some
brush that has been beaten down, as though someone had
entered the blackberries and other briars for about three
to four feet and then backed out.*

*Between Scene #2 and Scene #1, the body recovery
site, the north side of the haul road is a steep bank leading down to the Blue Slough Road, and there is thick
brush between the two roads. On the south side of the
road, there are mostly steep hills and one dead-end logging road just west of the condom location. With the
amount of light present, you can only see a few feet off
either side of the road. Visibility is next to nothing when
you enter the brush.*

Lane photographed and collected those items and
made a plaster cast of a tire track he found along the

south side of the road close to where the items were. There was an apparent acceleration mark in the gravel next to the condom, but not enough details to make a cast in that area. Unlike the McCollum crime scene, there was not much in the way of tire tracks on the roadway.

Lane later learned that the plaster cast he had made was of a common Sanyo tire brand, and it might have been left there at any time. But the condom and paper napkins were of better evidentiary value. From the liquid nature of the semen in the condom, and the lack of dirt and gravel on the napkins, it was clear they had not been there very long. He was sure they had been dropped there during the previous night and were part of the murder scene farther down the road. There was no other litter or items where he found the condom and napkins. Also, the body of the woman had not been there long, and it was apparent she had been killed sometime during the previous night. Probably sometime between the time the Weyerhauser trucks quit operating on the road the previous day and the early-morning hours when they started again.

Detectives checking the area found a stolen car from Seattle down an embankment on Blue Slough Road, about two miles from the crime scene on the Weyco Haul Road. It appeared that the driver had tried to make a turn on the narrow road and the vehicle had slipped down the embankment. When he couldn't get it unstuck, the person just abandoned it there. The interior of that vehicle had been cut up with a sharp knife. Whether the knifing of the car and the knifing of the woman had anything in common, the detectives couldn't tell at present.

The stolen vehicle was impounded and processed by Detectives Gary Parfitt and Matt Organ. The trash inside the vehicle was collected and then processed in Lane's lab. The car was also dusted for fingerprints that were sent to the Washington State Patrol Identification Section in Olympia to be run through the Automated Fingerprint Identification System (AFIS). Later it was determined that several fingerprints on the outside of the vehicle matched Deputy Tim Laur's. He had initially found the vehicle. Several other prints were run through AFIS but came back with no matching identification. The prints were also checked against the tow truck driver and the owner of the vehicle, with negative results. Even though McDonald's napkins were found in the vehicle, there was just not enough evidence to say that they belonged to the murdered woman's crime scene or not. McDonald's napkins were a pretty common item in that area. When the detectives left the crime scene, they still had no idea who the victim was, or if she was a local woman.

By the next morning after the body had been discovered, detectives had received information that a woman named Carol Leighton had been reported missing by her ex-husband. The woman in the mortuary seemed to match Carol's description. Carol's ex-husband, Robert "Bob" Leighton, had read an article in the *Daily World* about a woman murdered on the Weyco Haul Road. Even though Bob and Carol were no longer married, they were on good terms with each other, and he had driven her into Aberdeen on the day she was murdered. He had let her off at the city's public library, because she said she wanted to use a computer there to put a résumé together for future job opportunities. Carol told him she would take the transit bus back to Westport that evening, where they lived. She never arrived there, though.

Carol had been living in Arizona for a while, but she had recently returned to Grays Harbor County, and Bob

let her stay in a camper that sat behind his house in Westport. He told her she could stay in the camper until she
found a job and got back on her feet. Bob knew that Carol
had an addiction to heroin, but he still cared for her. He
just wasn't going to take her back in for good.

After hearing from Bob Leighton, the detectives
checked Carol's background and learned that she did
have an arrest record. Carol had turned to prostitution to
support her drug habit, and she had been arrested several
times in relation to that. Lane took some postmortem
prints from the Weyco Haul Road Jane Doe and matched
them to the fingerprints on file at the sheriff's office. The
dead woman was definitely Carol Leighton.

The article Bob Leighton had read in the *Daily World*
had run a headline declaring, BODY DISCOVERED NEAR COSI
(short for Cosmopolis). The article told of a woman, as
yet unidentified to the newspaper, being found on the
Weyco Haul Road. It noted that an autopsy would soon
be performed, and that preliminary investigation revealed
the woman had *"suffered wounds from some type of
cutting instrument,"* according to Undersheriff Rick Scott.

Undersheriff Scott revealed something else as well.
Scott told a reporter that the body had been discovered
about 8:30 A.M. by motorists taking a shortcut from the
Blue Slough Road down the Weyco Haul Road. They did
not work for the Weyerhauser Company as logging truck
drivers. These individuals drove into Cosmopolis and told
a police officer what they had discovered. The police officer followed them back to the body, and then they called
the GHSO, since this was in the sheriff's jurisdiction.

The article went on to report that the dead woman
was Caucasian, with shoulder-length brown hair and a
medium build. She was possibly in her late twenties or
early thirties. She had been wearing a red flannel shirt,

a blue sweatshirt or pullover blouse, blue jeans and
Birkenstock-style sandals. It was this description that
made Bob Leighton believe the dead woman might
have been his ex-wife, Carol. Unfortunately for Carol,
he was right.

Rick Scott added one more intriguing bit of information. He said the sheriff's office was trying to find out if
this murder had anything to do with a stolen vehicle they
had discovered a few miles from the scene on Blue
Slough Road. Nothing yet tied that vehicle to the murder
scene, except that it had occurred around the same time,
and was abandoned in the general area. Scott told a reporter: "We're treating them as separate incidents, but obviously we're being very attentive to see if there is a
connection."

The autopsy of Carol Leighton was performed by Dr.
Immanuel Lacsina who had been the medical examiner
for Pierce County, and was now a private forensic pathologist. The same procedures were followed as in the Elaine
McCollum case. Lane Youmans took photos of the
woman's body clothed, and as each item was removed.
Each article of clothing was documented, placed in a separate bag and tagged.

As the articles of clothing were removed, the pockets
were searched and all contents were packaged separately.
A total of $30 was removed from the right back pocket of
Carol's jeans. The bills had been folded in half and a
nickel was also found in the pocket. A small bar of motel
soap was found in the left back pocket. It was not
wrapped, and embossed upon it was the Camay logo. In
Carol's shirt pockets there were two opened packages of
GPC cigarettes, along with two disposable lighters.

After all the clothing was removed, and the items from the clothing catalogued, Lane took photographs of Carol's body. Meanwhile, Dr. Lacsina measured and examined each injury and spoke into a small recorder about each one. That procedure took over an hour as there were stab wounds on her front and back in an apparently random pattern. She had several stab wounds on her face, ten on her chest between her breasts, five in the area of her vagina and a scattering of other stab wounds on her stomach, legs, back and buttocks. The left side of her head was then shaved, revealing stab wounds there as well.

There was a deep cut across the front of Carol's throat that appeared to go from right to left in a sawing motion. The neck wound was the main source of the large pool of blood found at the murder scene on the road. That blood had also covered her face, chest and hands. Both Dr. Lacsina and Lane Youmans agreed that the neck wound had been one of the first inflicted, since the other wounds had not bled very much after that lethal injury. These other wounds were typified as perimortem and postmortem, meaning they were inflicted when she was dying or already dead.

Dr. Lacsina removed the paper bags Lane had placed on Carol's hands to see if there were any defensive wounds there. There was a bruise about the size of a quarter on the back of her left hand. She had probably been struck on the head at some point, and may have raised her left hand to try and protect her head area.

The knife used in the attack had probably not been very sharp, if judged by the wounds and the sawing effect upon Carol's throat. The majority of stab wounds were superficial, although one of the stab wounds to her chest had penetrated deeply enough to strike a lung. Dr. Lacsina concluded that Carol Leighton had died as a result of blood loss from the neck injury.

During the postmortem exam Dr. Lacsina also produced a rape kit, which consisted of hair samples; vaginal, oral and anal swabs; and fingernail clippings. Once the autopsy was completed, Lane took the evidence to the sheriff's office evidence room, where Carol's clothing was spread out on butcher paper to let them dry. All while the autopsy was going on, other GHSO detectives were contacting people who knew Carol Leighton. As they did so, a picture began to emerge about Carol's last hours.

After Bob Leighton had dropped Carol off at the library, she didn't use the library computer, as she told him she would. Instead, she contacted a friend of hers named Carol C and purchased some heroin. Leighton then went about collecting some more money in order to purchase more heroin. She went to various places around Aberdeen throughout the day, until about 10:00 P.M., and was last seen at the Time Out Tavern. She refused to pay the $2 cover charge, then left the tavern. Previous to that, she had been seen at Mac's, a downtown Aberdeen tavern, which was situated right across the street from the Smoke Shop, where Elaine McCollum had last been seen before her murder. It appeared that Carol Leighton may have been picked up by a driver in downtown Aberdeen, as Elaine had been, and was then taken out to the Weyco Haul Road. Unlike Elaine, who had to have wondered why she was being driven that way, Carol, who was a sometimes prostitute, probably assumed she was being taken out there for sex with a john.

As time went on, the detectives were able to put together a very accurate timeline of Carols' last movements. In a report Lane Youmans created, he noted:

> *12:42 P.M.: Bob Leighton drops off Carol at the Aberdeen Library. He then purchases eight-foot 4x4 lumber at Ernst. A receipt in his residence indicates time of purchase.*
>
> *Early afternoon: Carol visits Carol C on East Market Street, where she visits for twenty minutes.*
>
> *Between 1:00 and 2:30 P.M.: Carol Leighton purchases heroin from Dwight W, and they make arrangements to meet at 7 to 7:30 P.M. so she can purchase more.*
>
> *4:30 to 4:45 P.M.: Anita B sees Carol walking from Mac's Tavern to possibly the Silver Dollar Tavern.*
>
> *Between 5:00 and 7:00 P.M.: Carol C finds a message on her answering machine from Carol Leighton advising her that she would get ahold of her later.*
>
> *Between 7:00 and 7:30 P.M.: Leighton is supposed to have dinner with Nadine J at Nadine's house. But she does not show.*

The picture starting to come together for the GHSO detectives was that Carol had been driven about a mile and a half down the Weyco Haul Road, where the vehicle turned around, facing west. There was no shoulder on the road, so they parked in the middle of the road. At that time of night there was no traffic on the road, and the whole area was secluded, hidden by dense forest. Carol and her customer had sex, and either he or she dropped the used condom and condom wrapper onto the road, and cleaned themselves up with McDonald's napkins.

As they were heading back toward Aberdeen, the vehicle suddenly stopped. The detectives had learned by now that Carol sometimes ripped off her johns by stealing their wallets, and it was wondered if she had done that on the Weyco Haul Road. She was also known to carry a small knife in her purse. People who knew her said that she either carried that knife in her purse or strapped to a leg. It was wondered if Carol had pulled the knife on her john, but he had overpowered her and then killed her with her own weapon. In fact, he had not just killed her; he had slaughtered her in a towering rage.

Lane Youmans said later, "She was stuck a mile from civilization on a logging road with no escape. The suspect struck her several times on the head, and she put her hand up to protect herself. She was disarmed, and was probably on her hands and knees. The suspect took her knife, then cut her throat and began stabbing her in what could only be described as a frenzy. The scenario made sense, but we had to prove it with the evidence that was collected."

Lane later noted the work done by Detective Matt Organ, who started spending a lot of time in the downtown Aberdeen area, talking to bar patrons and especially prostitutes who knew Carol. Lane said, "Matt spent a lot of evenings with the prostitutes, buying them cigarettes and hamburgers to gain their confidence. He was able to identify a number of their regular customers. One of the most helpful on giving information about Carol was a prostitute named Nadine J. Nadine and Carol were friends."

Nadine told Matt that she would sometimes work with Carol and provide security for her. Nadine even said that sometimes she would hide underneath a bed at a local motel while Carol was with a john. Nadine added that Carol generally carried a knife for protection, either in her purse or in her pants.

Matt also found out from Aberdeen prostitutes that Carol did not permit oral sex or anal sex, and that generally she only had a few "dates" per night. But as Carol's heroin addiction progressed, she might have upped to ten clients per night, and her rules about oral and anal sex became less stringent if she was desperate for money.

Another article appeared in the *Daily World* reporting that the dead woman had been a resident of Westport. Rick Scott told the reporter, "I would say this is a very horrific crime. This woman was killed in a very brutal fashion and we're working very hard to determine who is responsible for this." Scott went on to say that he thought the woman had lain by the side of the road for about eight hours before being discovered. He asked that anyone with information about Carol Leighton's last movements call the sheriff's office.

Scott said that Carol did have a criminal record in Grays Harbor County, and that some of it was related to drugs. He added that he didn't know if that had anything to do with her death. And he told the reporter they were still looking into the matter of the stolen car left abandoned by the side of Blue Slough Road. That vehicle was determined to have been stolen in Seattle.

By the next day's newspaper there were a few more details about Carol Leighton. It was reported by her sister that "she had a good head on her shoulders, but a monkey on her back." When Carol had been murdered, she had been in the process of trying to get off welfare and kick her drug habit.

Carol's sister, Ruby, spoke of both their very traumatic childhoods. Ruby said that they had been molested and abused as children. As Carol grew older, she dealt with these problems in a more confrontational and combative style than Ruby. Carol would fight back, both verbally and physically in many situations in her life. Sometimes this anger in Carol would bubble to the surface at inappropriate times. For one so young, she had a lot of baggage to carry with her.

Things seemed to get better for Carol when she got married as a young woman and had a son. Carol was a loving mother and very protective of her son, knowing how harsh the world could be to a young person. But eventually the marriage failed, and part of the reason may have been Carol's new-found taste for illegal drugs. Drugs were Carol's way of escaping from her demons—demons that continued to haunt her from the things she had endured. Carol could overcome many things, but as time went by, drugs were not one of them.

Carol married again, this time to Bob Leighton, who was a good guy who loved her. But that marriage failed as well, mainly due to her drug use. Even though she tried several times to kick the habit and went to drug rehabilitation centers, she could never overcome that hurdle. By the 1990s, Carol was hooked on heroin.

Ruby said of Carol, "She was smart and caring. But she had these things she could not overcome. At least Carol was a good person and truly loved her son. She cared about others, too, and would stick up for them. But she had that battle with drugs that she just couldn't seem to win, no matter how hard she tried. It made her do things she wouldn't have otherwise done."

In this last reference, Ruby may have been referring to Carol becoming a prostitute in order to fund her drug use.

Carol's ex-husband, Bob, agreed with that assessment as well. The newspaper noted that Bob Leighton was not a suspect in Carol's murder. Bob said, "She wanted to be self-supporting. She didn't want to have to rely on other people." He added that she had been addicted to "opiates" for some years, but "she was doing better now, as far as I knew." Bob added that he didn't socialize much with his ex-wife around Aberdeen. He said that she was "free to come and go." Bob added that sometimes she would spend nights with her friends in Aberdeen, but when she did that, she almost always phoned and let him know she wasn't coming home for the night.

Another person who knew Carol was a former counselor who had met her when she got a DUI in the early 1980's in Washington state. This former counselor spoke of Carol being at an AA dance and about the charisma she radiated. "There was something in the way she walked. A rhythm, a kind of grace." He added, "Carol had a physical magnetism that was eventually her undoing. She told me that an AA counselor in California had once told her, 'The way you walk is a character defect.' She was puzzled. I knew what he meant by that, but I wouldn't have wanted it changed.

"What attracted me to Carol the most was a connection to her as an emotional being. There are only one or two other people I've known whose emotional vibrations I could feel as I did Carol's. Her pleasure, when she was happy was spontaneous and contagious. I'm sure that's what her husband, Robert (Leighton) saw in her. But the combination of the early trauma, her fatal attractiveness to the opposite sex, and the addiction were things she couldn't overcome."

One of Bob Leighton's last comments in the newspaper, gave a clue as to what might have happened on the Weyco Haul Road. He said, "She would stick up for herself. She wouldn't back down if somebody gave her a bad time." Rick Scott, Lane Youmans and the other detectives wondered if Carol had been given a bad time, not backed down, and been murdered for the consequence of sticking up for herself. The stab wounds on her body went far beyond what had been necessary to kill her.

9

STAKEOUT

Lane Youmans later signed out the evidence and took it to the old jail, which had been built during the early 1900s and was now used for GHSO storage. In the center of the three-story building, there was a large room that had once been the exercise yard. It provided Lane with a secure area where he could spread out the evidence and let it air-dry. In Aberdeen's wet, moist climate if that step wasn't taken, the items could easily mold, destroying key DNA evidence. Lane photographed every item of clothing once again on both sides, and after it had dried properly, each item was folded up with the butcher paper and returned to the evidence bag. The butcher paper was collected to insure that any trace evidence that had transferred from the clothing to the paper was collected as well. The photographs were essential so that if any questions arose about pieces of clothing, the photographs could be referred to without having to open up the collection bags every time. The less times they were opened, the better.

Once the initial examinations were done, Lane placed the collection bags into paper evidence bags and sealed each one with evidence tape, writing his initials and date on the tape. This was also important. If the evidence ever went to trial, a defense lawyer would want to know every person who ever looked within the bag and may have handled the item inside.

Lane knew that most items were going to be sent to the WSP Crime Lab, but some would be sent to the FBI Laboratory in Virginia. As the evidence bags made their way around the country, they would collect various colored evidence tape seals. GHSO seals were red; WSP seals were blue; FBI seals were yellow.

As Lane was photographing Carol's jeans, he noticed what appeared to be a bloody handprint on the upper left thigh. Lane surmised the handprint may have come from the perpetrator's right hand, with the fingers pointing toward Carol's head. This may have occurred when he spread Carol's legs apart so that he could stab her vaginal region.

Lane also noted a bloody finger mark on the back of the lower right leg of her pants. Carol had been moved around by her killer, and his hands were most likely covered with blood after he had slashed her throat. There were some small spots of blood on Carol's front pants legs that had either been caused by blood dripping from the knife, or the suspect may have even cut himself while butchering her, and it was his blood that had landed on her pants. This latter possibility would be a great help to Lane and the other detectives, if that were the case.

Lane processed the McDonald's napkins and Pepsi bottle that were found on the road, as well as the condom wrapper, looking for fingerprints. The wrapper and bottle were subjected to superglue fumes, which would adhere to any moisture contained in fingerprints and to a polymer, which caused fingerprints to become visible. If fingerprints did show up, they could be dusted with fingerprint powder and lifted with print tape. From that point the tape was placed onto fingerprint cards, and the case number, date and location written on the back.

Lane was able to lift ten prints off the Pepsi bottle, but on the Sheik condom wrapper all he could discern were several ridges that appeared to be part of a whorl pattern. The few ridges on those weren't enough for an AFIS search, let alone a comparison with a suspect's fingerprint card. The napkins that were found near Carol's body were processed with ninhydrin, a chemical that reacts with amino acids found in fingerprints, causing the print to turn purple. The napkins were then sprayed with the chemical and allowed to dry. Lane examined the napkins after this process, but he found no latent prints. He decided not to process the napkins found near the condom by chemical processing, because he surmised they probably contained the DNA of the suspected killer, and chemical processing would destroy that DNA. Lane was pretty sure the suspect had used those napkins to wipe himself off after sex, and then tossed the napkins onto the road.

After everything was dried, processed, photographed, repackaged and sealed with evidence tape, Lane returned all the items to the evidence room. The rape kit was put into the refrigerator to preserve any DNA, and Lane sent the prints he'd lifted from the Pepsi bottle, along with Carol Leighton's print card, to the Washington State Patrol Crime Lab in Olympia. He also sent the obscure print from the condom wrapper to them, knowing it was a long shot at best. Lane requested that they compare the prints and check any unidentified prints with AFIS.

Later, Lane Youmans received a report from the crime lab that all ten prints on the Pepsi bottle belonged to Carol, and the print from the Sheik condom wrapper was not identifiable. About a month after this happened, Lane received a report about the rape kit. The report stated that semen was present in the condom, on the panties, on the vaginal swab, anal swab and oral swab. By now, Lane knew that Carol had been a prostitute and there could be multiple sperm donors. As he said later, "I knew that the condom belonged to the killer, and the other semen found was probably from Leighton's other customers. We now had the suspect's DNA, and all we needed was to find someone to compare it with, because in 1996, the computer system that could compare DNA was still in its early stages. We did have some physical evidence, and [the names of] witnesses that saw Carol Leighton throughout the day before she was murdered. No one saw her after ten P.M., and we had no suspects yet. We had a possible scenario, based upon interviews and examination of evidence. I knew that it was probably not exact—they seldom are—but you continually fine-tune them as information comes in. The evidence is there, it doesn't lie. You have to be able to interpret the facts, and that comes from experience. The detectives will bounce ideas and theories off each other. We will often act out what we believe took place, and one detective portrays the suspect, while another portrays the victim. I know that someone watching us would think we were crazy."

Lane realized that the DNA database was still in its infancy, and it was going to be a matter of luck to get a match from the napkins and condom to an actual person. When the DNA computer system database began, it only had blood sample DNA from convicted sex offenders. Later this was expanded to all persons convicted of a felony. This, of course, left out anyone who had only been convicted of misdemeanors or had never been through the judicial system at all. As it turned out, the DNA from the napkins and condom did not come back with a match to anyone in the system.

Yet, as Lane Youmans stated, "There is no statute of limitation on murder. Although the results of the fingerprint and DNA analysis was disappointing, we continued working on the case, following up on leads and processing evidence. I watch a lot of crime shows, like *Cold Case Files,* on TV, and often I see a new technique or method for processing evidence. Then I start thinking how I can apply that technique to evidence in one of my cases. A mental list of evidence is constantly swirling in my mind, and I constantly pull items out of evidence to try different techniques.

"Every case helps refine what you've learned from experience. Although Virginia Barsic's and Robin Rose's cases had no apparent connection to Carol Leighton's case, what I learned on each helped me later on."

GHSO detective Matt Organ began talking to a lot of the prostitutes in downtown Aberdeen. From Organ's notes, and by talking with him, Lane was able to put together a report not only on Carol Leighton, but on her mode of prostitution as well. Lane Youmans wrote, *Carol was a forty-one-year-old woman who had been addicted to heroin for a number of years. Because of this addiction she turned to prostitution to support a $150 a day habit. She worked as a prostitute in Tacoma and also in Aberdeen. Her circle of friends were either involved in*

*prostitution or the drug trade. Carol started getting a
reputation for ripping off johns by stealing their money.
Most of her tricks were from $25 to $100. She always
demanded that the john wear a condom and preferred to
have straight sex with a customer.*

*The people she knew said that Carol was always care-
ful who she went out with. She would either notify a
friend, have that friend come along or at least call a
friend and give the license plate number of the person she
was going with.* (Apparently, Carol had not done this on
the evening of August 2.)

*She would spend some time with the john, talking to the
john before hand, to make sure they were okay. She would
never go to a strange location such as out in the woods,
but would go with the john to a local motel. She would
sometimes break this rule, if she was desperate for money
because of her addiction. The toxicology report indicated
that Carol had both cocaine and heroin in her blood-
stream when she died. There was one witness who said
that Carol was able to obtain heroin earlier in the evening
on August 2, 1996.*

*Carol had no close family members in the Grays
Harbor area. She and ex-husband Robert Leighton were
divorced around 1992, because of her drug usage. However, they were still friends, and she recently moved into
a mobile home on his property after returning from a
drug treatment center in Arizona. When Carol moved
back to Robert Leighton's place, he was not aware that
she was using illegal drugs once again.*

*When Carol worked as a prostitute, she dressed casu-
ally as do all of the prostitutes in the Aberdeen area, so
that they blend in. Carol normally wore blue jeans or
shorts, and a tee shirt with a long-sleeved shirt to hide the
track marks on her arms. The majority of her clothing*

consisted of those types of items; generally in blues, browns, and whites. She had very few personal possessions in the mobile home. There were no photographs, diaries or personal effects. Carol was an outgoing individual, but she was also street smart. She was not trusting of people. She normally carried a folding pocket knife with her that she would keep up her sleeve or taped to her pant leg when she [was] working, to protect herself. It is believed that this knife was used on her when she was killed.

While Carol was living on Robert Leighton's property, she would use his bathroom and kitchen, however, a search of her garbage revealed that she mostly existed on fast food. Although they were divorced, Bob Leighton still cared for his ex-wife.

Lane Youmans, once again, wrote of Carol's last-known movements. While much of this was the same as his previous report, he also added a few new wrinkles that highlighted certain aspects of new facts that had surfaced:

On August 2, 1996, Bob Leighton drove Carol from their home in Wesport, twenty miles into Aberdeen so that Carol could go to the Aberdeen Library and use their computer to construct her resume so that she could apply for a job. A check of the library computers shows that Carol did not use their facilities. Instead, she walked six blocks to a woman named Carol C's residence, where she made arrangements to purchase some heroin. She met a female named Teresa at a local 7-11 store, several blocks away where she purchased the heroin.

Carol then walked several blocks to the Asher Apartment Building and shot up the heroin in the laundry room. A short time later she walked three blocks to the downtown area around 4 PM. One subject saw her at

Mac's Tavern at 7 PM. At approximately 7:30 PM, a man named Ted called the tavern looking for an individual, and Carol answered the phone. Ted and Carol had a brief conversation and he was the last person to hear her voice besides the killer.

It is believed she met the suspect in the vicinity of Mac's shortly after 7:30 PM. At some time after that, Carol obtained a bottle of Pepsi Cola that was found on the Weyco Haul Road near her body. Her fingerprints were found on the bottle and it was approximately two-thirds full.

Lane Youmans began to believe that the Carol Leighton and Elaine McCollum murders had been perpetrated by the same individual. Not because the cases were close in time—they were not. Nor because Carol and Elaine knew each other. They may have met once or twice down at the taverns in Aberdeen, but they weren't friends. The connection in Lane's mind was because of the location of the murder sites on the Weyco Haul Road—one murder site within one mile of the other. And the savagery of both attacks. The murder weapons had been very different—one being a knife, and the other a large vehicle—but the frenzy of the scenes are what stayed with Lane. The driver who had killed Elaine had driven over her, backed up over her, and driven over her again, making sure she was dead. And the knife wielder had cut Carol's throat and then proceeded to stab her in the chest, stomach and vaginal area—many, many more times than it took to kill her. This absolute savagery on the killer's part made Lane believe the perp was the same man.

* * *

As the one-year anniversary of Carol Leighton's murder approached, Lane Youmans requested that GHSO perform a stakeout of officers on the Weyco Haul Road just in case the killer decided to savor that anniversary by driving down the road once more. Lane knew that some killers liked to remember the day and time they had murdered their victim. Most of the detectives in the Investigation Division at GHSO were behind the plan, and they even agreed not to put in for overtime, since the administration wouldn't approve the plan if they did.

The plan consisted of two-man teams—one man hidden in the woods near the murder site, and the other man hidden near where the condom had been found. It was decided they would work twelve-hour shifts on this, from Friday evening until Sunday afternoon, around the one-year anniversary of the murder. Matt Organ and Lane would work the Saturday-night shift; Lane at the murder scene and Matt at the condom scene.

They arrived at the locations around 8:00 P.M., and Lane parked his Jeep Cherokee at the end of a nearby spur road, well out of sight of the Weyco Haul Road. Both Lane and Matt were dressed in camouflage clothing, with camo makeup on their faces, and each carried a backpack filled with food, water, flashlight, portable radio and cell phone. Matt and Lane split up, and Lane walked down the logging road to the body site just as the sun was beginning to set.

Lane stepped off the road, into the brush, and settled down amongst small alder trees and ferns. Then he got out his bottle of bug repellent, to keep the mosquitos at bay, which were hovering all around. The sun set, and soon he was enveloped by total darkness. Lane took out his small night vision device and placed it on his backpack, along with the cell phone and radio. Then all was complete and utter stillness.

Lane recalled, "The hours slowly ticked by with nothing to see, nothing happening and nothing but quiet. I knew this plan was a gamble, but if we didn't sit out here, we would never know. Behind my position in the brush, I could see the headlights of vehicles passing by on Blue Slough Road, which was about one hundred fifty feet away, below me."

It was a very memorable experience for Matt Organ as well. He recalled, "The mosquitos were fierce that night and I wore my head net, but they still bit me through it because it was too close to the skin. It was very warm for nighttime in Grays Harbor and I was glad for that. I used a lot of insect repellent, but it tends to dissolve plastic. So everything I touched—my watch, pens, and canteen—were all smeared with the stuff.

"I made my 'hide' very comfortable, thinking about the guys who would follow me for the next few days. I set up a latrine a short distance away over a small ridge. And I tried making the 'hide position' not be very visible during daylight hours.

"The mystery of the stolen car that was discovered down the road from where Carol's body was found was still bothering me. I have never believed in coincidence in police work. I was certain the vehicle was somehow involved, but I just couldn't figure out why. Then I began to wonder if Elaine McCollum's murder on this same road had anything to do with Carol's murder. I believed it had to be.

"I thought about all the time I spent with the prostitutes in Aberdeen and Hoquiam and how the Aberdeen Police

Department could not give me the names of any prostitutes in their city because they said, 'We don't have prostitution here!' I found prostitutes there by picking them out in front of bars on the street. It had been pretty much no effort at all.

"I bought them meals or cigarettes to get them to talk to me about Carol and their patrons. It had been absolutely depressing getting to know these women. It had sucked the life out of me, talking to them. The dreams they once had were gone, and the hopelessness was depressing.

"As I sat there, I thought about the investigation I had done and wondered if I'd missed something important. I thought about the hours I had spent talking to others about it, boring them while I tried finding the missing piece. I read and re-read case reports and found nothing. I read the McCollum report and was not impressed by some of the work done on it. I hoped that no one in the future would read my report and think I was a moron. And I feared that there would be a need in the future for someone to review my work, because I did not believe that this killer was done, that sooner or later another body would be found on the Weyco Haul Road.

"I hoped this wasn't going to be my second unsolved homicide. I had worked on a case in eastern Washington in 1981 that was still unsolved, and very few days went by [that] I did not think about that case. I hoped against hope that the asshole who murdered Carol would show up and we could solve this case. I tried not to eat too much crap, but did, anyway, because I always do when I'm on surveillance.

"I worried that my wife would like me even less than she already did, because I was working all the time and becoming very detached from my family during times like this. She never appreciated that I was picking up hookers. I was thinking about my sergeant and his bullshit theories about this case and never wanting to be creative in police work. So I got comfortable and fought the mosquitos and checked with Lane now and then. And just waited."

Suddenly, around midnight, a vehicle approached on Blue Slough Road. As the vehicle passed Lane's position, the murder site, the driver slowed down to around thirty-five miles per hour and then, for no apparent reason, honked his horn twice. There were no other cars on the road, no houses nearby, no pedestrians. The only thing of significance anywhere in the area was the spot up the hill where Carol Leighton had been butchered one year before.

Lane jumped up from his hidden position and ran down the bank as quickly as he could to catch a glimpse of the license plate number. But by that time, the vehicle had moved on, and Lane's view was obscured by trees and bushes. Lane wanted to call dispatch immediately to send a patrol car out to detain this vehicle, but in his haste down the hill, he'd left his radio and cell phone sitting on his backpack.

Lane raced back uphill and then thought to himself that the dispatcher didn't even know that there were detectives out on the Weyco Haul Road in a stakeout. By the time he explained everything, it would be too late. His best hope now was that the driver, who had honked, would actually drive up to the Weyco Haul Road and come visit the spot of Carol's murder. Just to be on the safe side, Lane felt around on the ground and found his Model 870 pump shotgun. It had a short barrel and folding stock, because he'd used it on drug raids.

Lane said later, "I'd used that shotgun on raids because more than once, I was the first one through the door. Racking the slide on the shotgun in a dark room was what I called the universal sound of terror. It got people's attention right away. Luckily, I never had to use it on anyone.

"I remembered thinking up there on the Weyco Haul Road that I had to play it by ear. If that guy did drive up, should I confront him or just sit back and observe what he did and get his license plate number? I knew the smartest thing to do would be to get the guy's license plate number and call it in. But my inner voice was telling me that I couldn't let him get away. It was obvious to me, if that person stopped there with that car, then he was the one who had murdered Carol."

In the end all those thoughts were moot. The vehicle did not drive up onto the Weyco Haul Road, and Lane sat there until morning, observing nothing else of importance.

Matt said later, "In the morning when I was relieved, I decided not to carry all my stuff out and stashed it at the site. When I got back for the next shift, I found that someone had found it, eaten all my food, drank my water and had been through all my stuff. I was pissed!"

Lane and Matt worked their next shift Sunday night into Monday morning, but nothing of interest turned up. And yet something may have come of all this time sitting in the bush. Lane was sure that whoever honked near the murder site had been connected to Carol Leighton's death. Lane also believed that the person would kill again, or at least try to kill again. The savagery of Carol's murder pointed at a very angry individual who was not adverse to spilling blood when enraged. And Lane, like most in the sheriff's office, believed that the person who had butchered Carol Leighton had murdered Elaine McCollum as well.

Yet, as in the Elaine McCollum case and possible Rodriguez/McDonnell case, leads began to dry up about the Carol Leighton murder. One by one the detectives at GHSO started working on other cases. No one had bragged about killing Carol, just as no one had bragged about killing Elaine. Detective Matt Organ was promoted to chief criminal deputy and relinquished his role as primary detective. Sergeant Dave Pimentel was assigned to take charge of the Investigation Division.

About all of these changes, Lane said, "Life went on. I had by now inherited two murder cases that I believed were committed by the same person. Now I just had to prove it. The cases stayed with me, always hovering in the back of my mind. I began seeing the face of Carol Leighton in my bathroom mirror every morning as I shaved. Her face was covered with blood, her eyes partially open, staring at me as I spread shaving lather on my face. The sight would be there only for a few minutes and would be gone by the time I brushed my teeth. But it was there every morning, making sure that I didn't forget her. I don't know why I saw her face and not Elaine McCollum's. It was just Carol, lying on that muddy gravel road as I first saw her. I didn't tell anyone about her daily visits, and I never forgot."

The image of Carol Leighton did not leave Lane's thoughts, and in late 1996, he contacted the FBI's Behavioral Science Unit (BSU) in Virginia. He wanted them to take a look at the Elaine McCollum murder and Carol

Leighton murder, and see what characteristics they had in common, and perhaps provide a profile of the suspect or suspects. Lane had seen this done many times on television shows about the BSU, and he'd also read articles and books about that unit. Eventually Lane spoke with Special Agent Mark Safarik and asked him what they needed.

Agent Safarik told Lane that the FBI profilers needed complete copies of both cases, as well as 8×10 photos of the crime scenes and autopsy reports. Lane asked Jennifer Cowardin, a support specialist with GHSO, to provide this material for him. In time Lane had close to a hundred 8×10 copies made of relevant photos, and he produced a videotape of the two crime scenes and downtown Aberdeen area showing Mac's and the spot where the Smoke Shop had been. Lane narrated the tape, pointing out key locations, and where various evidence items had been found on the Weyco Haul Road. When he gathered all the material together, it filled a large archive box.

Lane took the archive box to the FBI field office in Seattle and turned it over to Special Agent Rick Mathers. Mathers then shipped the box to BSU in Quantico, Virginia, and then Lane waited.

In May 1997, he finally received a report from Special Agent Safarik. The report was disappointing, to say the least. In the opinion of the analysts, there was no connection between Elaine McCollum's murder and Carol Leighton's murder. They felt that in spite of the fact that the two women were murdered on the same isolated road in Grays Harbor County, the manners of death were too different, and too much time had elapsed between one murder and the other. And the "killer signature"—the thing a single killer did in common—was not evident in both cases. Worse than that, the BSU stated that since both victims had led fairly high-risk lifestyles, frequenting bars at night, and participated in prostitution in Carol's case, the BSU could not provide a profile of who the perpetrator might be, because there were just too many variables.

Lane recalled, "To say I was disappointed is an understatement. At the very bottom of the report was a 'just in case' line, stating that it was possible the killer of both women was the same man, but the BSU didn't think so. I at least expected them to point out some obscure detail that would show that the murders were committed by the same suspect. In a county of over nineteen hundred square miles, two women were murdered on the same logging road a mile apart, [it] was just too hard to believe that they were mere coincidence. Sure, they were killed by different means. Sure, they were killed five years apart. I didn't care what the experts said, I knew they were wrong!

"In the years I had been investigating murders in a county with a population of only sixty-six thousand, I had witnessed many ways people treat their fellow man. I've seen people who have been shot, stabbed, beaten to death, pushed off a cliff, drowned, burned, run over—you name it. In all of the murders I've investigated, there were only two that stuck out for their level of violence. They were the murders of those women on the Weyco Haul Road. The image of the two women stayed with me, lying on the gravel road, faces covered with their own blood. Faces distorted, with a look of panic in their eyes as they fought for their lives. Elaine McCollum and Carol Leighton had their problems, but they were people who laughed and cried, loved and hated, had their hopes and dreams. All of that ended on a gravel road late at night."

* * *

The FBI profile was a major setback for Lane's theory about Elaine and Carol, being killed by the same suspect. The GHSO sheriff and undersheriff both held great stock in what the BSU had to say. But Lane Youmans was adamant in sticking to his guns about his own theory. He later said, "The profilers didn't stand over those bodies. Theirs was the opinion of people who lived three thousand miles away."

Lane put the murders of Elaine McCollum and Carol Leighton way on the back burner, but he did not forget them. Almost every morning there was the brief image of Carol's face in his bathroom mirror, as if pleading with him to find her killer. One year turned into the next, with no real progress on the cases, and then out of the blue, on March 17, 1999, David Gerard struck Frankie Cochran in the head several times with a hammer and stabbed her in the neck as well. He was sure she would die, but Gerard did not count on Frankie's incredible will to live. And he especially did not count on her fingering him as her attacker, and setting off an epiphany in Lane Youman's mind that the attacker of Frankie Cochran and the killer of Elaine McCollum and Carol Leighton, and possibly Patty Rodriguez, Patricia McDonnell, Matthew Rodriguez and Joshua Rodriguez, were all the same person: David Allen Gerard.

10

PARALLEL LIVES

There is one inescapable fact about Aberdeen, Washington, and that is that the ghost of its most famous former resident, Kurt Cobain, lingers and permeates the place. Not unlike Elvis Presley and Tupelo, Mississippi, you cannot walk down a street or turn a corner without reminders that "Kurt was here." In Undersheriff Rick Scott's office, there is even a wry reminder of that fact with a picture of Kurt on the wall stating those very words: *Kurt was here!*

Kurt Cobain was born on February 20, 1967, at Grays Harbor Community Hospital when David Gerard was four years old. If anything, Kurt began his first years in a residence that was even more dilapidated than the Gerard household. In fact, Cobain's first home was little more than a shack on a back alley in Aberdeen. Charles R. Cross, Cobain's biographer, wrote of that place: *The residence was so tiny and decrepit, it made even Elvis Presley's birthplace in Tupelo, Mississippi, look palatial by contrast.*

Not unlike Gerard's, Kurt Cobain's parents divorced when Kurt was young, nine years old to be exact. And Cross wrote: *To Kurt it was an emotional holocaust. No other single event in his life had more of an effect on the shaping of his personality.*

It's hard to know what effect his parents' divorce had on young David Gerard, but apparently it was not good. Suddenly thrust into the role of the eldest male in the household, he became arrogant and angry. He argued with his mother and he fought with his siblings. Sometimes these arguments went beyond being just verbal. David spoke years later of being hit in the head by a frying pan wielded by his mother. Whether that was true or not is hard to tell. By that point there was as good a chance that Gerard was lying as he was telling the truth about his younger years. In fact, Frankie Cochran said that "David is a big liar."

For Kurt Cobain and his ruptured family, when his father moved out of the house, it was to a place only blocks away from where David Gerard and his mother and siblings were living at the time. By the time Kurt was nine and a half years old, he went to live with his father. Perhaps out of a feeling of guilt at the divorce, Kurt's father, Don, bought young Kurt a Yamaha motorized minibike, and Kurt became somewhat of a sensation in the neighborhood. He would ride the minibike in a nearby field, and it's a very good likelihood that David Gerard saw him there. Whether Gerard interacted with Cobain at that point is not known, but there is every possibility that he did. A woman named Nora, who lived in the area at the time, spoke later of Gerard hanging around young children in the area. She did not think it was heathy and she didn't have much respect for Gerard. Besides, Kurt was only four years younger than Gerard, and any kid with a minibike in that poor neighborhood was sure to attract attention.

In 1979, Wendy Cobain, Kurt's mother, granted her ex-husband, Don, sole custody of Kurt. Kurt and Don went to live in Montesano, not far from the sheriff's office and courthouse that would play such a prominent role in David Gerard's life in the coming years. And it was in Montesano that Kurt took two very crucial steps in his young life: First, his uncle bought him a secondhand cheap Japanese electric guitar. Second, Kurt started experimenting with drugs at the age of fourteen.

From that point on, the interaction and interweaving of locales that tied together parts of Kurt Cobain's life and David Gerard's bordered on the incredible. Kurt bounced around from his father's house to his mother's house to his grandparents' house to friends' homes. He even ended up spending a lot of time in downtown Aberdeen, where Gerard was now starting to hang out at taverns and cafés. Both Cobain and Gerard were constantly short of money during this period of time. And both sometimes took refuge in the Timberland Library, just to get out of the weather. Gerard was definitely not there to read books. He hated anything to do with education, and Frankie would later say that he wasn't into books or even movies.

Another thing Kurt and David had in common was a fascination with guns. With Kurt, it was more symbolic than functional. He really never was a hunter. But from the time Gerard was a boy, he often went out into the woods to hunt deer, elk and even bear. He was especially proud of his skills at hunting bear. Hunting was the one activity that Gerard was good at, and he also knew how to use a knife.

Kurt's fascination with guns started around the time that his mother, Wendy, had a huge argument with her boyfriend, Pat O'Connor. According to Charles R. Cross, Wendy became so mad at O'Connor for cheating on her, she threatened to kill him with his own guns. Afraid that she might actually go through with her threat, Wendy and Kurt's sister, Kim, hauled a sack of O'Connor's rifles down to the Wishkah River. Then they threw the sack into the murky waters of the river.

When Kurt found out about this, he made Kim show him the exact spot where they had thrown the guns into the river. Kurt was able to fish the rifles out of the water. He took them to a local pawnshop and bought an amplifier for his electric guitar with the proceeds. Guns would also become a big part of David Gerard's life. In fact, Lane would even look at the murder of a man in the woods and wonder if Gerard had killed the man and had taken his rifle.

The Wishkah River, and especially the Young Street Bridge over it, which was only a couple of blocks from Wendy Cobain's house, became inextricably tied in with Kurt's legend. It was a legend that he created from truths, half-truths and downright lies. In this regard he and David Gerard were very much the same. They both created stories about themselves, and over time came to believe the stories they created as being the absolute truth. Gerard, in particular, would create stories and alibis, and would stick with them no matter how outrageous they were. In regard to the Young Street Bridge, Kurt Cobain did the same thing. It became a part of his history, even though much of it was his own invention.

It was with the Young Street Bridge in mind that Cobain created one of his most autobiographical songs, "Something in the Way." The something in the way was him. He was always in the way of one parent or the other, filled with his own perception that they really didn't want him around.

In Kurt's mythmaking he would constantly tell others of being kicked out of his mother's house when he was seventeen years old, then going to live beneath the Young Street Bridge, only two blocks from her house. What was amazing, again, was the fact that this bridge was near the area where Gerard hung out all the time. There is no factual proof that Gerard and Cobain ran into each other in that area, but it would have been more than likely that they did. After all, Elaine McCollum and David Gerard were not exactly best friends, but several people after her death said that Gerard absolutely knew Elaine, just by the fact that they often frequented the same taverns of downtown Aberdeen.

In later years a reporter asked a patron who frequented Mac's Tavern, where David Gerard sometimes hung out, if Gerard ever hung out at the Young Street Bridge. The person related, "He went there sometimes. I wouldn't call it a hangout of his. But he definitely was around that area."

David and Kurt did diverge in one area. Over time, Kurt would take almost any illegal drug he could lay his hands on. By the time he was in his late teens, he was taking LSD on a continual basis and was smoking marijuana almost daily. But alcohol was always the drug of choice for David Gerard. He would go from slightly buzzed to downright drunk when he could afford it. He bragged about how on many occasions he drove around the area while drunk.

And for both young men, money was a continual problem. Neither one of them ever held down a steady job. Yet despite all his drug-taking, Cobain practiced on his guitar with almost a religious fervor, getting better all the time. For his part David Gerard just drifted from one low-paying job to another. Drifted from tavern to tavern, going nowhere.

There appeared to be a constant connection and a divergence of their lives that wound around and then took off in completely different directions. For David Gerard, the Young Street Bridge was just another place to drink; to Kurt Cobain, it was the very symbol of his life in Aberdeen, as he perceived it to be. Kurt might have been amazed and then cynical about a billboard that the city of Aberdeen eventually put up in a small park next to the Young Street Bridge. On the billboard was a large photo of Kurt at his most grungy, unkempt hair partially covering his eyes and almost a sneer on his lips. And in a strange way Kurt never quite knew what to think of Aberdeen—he both loved and hated it. And Aberdeen was both proud of its native son and embarrassed by him as well, knowing that he had such harsh words about the area at times.

The connection of Kurt Cobain and David Gerard took on its most improbable and amazing aspect because of what happened on the same banks of the Wishkah River. If Cobain was the most famous inhabitant of its muddy banks in the 1980s, then Billy Gohl was its most infamous resident in the early twentieth century. And once again, in that strange convergence of destiny, David Gerard had an incredible link to Billy Gohl. A link that would not come to light until Lane Youmans stumbled upon it many years later.

Billy Gohl (pronounced ghoul) drifted into Aberdeen after spending time in the Yukon goldfields. By 1903,

Billy had become a delegate of the Sailors Union of the Pacific. His office was a building that sat on pilings over the Wishkah River. The building had one curious addition to it, a chute that emptied directly into the river.

In his capacity as delegate for the Sailors Union, Billy helped sailors find jobs aboard oceangoing ships and often held their money and valuables until they got back from sea. At some point all that money and all those valuables must have become too much of a temptation for Billy. One by one, sailors that had no close family ties or ties to Aberdeen began to disappear. This was not too unusual in Aberdeen, considered one of the roughest ports on the West Coast. With its scores of saloons, brothels and street toughs, Aberdeen was a dangerous place in the early 1900s.

During an eight-month period while Billy Gohl was in the area, forty-three bodies were found floating in Grays Harbor and the Wishkah River. Some of the men had been beaten, others stabbed, and yet others looked as if they'd been clubbed over the head, perhaps while intoxicated. The bodies started being cynically nicknamed the Floater Fleet. Not too much attention was paid to all of this, since these men were at the lowest economic rung in the county, and given to alcoholism and fits of violence. It was assumed that many of them had gotten into fights with one another, and the winner would deposit the loser into the harbor or Wishkah River.

In point of fact, there is a very good possibility that Billy Gohl was killing some of his clients and dumping their bodies down the chute directly into the Wishkah River, which drained into Grays Harbor. He might have gotten away with more killings, except that in 1909 he went too far and was fingered for the murder of a man named Charley Hatberg.

Despite so much evidence against him, Billy Gohl was not unlike David Gerard, in that he created an alibi and then stuck with it no matter what. Gohl testified that Charley Hatberg was alive and up in Alaska. Gohl said that the body the sheriff's office found on the sandbar was not that of Hatberg. It was just some poor unfortunate, and he had no idea who that person was.

Then the prosecution brought in a severed arm that had been pickled; they showed it to the jury. The arm had a distinctive tattoo on it. The same tattoo that Charley Hatberg had on his arm. With this evidence, Billy Gohl was convicted of murder and sentenced to prison for the rest of his life. Eventually Gohl was transferred to a facility for the criminally insane and died there in 1928.

Even though Billy Gohl was convicted only for this murder, many people believed some of the bodies of the Floater Fleet had been Gohl's victims. They were sure he had murdered them, dumped their bodies down the chute into the Wishkah River, and then took their belongings. Like many in law enforcement in the 1990s, there were some that thought what was known about the crimes of Billy Gohl were just the tip of the iceberg. In fact, some thought that David Gerard was Grays Harbor's most prolific killer since the days of Billy Gohl.

The amazing part of all this was that in the 1980s, David Gerard began hanging around with one of Billy Gohl's great-nieces. In fact, she would become one of Gerard's staunchest advocates, still believing in him while many, many others only thought of him as a man who became enraged and then murdered. This young woman would maintain these feelings toward Gerard even after the news about Frankie Cochran became public knowledge. She spoke of him as being a "good person. Fun to be with, and a nice guy." Information about this

great-niece of Billy Gohl's eventually was passed on to
Lane, and he found it remarkable that David Gerard
always seemed to have connections to so many various
people, living and dead, around the area. Lane Youmans
said, "Lots and lots of people I spoke with said they
knew of David Gerard. But very few said that they knew
him very well. He was like a shadow moving through
the area."

If the Young Street Bridge was emblematic of Kurt
Cobain, and one of his most frequent haunts, then the
Red Barn Restaurant in Grand Mound became that place
of choice for David Gerard. He spoke later of getting
alcoholic drinks there by the time he was fourteen years
old. Due to his exaggeration at times, this probably isn't
true, but he certainly was drinking beers there a few years
later. The Red Barn became Gerard's home away from
home. It would also become his hunting ground for fe-
males. In fact, he would meet Frankie Cochran there and
possibly one other girlfriend before her.

It was certainly the location where he met Frankie
Cochran when she was working as a waitress. But even
more intriguingly, it was also the place where a family
named Strasbaugh ran that restaurant during the 1980s.
And it just so happened that one of the Strasbaugh daughters named Roberta would go missing for a few weeks in
the surrounding area. Only later would her remains be
found on an isolated road in Lewis County. Just the type
of isolated road where Frankie told Lane Youmans that
Gerard was always driving on. Just the type of road
where female bodies started showing up with some reg-
ularity.

Another location of extreme importance for Kurt

Cobain and David Gerard was the Thriftway store in
Montesano. In 1983, as Kurt recalled later, he showed up
there one day to be given a flyer for a free rock concert
behind the store in a parking lot. The band turned out to
be the Melvins, playing their version of punk rock. Kurt
was absolutely entranced by the hard-driving sound.
Within a few years, the Melvins would be one of the first
important bands playing the "Northwest sound." What
was remarkable was the fact that David Gerard, in 1998,
would pull off one of his most audacious crimes at that
very same Thriftway store. It would take a combination
of Lane Youmans and Frankie Cochran to detail just what
Gerard had done there. And when Lane learned about
this, he shook his head at Gerard's audacity.

While Kurt Cobain honed his skills on guitar, David
Gerard stumbled on from one low-paying job to another.
Then in July 1985, both Gerard and Cobain would have
an intersection of importance that concerned law enforcement. Gerard was constantly being cited for misdemeanors concerning DUIs, public drunkenness and other
"nuisance crimes." On July 23, 1985, Kurt had his own
run-in with the Aberdeen Police Department. Unlike
Gerard, Kurt did not graduate to felonies, but he certainly
had his run-ins with local law enforcement.

Kurt and three other guys were on Market Street in
Aberdeen, marking graffiti on the wall of a business
building. It was not the smartest place to be doing something like this, since the building was only one block
from the police department. APD detective Michael Bens
just happened to be driving by and spotted the foursome.
The four young men spotted Bens jumping out of his vehicle, and three of them took off. Kurt, though, was
rooted in place, perhaps shocked by the sudden appearance of the detective. Arrested and booked at the police

department, Kurt was let go when he promised to pay a $180 fine.

Chronically short of cash, Cobain had not paid the $180 by May 18, 1986, when he was arrested again. This time it was for public intoxication while he was stumbling around on top of a downtown Aberdeen building. Since he hadn't paid the fine, Kurt was booked into the jail. Since he had no money at all, Kurt spent the next eight days in jail.

What is intriguing with both Kurt Cobain and David Gerard was what they didn't get arrested for. Tavern patrons who knew Gerard very well would later tell of his "light-fingered" ways. Wanting only to tell their first names, bar patron Larry said, "David was always stealing stuff. When he was drunk, he'd brag about it. I didn't doubt that he was doing it. He didn't make a lot of money from his jobs." Fellow customer Ed agreed with this assessment. He said, "Gerard was a scrounger. He was always getting into stupid situations."

Jeff Myers, who would later become Hoquiam's police chief, also picked up on this theme of stealing by David Gerard. Myers said, "Gerard was a suspect in a 1982 robbery and 1984 burglary. In 1990, he was the suspect in a theft. He always seemed to be getting into some kind of trouble. But it wasn't learned until much later, what kind of really serious trouble he could get into." And Lane later would learn of Gerard's most boneheaded theft. Gerard was working for Ocean Spray when a bunch of their Thanksgiving turkeys were stolen. The trail led back to Gerard as the thief, and he was fired.

Stupid situations were the hallmarks of Kurt Cobain's life in Aberdeen and Hoquiam. For both Kurt and David, there was always an aspect of not thinking things through, but rather just acting on impulse. For Kurt, it would lead to flights of inspiration and insight. For David, it would often just lead to violence.

In 1987, Kurt took a huge step that would change his life and that of the rock world. He left for Olympia, Washington, with its college-town atmosphere and milieu of progressive bands. Kurt would never live in Grays Harbor County again. Within a few years, Kurt and the band Nirvana would take the music scene by storm and, arguably, become the most important rock band of the early 1990s.

On February 6, 1994, on the day that Elaine McCollum was murdered, Kurt Cobain was in a reflective mood and writing lyrics for his upcoming album. He also wrote a few pages of autobiographical material that covered his younger years in Aberdeen, Hoquiam and Montesano. On the same day that Elaine died beneath the wheels of a car, Kurt penned, *Thanks to unencouraging parents everywhere, for giving their children the will to show them up.* By that point Kurt was indeed showing his parents up, by being at the height of worldwide fame. David Gerard would also show his parents up, not by music but by murder.

In later years there was one word that more than any other would be repeated by ordinary people who knew Kurt Cobain and David Gerard in downtown Aberdeen. The word was "weird." They spoke of Kurt as being a "weird kid" and David as being a "weird guy." Both of them were constantly prowling the streets of downtown Aberdeen, day and night, like alley cats. They both seemed to be restless, searching for something. Even now, there were still plenty of people in downtown Aberdeen who had known both young men. For Kurt, his journey would take him to the heights of stardom and eventually suicide. For David, it would take him to murder and a life behind prison bars.

Just as Kurt Cobain was in so many places on Aberdeen's streets and on Grays Harbor County's back roads, so was David Gerard. In fact, their paths intertwined and melded and ran in parallel lines. Kurt bounced between homes in Aberdeen, Hoquiam, Montesano and Cosmopolis. And if anything, David Gerard bounced around even more, as if he were being pushed around by a strong wind.

Lane always liked to believe that an enormous storm, known as the Columbus Day Storm of 1962, presaged the advent of David Allen Gerard into the world. In mid October of that year, Typhoon Frieda developed in the tropical western Pacific. As it moved northward, it veered around a very cold air mass moving down from the Gulf of Alaska. Once it did this, wind speeds started picking up and Frieda slammed into the Oregon and Washington Coasts. Sustained winds were clocked at 150 miles per hour, and one gust reached 179 miles per hour near Cape Blanco.

By the time Frieda ripped through the area, forty-eight people had perished, and damage costing over $6 billion in today's terms had occurred. It was a storm the National Weather Service considered to be "the benchmark of all Pacific Coast windstorms, against which all others are compared." Two weeks later, on November 23, 1962, David Gerard was born.

The Gerard home, not unlike that of the Cobain home, became unglued at some point. Most of the reporting on this came from David himself, so it had to be taken with a grain of salt. He later spoke of abuse by both parents, though his siblings did not. Of course, by the time he spoke of this abuse, he was trying to mitigate actions he had taken, especially concerning murder and attempted murder.

What is known is that once his father left home, David and his siblings lived with their mother in a housing project in Aberdeen. And something occurred there when David was a teenager that was dark and half-hidden in rumor. A woman named Nora, who lived near the Gerards, heard a story that David had molested a very young girl in the projects. Nora didn't know this for a certainty, but she didn't discount it. Nora considered David to be "weird." She also thought he was a bully to those who were smaller than him and a coward toward those who were larger than him. To say the least, she did not like him, even when he was a teenager.

David certainly did not like school. He never did well in any subject, and by the time he was in the eighth grade, he dropped out of school for good. Neither he nor Kurt Cobain ever got a high-school diploma. What followed for Gerard was a long line of low-paying jobs all around the area. Later court documents would tell of his low IQ, and even friends would describe him as "slow." The one thing that Gerard liked to do more than anything else was to go hunting. He was good at it, and bagged his share of deer, elk and even bear. And true to form, more often than not, he didn't bother buying a hunting license. Instead, he just sneaked off into the woods somewhere.

Next to hunting, his other passion was driving. Not to any specific location—just driving. The roads took him up north to Forks and Olympic National Park. West to Ocean Shores, and east to Elma and Olympia. South to Pacific County and down to Lewis County. He could do it for hours on end, almost in a trance. Being inside his vehicle might have been the one place he felt safe and not put upon by others. And when he drove, it would be from cafés to bars to roads, out into the most distant parts of the county and beyond. Isolated roads that only locals seemed to know about. Frankie would later say that she lost all sense of direction while riding around with him. She added, "I don't know if he was looking for something or hiding from something."

On September 11, 1984, the Hoquiam Police Department (HPD) received a phone call about a domestic disturbance at a residence on Arnold Street. Officer S. Wood drove to that location and talked with Donna Gerard, who told him that her son David had struck her son Donald with his fists. In fact, David had hit Donald so hard, that Donald was now hiding out in a bathroom, behind a locked door. Donna also indicated that she had been shoved against a wall by David when she tried to intervene.

Officer Wood, Officer Kinney and Sergeant Maloney all walked into the house to the back portion of the residence, where David was standing outside a bathroom yelling, "I'm going to get you!"

Officer Wood asked who David was talking about, but he would not state a name, or even look at Officer Wood. Wood wrote later: *His eyes were fixed on the bathroom door. He also appeared to be very angry and tense.*

Because of the things Donna Gerard had told Officer Wood, and David's continued bizarre and angry behavior, David was placed under arrest. In fact, David was so intent upon his mission of beating his brother, he barely acknowledged the officers at all. At first, he would not respond, but eventually submitted to being arrested when the fairly new domestic violence law was explained to him. Without any further trouble David was taken to the station by Officer Kinney and booked into jail.

Meanwhile, Officer Wood took a statement by Donald Gerard of what had just occurred. Donald was so rattled by the incident, he was still shaking when he spoke with Wood. Donald said that he and David were watching television, and David left the room. When David left, Donald changed the channel to HBO. David came back into the living room and turned the channel back to where it had been before, telling Donald that if he changed the channel again without asking, he'd "knock" his brother's "block off."

Maybe just to irk David, Donald did get up and changed the television channel once again. Without a word David walked over and struck Donald in the head twice. Donald was not only stunned by this, but angry as well. He went over and unplugged the cable attached to the television. When that occurred, David became extremely angry and punched Donald in the nose, making it bleed. In fact, he hit him so hard that Donald fell down and the television crashed to the floor. Then David started striking Donald in the side as his brother lay on the floor. Mrs. Gerard heard all the commotion and ran into the room to restrain David. While she did so, Donald got up and ran into the bathroom, where he locked himself inside.

Taking a statement from Donna, Officer Wood learned that Donna heard a crash in the living room and ran there to see the television set on the floor, and David striking Donald with his fists. When Donald got up and ran to the bathroom, David followed him. Donna tried restraining David in the hallway, but he pushed her up against a wall.

While that was going on, Donald managed to lock the bathroom door.

David didn't help his cause any by telling Officer Kinney in the police department booking room that he had planned on going bear hunting that day, but now his day had been ruined. David said that if he had to spend time in jail, he was going back and "get Donald." At the booking room David's height was measured at five-ten and his weight as 205 pounds. In bulk he held a substantial advantage over his mother, Donna, and brother Donald.

In the end neither Donald nor Donna wanted to press charges against David. They signed waivers, which were sent on to the County Prosecutor's office. Officer Wood told them about restraining orders, which could be placed against David, which would make him keep his distance from them, or be arrested all over again if he disobeyed the order. But it did not appear that they wanted a restraining order.

Eventually Donald filled out a form that stated in part: *I, Donald Gerard, do hereby authorize the Hoquiam Police Department not to prosecute David Gerard regarding my complaint. I am satisfied with the manner in which the investigation was conducted. I release the City of Hoquiam, its officers and agents and the Police Department of any responsibility regarding this complaint.*

This was the only official incident to come to light about David Gerard's younger years and trouble with the law. But there were rumors that went around his neighborhood about David and his strange ways. Detective Parfitt later said, "I talked to some 'tavern girls' in downtown Aberdeen. Some of them knew Gerard. The common theme was how 'weird' he was. They recalled him mostly sitting alone at the bar and staring at them. He gave them the creeps."

Gerard also gave Jeff Myers the "creeps." Myers would one day become Hoquiam's police chief. Before he was with the HPD, Myers recalled, he worked as a sheriff's office deputy. Myers often patrolled the back roads of Grays Harbor County. On several occasions he gave David Gerard speeding tickets. These occurred in the late 1980s and early 1990s. Myers recollected, "When he was pulled over, he always seemed to be in a different vehicle and on a different road. He had an odd way of looking right through you. He was one of those guys I would not turn my back on. Literally. After giving him the ticket, I would walk backward to my patrol car, never turning my back on him. I just didn't trust what he might do."

In time Jeff Myers and the other cops would learn that David Gerard had a habit of wrecking his vehicles over the years. He wrecked his T-Bird when he lost control of it and ran into a ditch. Frankie said that he was always drinking and driving. He wrecked his Metro when he hit a deer. When Lane Youmans saw the insurance photos on the Metro, he said, "He really smacked something."

Gerard was just as careless with his employment as he was with his vehicles. According to Lane, Gerard lost a job at Kmart for stealing and another job at Ocean Spray for stealing. In both cases the police weren't called. Gerard was just terminated for his habit of taking things that weren't his. In time the taking of things would include taking people's lives.

11

LANE

David Gerard and Lane Youmans had two things in common; both their parents had divorced when the boys were teenagers, and both teens went to Hoquiam High School. But that was where the similarities ended. Lane's family had all been involved in public service in the area. Lane's dad, Rolland "Omar" Youmans, was mayor of Hoquiam at one point, and later a Grays Harbor County commissioner. Lane's mother, Jackie Youmans, worked as a retail clerk at LaVogues store in Hoquiam, and she also worked on election boards and was a senior companion. Lane's brother, Paul, was the head of the Community Action Program in Aberdeen for many years, and later worked for the Cowlitz County Economic Development Council.

Lane related, "I wanted to get into law enforcement ever since the fifth grade at Central Grade School. I was a patrol boy, working as a crossing guard, and the Hoquiam police officers would drive by and wave. I'd picture myself driving in one of those cars and being a police officer someday. When I was seventeen, I became a Police Explorer for the Aberdeen Police Department, which gave me my first real taste of police work. After graduation from Hoquiam High School in 1971, I attended Grays Harbor College, where I met and fell in love with Terri, who would become my wife."

Lane did one more interesting thing at college, which had nothing to do with police work and took him in quite an opposite direction. Lane and three buddies formed a rock band called Nation. Besides Lane, there was Gary Jarbo, Stan Sliva and Jim Beeman. Lane was on drums, and they started playing at high-school dances, local taverns, weddings and outdoor functions. Since the college didn't have classes that would prepare Lane for a career in law enforcement, he quit college and devoted most of his time to playing in the band. At high-school dances they would play for three or four hours, often after a football game. Lane recalled, "We played Mount Si High in Snoqualmie, the night they won their big game. You could feel the energy and excitement from the crowd, and they really enjoyed themselves. It was one of our best nights."

Lane related, "The band members and I moved to Seattle in 1973. We were a hard-rock band performing songs by the Rolling Stones, Black Sabbath, Jethro Tull and Alice Cooper." Not unlike Kurt Cobain and Nirvana, Lane and his band members knew that Seattle had much more to offer, as far as bands went, than provincial Grays Harbor County. Nation played a lot of the local venues around Seattle with the same hard-driving music. But unlike Kurt Cobain and his Nirvana bandmate Krist Novoselic, Lane said that he and his bandmates realized that playing in a rock band was only going to take them so far. They were good, but they weren't extraordinary.

Nontheless, Lane recounted, "we all knew we weren't

going to get rich, but it was fun while it lasted. One of our most memorable shows was in Forks, out on the Olympic Peninsula." (This was the same Forks that David Gerard would later try to claim as an alibi when he attacked Frankie Cochran with a hammer.)

Lane recalled, "The most classic small-town hotel our band ever stayed in and played in was the Antlers Inn in Forks. Forks was a real logging town, with everything that goes with that. The bathroom was at the end of the hall, and there was a flashing red sign right outside our window. The beds were tubular metal hospital-type beds. Playing music in the Antler Room was like that scene in the Blues Brothers movie. There were drunken loggers, logging trucks rumbling by at four A.M., constant noise and fights.

"We even did tours all over the Northwest. One tour took us to all the lodges in Yellowstone National Park and surrounding towns. Our last gig was in Cody, Wyoming. I remember sitting on the ground in a parking lot before the show, eating a can of cold Spam and coming to the re-alization that I needed to leave the music business and pursue my goal of becoming a law enforcement officer."

In late 1974, Lane quit the band and started looking around for jobs that would help him to become a police officer. By this time his girlfriend, Terri, was going to college in the Seattle area, so Lane started looking for work there. He got a job doing security at the State Liquor Warehouse in Seattle, and he and Terri were married in 1975.

Lane's next job would bring him into contact with an-other site that would have its moments of fame. It was the large Weyerhauser mill in Snoqualmie, and this mill eventually would be the setting for David Lynch's televi-sion series *Twin Peaks*. Lane related, "I became a big fan of that show. The Weyerhauser mill was a huge facility. Our main job in security there was fire watch. We carried a watch clock that looked like a round canteen. There was a clock and key hole on the front, and on the inside a paper tape. A number of large keys are located throughout the mill, and when you got to a station, you inserted the key into the watch clock and gave it a quarter turn. The key had a number on it, and that number was pressed onto the tape. At the end of the day, the boss could look at the tape, and know where the security officer had been at any given time. It was pretty primitive by today's technology, but it worked.

"Being in charge, since I was a lieutenant of security at that point, I had to work all three shifts. So my work week consisted of two swings, two graveyards and one day shift. After a few weeks of that, I lost all track of time. I woke up once, sitting on the edge of my bed, and I couldn't remember if I was getting up or going to bed."

Lane knew that this job was only a temporary one, and he started putting in résumés to various police departments around the area. He also taught classes concerning security work, to bolster his résumé. Terri got a job working for the city of Hoquiam, and the Youmans moved back to that city, where Lane worked security at several stores. Lane's main goal was to be hired as a state police trooper.

Then on January 1, 1977, Lane's dream of being in law enforcement finally came true. He was hired as a deputy by the Grays Harbor County Sheriff's Office. In that era new deputies worked at the jail unit until they were ready to go out on patrol. Lane recounted, "One morning in July 1977, the chief criminal deputy issued me a worn-out Colt .357, a ticket book, deputy's badge, and told me I could go out on patrol. The problem was, I had no police training at all, since I didn't go to the academy until March 1978. There was no field-training officer or standard operating procedure manual back then. I was literally on my own. Luckily, I was able to BS my way through a lot of situations. It was helpful having watched so many episodes of *Dragnet, Adam-12* and similar TV shows. I usually worked on the west end of the county, so I knew the roads, and I knew many of the people, or knew someone who knew them. Every time I got a call on the radio, I felt a tightness in my stomach.

"I'm not a big guy—so, many times I could diffuse a tense situation with some humor and common sense. It was shocking that they basically had a person with no law enforcement experience with a gun, enforcing state laws. I was always eager to go to work, and, at the same time, scared to death. I enjoyed working crime scenes, whereas most deputies didn't. They were much more aggressive and interested in pursuing bad guys. They liked to be in on the action. I liked the details of a crime scene. I liked the evidence aspect—being able to prove that someone committed a crime.

"Victims also appreciated the extra effort, and many times would invite their neighbors over to watch me work. I dusted many rocks that had been thrown through windows, more for the benefit of the victims, but sometimes I could raise prints off the surfaces that I never thought possible.

"When I went to the academy, it had a course of eight hours of evidence collection. That was it. I gained most of my experience from being on what I called five-dollar burglaries, where a window was broken and some small item stolen. I'd pull out my print kit and spend some time looking for prints and evidence. If I screwed up, I learned from that experience."

As Lane spent his years with the Grays Harbor County Sheriff's Office, he helped start a Police Explorers post for young people interested in law enforcement, and he joined the dive team. Later he became a member of the SWAT team, Search and Rescue, and eventually a detective in the Investigation Division. As the years progressed, Lane became GHSO's crime scene specialist and fingerprint expert. He said, "I also became the Cold Case Squad because detectives who had been assigned to [working] homicides would get promoted, while I remained in Investigations. As in a Cold Case Squad of one. I wanted to remain detective, because I was good at it, and I looked forward to going to work. Early in my career I had the same lofty goal most cops have of saving the world. I soon realized that was unrealistic, but I knew I could save small pieces of it."

And then February 6, 1991, rolled around. Lane didn't know it yet, but his life and that of David Gerard's were going to converge. The convergence would have a profound effect on both of their lives, and they were never going to be the same afterward.

12

HUNTING EVIDENCE

After David Gerard pled guilty in the Frankie Cochran case in 1999, Lane Youmans had Jennifer Cowardin, at GHSO, make a working copy of the Carol Leighton murder investigation. The archive box by now held three large three-ring binders full of material about the case. Lane's first task was to read the other officers' reports, notes, statements and lab reports to reacquaint himself with the details about the murder. Lane also wanted to see if the name David Gerard was mentioned anywhere in the reports by other officers. As Lane read along, he discovered that David Gerard's name had never been mentioned at all by various people who had been interviewed by detectives concerning Carol Leighton, including numerous interviews of prostitutes in the Aberdeen area. Yet, that seemed to be a pattern with Gerard. He was always in some kind of trouble or predicament, but rarely to the level of it being a felony. Or at least the things that had come to light, by that point, were below the level of felonies. Lots of people knew David Gerard, but only in a cursory manner—they'd seen him sitting at a bar or walking down the street. But Lane couldn't find anyone who said they were good friends with Gerard. He just seemed to be one of those guys that others knew on sight, and that was about it.

On April 19, 1999, Lane obtained one of the two blood samples of Gerard's blood and sent it to the WSP Crime Lab in Seattle. He asked them to extract Gerard's DNA and compare it to the semen found in the condom that Lane had discovered on the Weyco Haul Road, not far from where Carol Leighton had been murdered in 1996. Four months later, Lane received a phone call from Jodie Fass, who worked in the DNA section at the WSP Crime Lab. Fass told Lane that four out of six bands matched Gerard's sample, but they would have to switch to a different type of testing for a more definitive result. Fass also said that the condom itself might have to be submitted for testing.

Lane immediately contacted evidence custodian Bill Pelesky to make sure the condom was still in evidence. Pelesky called Lane back and told him the condom was still there. Later, Lane recalled, "I didn't tell anyone about my call to the crime lab at the time. I was afraid I would tell them about a possible match, only to find out later that further testing showed there was no match. While I waited for the results, I asked Jennifer Cowardin to pull the sheriff's case file on the Elaine McCollum case."

Even though the FBI profilers didn't think that Elaine McCollum's murder and Carol Leighton's murder were connected, Lane still held a strong belief that they were. He took the evidence box on McCollum and read through all the reports and files, just as he had done with Carol Leighton. Lane once again looked for any report that mentioned David Gerard's name in connection with all the people the officers had spoken with concerning McCollum's murder. Way down at the bottom of the box was a list of people who had bought Classic Premium tires from the Les Scwhab store in Aberdeen. There were 213 customers named on the list, and on the last page of the list, Lane found the name at number 207: David Gerard, at a post office box in Aberdeen. Gerard had purchased four Classic Premium tires on September 10, 1990, five months before the murder of Elaine McCollum.

Lane learned that after the murder of McCollum, Detective Stocks had checked the phone book and found a David Gerard who lived in Montesano. Stocks contacted this person, and it was proven he had nothing to do with the murder of Elaine McCollum. What Detective Stocks didn't know at the time was that David Gerard, of Montesano, was not the same David Gerard who had the POB in Aberdeen, nor was the Montesano David Gerard the same David Gerard who had attacked Frankie Cochran. Incredibly, there were two David Gerards who lived within fifteen miles of each other in Grays Harbor County in 1991. Because of this twist of fate, Detective Stocks never did contact David Gerard, of Aberdeen, nor see his brown Ford Thunderbird, which might still have had damage to the front-end undercarriage after running over Elaine McCollum.

On September 22, 1999, Lane received a phone call from Jodie Fass at the crime lab. Fass told Lane that she had completed a new test on the DNA found in the condom, discovered at the Leighton murder scene, and it matched to David Gerard, the same David Gerard who had pled guilty in Frankie Cochran's case. Fass told Lane that the official report hadn't been written yet, but the chances that the DNA from the condom was someone else's DNA was one in several billion.

Lane recalled, "A rush came over me, but I was in my office alone when I got the call, which was good, because when I hung up the phone, I let out a yell. The other detectives and several administrators were in superior court for the trial of a man that had kidnapped an eight-year-old girl from her bed, carried her to a tent nearby and raped her. I had worked that crime scene and had already testified. I walked over to the courtroom, and several detectives and Undersheriff Rick Scott were standing around the hallway outside the courtroom. Some were waiting to testify, and witnesses had been excluded from the courtroom until they were called. There were several civilians standing around, so I motioned for the officers to come over to me. Undersheriff Scott, Detective Parfitt, Sergeant Pimentel, and Deputy Patrick walked up to me. I told them the crime lab had called and they had a one hundred percent match with David Gerard to Carol Leighton. They all said nothing, just stood and stared."

No wonder they all stared. It had been three years since the Carol Leighton case, and it had grown ice cold. And suddenly here was Detective Lane Youmans standing in front of them, telling them that the WSP Crime Lab had a 100 percent match to David Gerard and Carol's murder case. The same David Gerard who had recently tried murdering his girlfriend, Frankie Cochran.

Lane said later, "I needed to know everything I could learn about David Allen Gerard. I already knew that he had tried beating someone he loved to death with a claw hammer. I knew he had a 'little spat' with another girlfriend, Patty Rodriguez, and she was dead before dawn

David Allen Gerard had brushes with the law even as a young man.
(Mug shot)

As a young girl, Frankie Cochran was bright, inquisitive, and adventurous. *(Photo courtesy of Frankie Cochran)*

Frankie was a proud mother when her first child, a daughter, was born. She would eventually have two sons as well. *(Photo courtesy of Frankie Cochran)*

One day, in the town of Montesano, Gerard told Frankie that he had stolen a bank bag from a local Thriftway store and that he would hurt her if she ever told anyone. In a strange coincidence, Kurt Cobain jammed with his buddies behind the store. (Author photo)

When Frankie decided she wanted to work part time, Gerard became so upset about losing total control of her that he smashed most of her personal belongings. (Photo courtesy of Gray's Harbor Sherriff's Office)

Gerard grabbed Frankie and violently pulled her out of his vehicle during an argument. In response, Frankie threw hot coffee on Gerard's chest. *(Photo courtesy of Grays Harbor Sheriff's Office)*

The deputy who took this photo believed that Gerard had bitten his own lips to make the injury look worse than it was. *(Photo courtesy of Grays Harbor Sheriff's Office)*

After Frankie threw coffee on Gerard, he took a hammer from a tool shed and threatened to kill her with it. A week later, he attempted to do just that. *(Photo courtesy of Grays Harbor Sheriff's Office)*

On March 17, 1999, Frankie was alone in the milking parlor at Clark's Dairy, milking cows. Gerard sneaked in, hit Frankie in the head at least five times, and stabbed her in the neck. *(Author photo)*

A long streak of blood trailed down a concrete ramp in the milking barn where Frankie lay for hours before help arrived. *(Photo courtesy of Grays Harbor Sheriff's Office)*

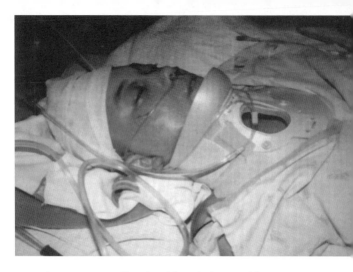

The injuries to Frankie's head from the hammer blows were massive. Few expected her to live through the ordeal. *(Photo courtesy of Grays Harbor Sheriff's Office)*

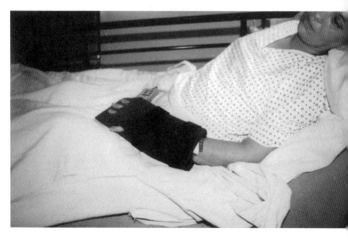

Frankie miraculously survived the attack, but it would take years of painful recovery to learn to walk again and use her arms. *(Photo courtesy of Grays Harbor Sheriff's Office)*

Gerard's girlfriend, Patty Rodriguez, had two boys, Matthew and Joshua. *(Photo courtesy of Matthew B. McDonnell)*

Patty broke up with Gerard on February 14, 1995, at Muddy Waters Tavern in Aberdeen and threw some of his clothing at him in the parking lot. Hours later, Patty, her sons, and her mother Patricia McDonnell were dead. *(Photo courtesy of Lane Youmans)*

The remains of the house where Patty, her sons, and her mother died in a mysterious fire. *(Photo courtesy of Matthew B. McDonnell)*

Patty never made it down this burned-out hallway. Detective Lane Youmans believes that Gerard murdered Patty, her two boys, and her mother, and then set the house on fire to cover up his crimes.
(Photo courtesy of Matthew B. McDonnell)

Elaine McCollum of Aberdeen had a typical childhood and attended Aberdeen High School. Although not a good friend of Gerard's, she knew him. *(Yearbook photo)*

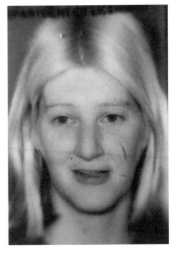

After an emotional breakdown, Elaine got back into the city life and often went to downtown taverns with her boyfriend, Dave Simmons. *(DMV photo)*

On February 5, 1991, Elaine went missing from a downtown Aberdeen tavern. The next day, her body was discovered on the Weyco (Timber Company) Haul Road outside of Aberdeen. She had been run over and crushed by the same type of large vehicle that Gerard owned at the time. *(Author photo)*

Carol Leighton's sister said she was courageous and had an adventurous streak. *(Yearbook photo)*

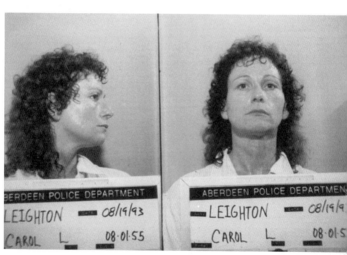

Carol was arrested on August 19, 1993, in Aberdeen. *(Photo courtesy of Grays Harbor Sheriff's Office)*

Carol was last seen at Mac's Tavern in downtown Aberdeen on the night of August 2, 1996. Elaine McCollum had been last seen across the street from Mac's on the night she was murdered. (Author photo)

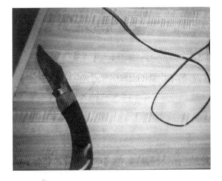

After the assault on Frankie Cochran, Detective Lane Youmans saw a photograph of a knife that Gerard had owned, according to Cochran. It looked like the same kind of knife that Carol had once owned. (Photo courtesy of Grays Harbor Sheriff's Office)

Detectives discovered that Gerard bought tires at the Aberdeen Les Schwab store, the same kind of tires that matched plaster casts of tread marks found on the Weyco Haul Road. (Author photo)

Detective Lane Youmans and Detective Matt Organ did a stakeout on the one-year anniversary of Carol's murder. At midnight, someone drove by and honked their horn at the spot where Carol had died. Lane later showed the place where he'd made his observation post by the side of Weyco Haul Road. *(Author photo)*

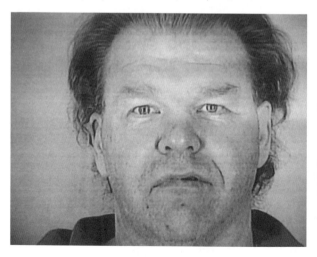

Gerard was convicted of murder in 2005, after pleading guilty to the second-degree murder of Carol Leighton. *(Mug shot)*

Rumors would surface that Gerard buried a box of "keepsakes" near Lake Quinault, adjacent to Olympic National Park. According to Frankie Cochran, the box contained numerous photographs of women unknown to her, as well as women's jewelry. *(Author photo)*

Eighteen-year-old Roberta Strasbaugh went missing in October 1985. Her parents owned the Little Red Barn Restaurant, one of Gerard's favorite hangouts. Months later, her remains were found in a wooded area of Lewis County. *(Author photo)*

Seventeen-year-old Tracy West went missing while riding her motorbike to work on October 26, 1988. The following year, her skull was found two miles from where her motorbike had been discovered. Years later, Gerard became a suspect in her abduction and murder. *(Yearbook photo)*

Connie Rolls was a music fan and an accomplished artist. In January 1984, she disappeared from the streets of Aberdeen. A year later, her skull was found in a neighboring county. *(Photo courtesy of Rebecca Hansen)*

Lane Youmans worked tirelessly to connect the murders of Carol Leighton, Elaine McCollum, Patty Rodriguez, Matthew Rodriguez, Joshua Rodriguez and Patricia McDonnell to David Gerard. *(Photo courtesy of Terri Youmans)*

The one person whom Gerard would talk to was Undersheriff Rick Scott. Both Gerard and Scott knew many people on the same farms and dairies of Grays Harbor County. *(Photo courtesy of Grays Harbor Sheriff's Office)*

Frankie and her caregiver Steve Jones fell in love and planned to get married, but Steve got cancer and it was Frankie, in a reversal of roles, who tended to him before he died. *(Photo courtesy of Frankie Cochran)*

Elaine McCollum is buried not far up the hill from Patty and the others in the same Aberdeen cemetery. *(Author photo)*

the next day, as well as her sons and mother. And now I could put him on the Weyco Haul Road on the same evening, two-tenths of a mile from a woman who had been slaughtered." The two-tenths of a mile away was, of course, the spot where Gerard had dropped a used condom on the road.

Lane set up a filing system from all the various cases into one handy reference system, where he could pull out information in a regulated and concise manner. There was one file box for all the various police reports and criminal history, another for all the vehicles Gerard had ever owned, a third for all his past girlfriends, another for family members and friends. The criminal history and police report section alone grew to three large binders. This section went clear back to 1984.

From the police reports Lane found the names of six former girlfriends of Gerard's, the last one being Frankie Cochran. As far as family went, Lane discovered that Gerard's mother had died in 1986 and his father in 1992. David had a sister, Kathy, and three brothers, Donnie, Dennis and Kevin. Lane also learned that David was the oldest, and his parents had divorced when he was still in his teens. When his father left home, David's mother was saddled with raising all the children in a low-income housing project in Hoquiam's west end. His mother went on Social Security, and had to take medication for several medical problems.

What really perked up Lane's interest was the fact that David Gerard's mother was a diabetic and was found in bed unconscious one day in 1986. Since it was part of David's duty to watch over her, and make sure she took her meds, this set off alarm bells in Lane's head. Mrs. Gerard was rushed to Community Hospital in Aberdeen one day in 1986, but she was dead on arrival (DOA). The cause of death was determined to be acid ketosis, or very high blood sugar, due to lack of insulin.

After Donna Gerard died, coroner John Bebich conducted a death investigation into the circumstances leading up to her death. Bebich learned that a month prior to her death, Donna had been admitted to Community Hospital with numbness in one arm and slurred speech. She was complaining of a severe headache, and claimed that while driving her Volvo, she had been rear-ended by a pickup truck at a stop sign next to Aberdeen's Honda dealership. The emergency room doctor concluded she had sustained a head injury in the accident, and she was admitted to a nearby nursing home to recover.

Within a short period of time, Donna Gerard was removed from the facility by family members against doctor's recommendations. Two weeks later her daughter discovered her lying in bed and unresponsive. Kathy Gerard immediately called for an ambulance. After Donna was pronounced dead at the hospital, an autopsy was performed and blood samples were taken. A test of the blood revealed the high glucose level, and it was obvious she hadn't taken her insulin. When asked about this, family members said that she wasn't good about taking it regularly. David was supposed to help her with that chore.

Coroner Bebich was still suspicious enough about this situation that he looked into the car accident story and inspected Donna Gerard's Volvo. He found no damage to the Volvo and there was no indication of an accident in front of the Honda dealership in Aberdeen, as she had claimed. Certainly, no accident report had ever been made by the Aberdeen Police Department. Bebich interviewed the staff at the car dealership, and no one there recalled any accident in front of the dealership.

Looking further into the matter, Bebich talked with

several friends of Donna Gerard and learned from one that Donna had indicated she was afraid of one of her boys, although which boy's name didn't come up. This friend believed that Donna hadn't been in any car accident, but rather had been assaulted by this particular son. The friend also believed that Donna had concocted the car accident story, either out of love or fear of this son.

When all was said and done, Coroner Bebich took his autopsy report and showed it to another pathologist. After looking it over, the other pathologist agreed that Donna Gerard had died from complications due to diabetes. Whether there were other circumstances involved in her death couldn't be determined. No more investigation was done about a son who may have assaulted Donna a few weeks before her death—a son she was so afraid of that she concocted a false report about a vehicle accident.

Lane Youmans started gathering more and more files about David Gerard's criminal history. These reports came in from GHSO, HPD, APD, Montesano Police Department (MPD), Olympia Police Department (OPD), Lewis County Sheriff's Office (LCSO), Thurston County Sheriff's Office (TCSO), Pierce County Sheriff's Department (PCSD), Washington State Game Department and WSP. Despite all these arrests and citations, Gerard had never served any prison time before his conviction of the assault on Frankie Cochran. Nonetheless, Gerard had obviously been in a lot of trouble in numerous counties around Washington State.

It surprised Lane to learn that Gerard had been a suspect in a 1997 rape case in Grays Harbor County. Lane had been working on other cases at the time, and the name David Gerard didn't mean anything to him then, other than a connection to Patty Rodriguez and a house fire that had been ruled as accidental. A woman reported that she had been raped on a logging road outside the small town of McCleary in the eastern part of the county. Detective Ed McGowan was the on-call detective then, and he responded to the hospital to contact the victim. McGowan learned that the victim, Julie, had been drinking at a tavern in Elma, and at the time she carried a fanny pack with a .38 revolver inside for protection.

Having a revolver didn't help Julie much when she started drinking on the evening in question. A man sat down next to her at the bar and struck up a conversation with her. At some point she must have either talked about or shown the man the revolver in her fanny pack, although she didn't recall this later. Apparently the man conveyed this information to the bartender about the revolver in Julie's fanny pack, and the bartender told her she had to leave the tavern. Julie began staggering toward the door, angry and upset that her night of drinking had been cut short. The man sitting next to her got up and helped her to the door. What was odd was that Julie had not drunk that much alcohol to make her so woozy and unstable.

Julie didn't get far, but, rather, fell down near the doorway just as an Elma police officer arrived. The officer removed the revolver from Julie's fanny pack and called for an ambulance. When the ambulance arrived, Julie was transported to Mark Reed Hospital in McCleary, about ten miles away. The man who had helped Julie to the doorway followed the ambulance to the hospital.

At the emergency room Julie was combative and uncooperative with the hospital staff, and they released her to the custody of the man who had followed her to the hospital. It was at that point that things went from bad to worse for Julie. She was still fairly intoxicated, but she recalled being driven by the man for several miles into some dark woods. The vehicle stopped, and Julie tried opening the door, but it wouldn't open. She then rolled down a window and pulled the outside door handle. Once the door opened, she staggered out into the inky darkness. Julie felt her way to the back of the car, where the man was standing.

Without saying a word to her, the man suddenly pushed her down onto the vehicle's trunk. He savagely pulled her pants down while holding her body against the trunk lid. He then entered her from behind. She wasn't sure how long the rape lasted, but when the man was done, he pushed her off the trunk lid and onto the gravel road. He told her if she ever told anyone about this, he would find her and kill her. Then he climbed back into his car and drove away, leaving her lying in the gravel road, alone in the cold, dark woods.

Julie was found the next morning, lying naked and still intoxicated, in a fetal position, where she had been pushed to the ground. Taken by ambulance once again to Mark Reed Hospital, deputies returned to the scene where she had been discovered and found her jacket, jean shorts, some keys and change lying on the ground. It was hard to tell if these latter items were connected to the crime or not. Some locals used the spot to dump their unwanted garbage and other items.

It was after this second trip to the hospital that Detective McGowan contacted Julie and interviewed her. McGowan also obtained copies of the medical forms from Julie's first trip to the hospital. At the bottom of a release form was the signature of the man who had accompanied Julie to the hospital from the tavern. The signature was that of a man named David Gerard.

After reading that, Detective McGowan discovered that David Gerard had been booked into the county jail on a previous occasion, and McGowan obtained a mug shot of Gerard. McGowan then put together a photo array of six mug shots of different individuals, one of them being Gerard, and showed the array to Julie. Within seconds Julie pointed to the fourth photo and said that he was the man who sat next to her at the tavern. The fourth photo was David Gerard.

Detective McGowan had a female police officer take photographs of the bruises, cuts and abrasions on Julie's arms, thighs, shoulders, buttocks and back. While none were serious, it was obvious from them that she had been manhandled pretty roughly. When the photos were taken, a scale was placed next to the bruise or cut to show how large they were.

Detective McGowan went to Merino's Seafood restaurant in the town of Westport, where David Gerard was working at the time, and contacted him there. Gerard admitted that he'd been at the bar in Mary's Kitchen on a previous night and met a woman there who had been drunk. In fact, he said he'd met her once before at Sidney's Lounge in Aberdeen. Gerard admitted he helped the woman to the door at a tavern and followed her to Mark Reed Hospital. Gerard spoke of Julie trying to assault the staff, and he had told the staff he would drive Julie home. He said they drove a few blocks to a downtown park, where he got out of the car to use a public restroom. According to Gerard, Julie also got out and started walking toward the women's restroom there.

Gerard said, as he was going into the men's room, he noticed a brown van parked nearby that had several

Hispanic men inside it. When he was done urinating, Gerard added that the van was gone, the Hispanic men were gone, and so was Julie. He assumed at that point she had left with them. He went home to Aberdeen, got a few hours' sleep, then went to work at Merino's Seafood restaurant.

At that point Gerard added one more bit of unexpected information. He said he wouldn't have raped Julie because he had a rash on his penis and it made sex painful. He even said he'd be willing to take a polygraph test to prove his innocence.

Lane said later, "Detective McGowan was a good interviewer, since he handled most of the sex abuse cases that came in. But he didn't examine Gerard's vehicle. McGowan didn't realize that by dusting the trunk lid of Gerard's car, he could have confirmed Julie's story by finding her handprints on it, as she was pressed down on it. An exam of the car would have also confirmed that the inside door handle on the passenger side didn't work."

Detective McGowan later found out that the doors to the restrooms at the park, where Gerard claimed he and Julie had gone, were locked by the McCleary Police Department every night at ten. The doors had been locked several hours before Gerard said that he and Julie used them. After getting this information, Detective McGowan tried to contact David Gerard once again, only to discover that Gerard had quit his job at Merino's Seafood shortly after being questioned and hadn't even gone back there to pick up his final paycheck. Julie's rape kit was sent to the Washington State Patrol Crime Lab, but no semen was found. After that, the investigation stalled.

* * *

On October 15, 1999, Lane Youmans contacted Julie, and she still remembered some details about the night she was raped. Lane asked her if she had met David Gerard before that night at Sidney's in Aberdeen. Julie responded that she was a member of a pool-playing team, and she shot pool at various taverns around the area, but never at Sidney's. She had once been to an office party there, but she did not believe she had met Gerard at the time.

One thing had bothered Lane for a long time—he noticed by looking at old files that Julie's panties had never been collected for the rape kit. He said later, "They weren't in the rape kit and weren't found on the road. Rape kits have a bag marked 'Undergarments,' and the bag in Julie's case was empty. I felt uncomfortable asking a woman such personal questions like that, but I asked, anyway, knowing it might be important. She told me she didn't wear panties, and that's why none had been collected."

Lane was also troubled by one other thing. When he had looked at the photos taken of Julie after she reported the incident, he noticed that even though they had scale markings as to size, there were none to indicate how far up the body the cuts and bruises began. This could have been helpful to place them in relation to Gerard's vehicle trunk and bumper.

Lane now took some more photos of Julie as she stood next to a large measuring stick. Even though the bruises were long gone, and she was now fully clothed, Lane could estimate where some of the bruises had occurred in relation to the height of the vehicle's bumper and trunk lid. It was a long shot he would ever find that vehicle again, since he already knew that Gerard had sold it long ago. The current owner of the Chevrolet sedan had moved and the license had expired, but there was no indication from the licensing bureau in Olympia that the vehicle had ever been destroyed. Finding it would be like finding a needle in a haystack, but Lane was determined to try.

Lane didn't tell Julie all he knew about Gerard up to that point, except to say that he was now in prison for trying to kill his girlfriend. Lane added that they might proceed with charges about David Gerard raping Julie in 1997. As Lane noted later, "I didn't want to freak her out. I wanted to protect her for as long as possible from knowing she must have been one of Gerard's few living victims. I knew that the only thing that had saved her that night was her highly intoxicated state. She was too drunk to put up much of a fight. I guessed that normally she was the kind of woman who would have put up a fight. Fighting off Gerard's advances would have just pissed him off, and most women who did that didn't live very long. Julie would have to know eventually, but for now I decided to keep it a secret."

And Lane began to wonder if Julie had been drunk at all when she staggered toward the door of the tavern. Lane noted that Rohypnol, the date rape drug, was odorless and colorless. Gerard could have easily slipped it into Julie's drink when she wasn't looking. In the past she had never become so "intoxicated" on so few drinks. That night she displayed all the symptoms of someone who had been given Rohypnol.

One reason for keeping all of this a secret was that Lane Youmans was sure by now that David Gerard had been the one who had killed Carol Leighton, and maybe Elaine McCollum as well. He wanted to keep those ideas in his back pocket for now, not tipping off Gerard or his defense lawyer until things were further along in the investigation. Lane believed that if Gerard knew he was a suspect in Carol or Elaine's murder, he would begin concocting an alibi. An alibi more airtight than the one he had tried to concoct about Frankie Cochran and his supposed drive around the Loop when she was attacked. The detectives needed the element of surprise when they confronted Gerard with these new allegations. And they needed more evidence. One thing Lane had learned about Gerard so far was that once he concocted a story, he stuck with it, no matter what. He couldn't be bulldozed or frightened into confessing to things he had done.

Since the cases David Gerard might have been involved in now included the rape of Julie and the murders of Carol Leighton and Elaine McCollum, Lane hauled all the evidence boxes that had been in storage to an empty room on the old jail's second floor. This area had once been used as a records area until a new building was built. With the help of evidence custodian Bill Pelesky, Lane moved all of the evidence of these three cases to the former archives room. Lane made separate piles of material along one wall, one for each case, and then signed the evidence transfer sheets for all of the items after he and Pelesky inventoried everything to make sure all the items were there. Lane placed a padlock on the front door, so that he would be the only one to enter the room. And then he placed a sign-in sheet near the door, which he wrote upon every time he entered the room, stating date and time.

To some of the detectives at GHSO it became sort of an in joke: "Lane Youmans, the one-man David Gerard Task Force." They gave him good-natured kidding about it and even took up some of the slack when Lane was working on aspects of the different cases. Lane mostly worked on all of this on his own time.

Over the course of the next year, when he had time, Lane examined every piece of evidence that had been collected concerning the cases. He photographed many of the items once again, collected trace evidence from them, and submitted numerous items to the Washington State Patrol Crime Lab. He also contacted the FBI Laboratory to see if they would conduct mitochondrial DNA exams on the hairs found on the condom and on the tissue paper lying next to it, which had been found two-tenths of a mile from where Carol Leighton's body lay. Those hairs had already been sent to the WSP Crime Lab, and the results from them had been that the hairs were "similar to Carol Leighton's hairs." The WSP lab with their testing couldn't be any more specific than that. This evidence would be crucial if the hairs in and on the condom came back as a hit to Carol Leighton. It was already proven that David Gerard was the donor of the sperm inside the condom. If Carol Leighton's DNA matched the hairs found on the condom, then it could be proven that Gerard and Leighton had sex on the Weyco Haul Road around the time she was murdered.

On July 10, 2000, Lane was finally able to send the hairs to Alice Eisenberg, at the FBI Laboratory in Quantico, Virginia. On January 19, 2001, Lane received a reply from the FBI Laboratory. The DNA from the hairs didn't match Carol Leighton's. Lane said later, "This was a real blow. It would have been the evidence to put David and Carol together."

Lane was still sure that David Gerard had murdered Carol Leighton, however, and he sent the McDonald's napkins, once again, to the state lab to check them for DNA. He also sent the lab the actual condom and asked them to swab it for Carol Leighton's DNA. The lab reported back that there was no DNA found on the outside of the condom. At least none they could trace.

The weeks went by again, with other cases beginning to take up Lane's time. Then Lane got more news that he'd been waiting for. He received a report from the WSP Crime Lab indicating that the DNA found on the vaginal swab taken from Carol Leighton, the DNA found on her panties and the DNA from the napkins all came from David Gerard. The lab stated that the chances of the DNA belonging to someone other than David Gerard was one in several trillion. There weren't that many people living on Earth. To make things even better, there was a mixture of Gerard's and Carol's DNA on the napkins. Now, once and for all, it could be proven that David and Carol had been together, having sex, on the Weyco Haul Road, not long before she was murdered. And this sex had occurred only two-tenths of a mile from where her body was discovered. This magnified what he already had learned on the DNA trail to David Gerard.

Lane quickly notified Sergeant Pimentel, Detective Matt Organ and Undersheriff Rick Scott. At 9:00 A.M. that same day, Undersheriff Scott and Lane Youmans met with county prosecutor Steward Menefee and deputy prosecutor Gerald Fuller. Lane briefed these prosecutors on the evidence he now had concerning Carol Leighton's murder, and also told them that he believed that David Gerard had murdered Elaine McCollum in 1991. He backed this up by saying that he'd already sent Elaine McCollum's panties to the Washington State Patrol Crime Lab, but they had not returned a report to him, because they were so backed up with work concerning the infamous Green River cases and "Green River Killer" Gary Ridgway.

Once Lane presented his evidence, County Prosecutor Menefee told him they should wait before arresting David Gerard on either the Carol Leighton murder or Elaine McCollum murder. He wanted Lane to gather more evidence and wait for the McCollum lab report to come back in about Elaine's panties. Menefee knew they would only have one chance in court concerning Carol and Elaine's murders. If a jury did not convict David Gerard, then he could never be prosecuted again on those cases.

Disappointed, and waiting for the lab reports to come back about Elaine McCollum, Lane became determined to dig even deeper into David Gerard's background. Lane decided to talk to every person he could find who knew Gerard, and he concocted a cover story that he was conducting a study of domestic violence offenders. As Lane recalled, "I would explain that Gerard exhibited some of the same characteristics as the other offenders I had dealt with, although most of them wouldn't go so far as to try and kill their loved ones. I would say I wanted to find out if there was something in their past that would lead them to become abusers. Hearing that explanation, people might be helpful in filling me in about Gerard's background. I knew of all these people, Frankie Cochran would be the biggest help of all."

13

FRANKIE'S TALE

Frankie Cochran's recovery after the assault was a slow and painful one. She had spent six months at a rehabilitation center in Bakersfield, California. Frankie later said of this experience, "I was in constant pain. I took every kind of medication they had, from low to high. Nothing seemed to work. Then I took something that was the last on the list. It finally helped with the pain some."

A lot of rehabilitation work there centered on the use of her legs. After months and months of therapy, Frankie was able to get out of her wheelchair. Even then, when she began to walk, there were other problems. One day she was walking down the hall with some of the staff. Even though they were near her and talking, she could hear them but not see them. It freaked her out, and it was discovered that her peripheral vision was nearly gone. This added to Frankie's anxiety, because Gerard had sneaked up on her and she only saw him at the last second. This lack of peripheral vision made her hyper-alert because of the fear of not being able to see anyone coming toward her from outside of her line of sight.

There were so many things to work on at the Centre for Neuro Skills (CNS): Frankie's vision, motor skills, memory skills, use of her arms, use of her legs. The list went on and on. Slowly she got better and more independent in her ability to take care of herself. For someone who was not even supposed to live, she was making a remarkable recovery.

Lane Youmans kept in touch with Frankie often by mail when she was in California and he also kept in touch with her mother, MaryLou. When the Department of Labor Industries refused to cover Frankie's medical bills, Lane made sure the department knew that Frankie had been working at the time she was assaulted. With that, and a few well-placed phone calls by Lane, the department began covering Frankie's medical expenses.

Eventually Frankie returned to Washington State, and was walking with the help of a leg brace and cane. When she spotted Lane for the first time, after her return from California, she went up to him as fast as she could and gave him a big hug.

Frankie spoke to a reporter for Aberdeen's newspaper, the *Daily World*. A lengthy article was about domestic violence, and Frankie admitted, "Never in my wildest dreams did I expect him (Gerard) to do something like that." She once again reiterated she wasn't sure what had attracted her to him in the first place, but she said in the beginning "he was a great guy."

They went out dancing, drinking and shooting pool. After they moved in together, Gerard sold off a few cows that he owned and bought a new car for Frankie with the money. Or at least that's what he told her about how he had gotten the money. Frankie was impressed, but she didn't realize that there were strings attached.

With the gift of the car to Frankie, Gerard became more and more possessive of her. He kept the car documents in his name, and would threaten to report her to police. If she ever left him, he would claim she had stolen the car. Things only got worse when David learned that he was diagnosed with diabetes. This was the ailment that had killed his mother, and Lane always wondered if it was because David had withheld her insulin. David began drinking even more and went into dark moods.

When Frankie left Gerard for a week at one point, her cat was killed and its body was left in her mother's pickup truck. She immediately suspected Gerard of killing her cat. But having no job, and little money, Frankie came back to Gerard despite this incident.

Frankie told the reporter her reasoning for this was "He had already destroyed everything of value that I had. I never believed he would seriously injure me. And besides, I was worried about losing the mobile home we were buying together."

Despite her mother's warning that David would seriously hurt her, Frankie stuck with him. Frankie's mom, MaryLou, told the reporter, "I don't know the true definition of violent rage, but that's what David's all about."

And that rage surfaced right to the top when Gerard accused Frankie of cheating on him with her boss at the dairy, Eugene Clark. When Frankie threw coffee on him, and he was fired from his job as a handyman at the dairy, it only fueled that rage. And yet with Gerard it was generally a controlled rage. When he struck her with the hammer in the milking shed, it was in a calculated, methodical manner. He wasn't yelling. He wasn't screaming. He was totally silent, focused and determined to finish her off. (Which once again made it hard to "type" Gerard. He had been so methodical and cold in trying to kill Frankie with the hammer; whereas with Carol Leighton, Lane believed, he flew into an uncontrollable rage as he stabbed her.)

In the same article the reporter spoke with Aggie Eldred, director of the Domestic Violence Center of Grays Harbor. Eldred said that Frankie's story was not uncommon, except for the fact that she had survived such a brutal attack. Eldred added that in the year 1999, alone, more than 250 women had become new clients at the Domestic Violence Center. Eldred stated that they came in with broken arms, broken ribs, bruises, cuts and scrapes.

Speaking directly about Frankie Cochran, Eldred said, "She has a very typical case. The extent of her injuries is the only major difference. Any one of those other women could end up that way, whether it's the first time or the tenth time they're attacked. Domestic violence victims invariably think there are many compelling reasons not to leave their abusive partners. The largest factor, by both the abuser and victim, is denial."

Turning back to Frankie, the article told of the immediate aftermath of her almost fatal assault. Frankie recalled being struck in the head three times, but she was actually struck five times. And she said, "It didn't hurt at the time. You'd think getting hit with something that hard would hurt. It only hurt later."

Frankie recalled lying on the cold, wet floor, slipping in and out of consciousness for two hours. She also recalled the moment that Eugene Clark found her, and she clutched his arm, begging him not to leave her. He, of course, had to do so, to call 911.

The article went on to relate the flight to Harborview Medical Center and surgery, followed by months and years of rehabilitation. Frankie's cheekbone and jaw had been broken. Her eye socket was crushed. The fist-sized piece of skull had to be removed because her brain was so swollen. She had a stroke, causing paralysis in her left side. As she lay in bed, there would be episodes of excruciating pain. She went through anger and depression, and at times she wished she could just die. Even now, her left eye tended to wander, and she had to help move her left arm by the use of her right arm.

And despite all those things, something good had happened to Frankie. She had met a decent man, who now cared for her and helped her in the most positive ways— her physical therapist, Steven Jones. Steven, called Steve, helped her through her pain, depression and the nightmarish flashbacks that had haunted her since March 17, 1999. He helped her overcome her fear of men in general. Steve was a caring and sympathetic individual and he helped Frankie during her days and nights of despair. Lane Youmans liked Steve as well. He called him a "caring, compassionate person. He was good for Frankie."

Frankie told the reporter, "The girl David Gerard beat up with the hammer, she's dead. She's never coming back. But I'm here. I'm alive and walking again. I'm doing the best I can."

Frankie went to the KBKW radio studios in Aberdeen with Gray Harbor County sheriff Mike Whelan. A reporter on the station generally spoke about topics that concerned Grays Harbor County. The topic of the day was domestic violence. The reporter said, "This is a lady with as much courage as anyone you're going to find anywhere. This lady is a survivor!"

From a legal standpoint, the reporter reviewed with the sheriff what had happened to Frankie. Sheriff Whelan said it was one of the most brutal attacks he'd ever seen in his twenty-three years of law enforcement. Then the reporter said it was amazing that she had survived such a brutal attack.

The reporter turned to Frankie and said that it was incredible that she was still alive. She agreed by saying that none of her doctors or surgeons had expected her to survive the ordeal. She added that she was walking again, but it was taking a long time.

The reporter apologized to her for dredging up such painful memories and asked if she ever suspected that anything like this would happen in her relationship with David Gerard. Frankie admitted that she never thought it would go to that extreme. In fact, she was more adamant than that. She said in her wildest nightmares she never expected anything like that would ever happen to her.

They touched on Gerard's lengthy sentence, and the reporter said that Gerard would be behind bars until he was seventy years old. Frankie corrected him and said that Gerard would be seventy-four. But even at that age, if he got out, she believed he would try to finish what he started. In other words, kill her. At least she took comfort in her belief that Gerard would never make it all the way through his time, because of his diabetes. She was certain that he would eventually die in prison.

Sheriff Whelan brought up the fact that Frankie's relationship with David Gerard was initially a good one, and that was often the case with victims of domestic violence. And then Whelan cited all the promises Gerard had made to Frankie in the beginning, and his supposed gift of a car to her. Whelan said this was typical of the way a lot of domestic violence relationships started. There would be good conduct from the abuser, which changed over time as he settled into the relationship. The one primary factor was that the abuser started calling more and more of the shots, and if he deemed that the other person had stepped out of line, he would "punish" that person.

The reporter asked if Gerard's violence against her had escalated. Frankie admitted that it hadn't been the norm of a lot of domestic violence situations, where arguments often led to the man hitting the woman. Frankie said that Gerard had never done that. The most he had done in that regard was to raise his voice. She said there was a lot of mental abuse, but he never got to the point of hitting her. All that, of course, was before the attack with the hammer, where he nearly killed her.

And then typical of Frankie's sense of humor, she said that Gerard hadn't struck her before because he knew "she could take him down."

The reporter laughed and replied, "That's probably why he went and got the hammer."

Frankie laughed as well and said, "Exactly!" Then she added, "Look for dramatic behavioral changes. To you women out there, when you see those, run like hell and don't look back!"

The reporter spoke of the "noose being tightened" in the relationship, and asked Sheriff Whelan if that was what this was all about. Sheriff Whelan said that it was very typical of the cycle of abuse, and that exerting control was one of the first things that happened in an abusive relationship. He said that the situation with the car that Gerard supposedly "bought" Frankie, and then retained control, was a classic example.

The reporter asked why she went back with him, and if he had worn her down with time. She said that was basically the case. Then Frankie added that she really wasn't sure why she went back with him. She thought one of the main reasons was security. She said he had the job, and she wasn't allowed to have a job. He had all the money, and she had none.

Sheriff Whelan said that reasoning occurred with victims of abuse because "the perpetrator controlled the situation by controlling finances." This aspect made the victim depend upon the abuser to a great degree. And then Sheriff Whelan added that this situation was so common amongst women who had children and depended upon an abuser, there were probably some of them out in the radio audience at the present moment, listening to the program. Whelan stated that these women felt that for their own security, and the security of their children, that there was no way they could leave the abuser. They felt trapped and powerless.

The reporter asked if late in the relationship, if someone had given her a phone number for the local domestic violence center, if she would have called them. Frankie replied that, honestly, she probably wouldn't have done so then. The reporter asked her why, and she said she wasn't mentally prepared to do it at the time.

The reporter then asked an interesting and pointed question of the sheriff. He wondered if things had turned so violent because David Gerard wanted Frankie to fear him, and she wouldn't. Sheriff Whelan replied that he didn't really know what was going through David Gerard's mind when he hit Frankie with a hammer and attempted to kill her. Whelan said that he and Frankie had talked about that very point, and that it was never an excuse for what Gerard did. But one reason that Frankie had told him was that David came from an abusive household. He had been an abused child, according to David. All three agreed that these things could be generational, and the cycle had to be broken if things were to get better.

The reporter brought up the fact that Frankie had worked very hard to try and get back to a life that she used to have. If she hadn't done so, then David Gerard would have won. Frankie absolutely agreed and replied that there was no way she was going to let Gerard win in this contest of wills. It was the one thing that had kept her going, pulling herself through the pain of her recovery.

Sheriff Whelan added that it was a credit to Frankie's courage at how much of her life she had reassembled through very difficult physical and mental work. Whelan said that six months in the past, Frankie could barely walk. She was still confined to a wheelchair at that point. He also brought up her painful rehabilitation in southern California, and spoke of how progress was slow and measured in small steps forward.

The reporter asked what was now in store for Frankie. She sighed and said that she had a lot more intense therapy to endure. She said it didn't hurt to walk now, but she still had trouble doing so. Then she said that her brain didn't know how to "manipulate" many situations anymore. It was more than just memory. It was putting together things of what she saw and felt, and how she had trouble making sense of situations she encountered. What other people took for granted was now a struggle for her.

The reporter wondered if Frankie had spoken with any other women who had been in her situation. She said no, and the fact was, most women who suffered injuries that Frankie had did not live. Sheriff Whelan added, however, that all of the volunteers at the domestic abuse center had been abused women. They knew exactly where a new client was coming from. They had been there themselves. And Whelan thanked Frankie for having the courage that day to come speak on the radio, because he knew it dredged up very painful memories for her. But if those memories helped one woman break out of a domestic abuse situation, then it was worthwhile. He spoke of Frankie as having been at "death's door," and nothing else could highlight just how dangerous these situations could become.

The reporter asked if she could get any of David Gerard's assets and sue him in a wrongful harm civil suit. Frankie didn't think she would do so, or that it would even be feasible. In fact, Frankie said that the judge and her mom had urged her not to go to Gerard's trial for his attempted murder of her. They thought it would be too emotional and upsetting for her. And then Frankie added, "The day he gets out of prison, I will have two hammers in my hand. Not one, but two!"

The reporter laughed and said that Gerard would be seventy-four by that point, so maybe she would only need a little hammer. Then he added that he could certainly understand the anger she still had at David Gerard for destroying the life she had known.

And then the reporter ended with a fact that was near and dear to Frankie's heart. By her attitude and hard work, she was determined not to let David Gerard win. Every day that she got better diminished his power over her. Every day diminished the evil that he had done.

After the radio interview and newspaper article, Lane Youmans began asking Frankie various questions, but he kept the number of questions limited. Lane said later, "She was still having trouble remembering details about what she called her 'former life.' Frankie was convinced that the old Frankie was dead, left bleeding on the floor of that milking parlor. She had to make do with what was left."

Frankie told Lane that she had met Gerard at the Red Barn Restaurant and Lounge in Grand Mound. Her recollection of dates now was very foggy, so she thought it was in 1997 or very early 1998. Frankie said, "One day I met him, and before I knew it, we were living together. It's like one day he wasn't there, and the next day he was. I hadn't had anything like that happen to me before. I'm not even sure how he suddenly was in my life."

Frankie and Gerard moved into a mobile home in Lewis County, and everything at first was fine. David was working, while Frankie stayed home and kept house. They would go out sometimes to shoot pool, go dancing and take long drives in the countryside. David seemed to like doing that a lot. He drove all over the area, with no place in particular as a destination. He seemed to know a lot of back roads and was familiar with the areas where he drove. Frankie thought nothing of it at the time, except that Gerard seemed to know a lot of roads that were off the beaten track. He wandered here and there, often silent as he drove along, but attentive. Only in retrospect did Frankie wonder if he was scouting out locations, or even going to locations that had some important memory for him. Memories of places where he had harmed someone, or even had murdered them.

After a few months Frankie started noticing a change in David Gerard. He was becoming more and more possessive and jealous. He would explode if Frankie danced with, or even talked to, another man. This wasn't directed at strangers, but rather friends that Frankie had known for a long time. David's reaction would go way beyond what was called for in the situation.

David was also becoming more and more adamant that

he and Frankie have a child; something she did not want
to do, already having three children and not wanting any
more. David told Frankie that he had twins by a former
girlfriend, but Frankie never met them and wondered if it
was the truth. Lane Youmans wondered as well, since he
could find no record of Gerard ever having fathered any
children. This was a constant theme, however, and Lane
would hear stories from other people about Gerard claim-
ing to be a parent. In one story Gerard would claim to
have a son; in another story a daughter. And in one story,
as Frankie noted, Gerard claimed to be the father of
twins. Despite all of these claims by David Gerard, Lane
could find no record that Gerard was a father at all.

Frankie also told Lane about Gerard's almost compul-
sive obsession with sex. Lane related, "She told me that
he had sex with her twice a day, every day. Nothing fancy,
nothing kinky. It was always in the missionary position,
and he expected her to be ready when he was. He also
wanted to marry her—something she didn't want, since
she'd already been married, and didn't want to marry him
or anyone else at that point. Their days got into a definite
pattern. They would go away on long drives, shoot pool,
and she would wait around for him to come home and
have sex with her. She wanted more from life than that."

One day, fed up with the unvarying—and what she
considered selfish—routine on Gerard's part, Frankie
went to a store located near the mobile home park and put
in a job application there. When Gerard found out about
this, he walked into the mobile home they shared and
began destroying every item Frankie owned that he could
lay his hands on. She told Lane that while David was
doing this, he showed absolutely no emotion, nor did he
say a thing to her. He just destroyed her things, slowly and

methodically. Anything she held of value was completely wrecked. Then he left without a word.

Once David was gone, Frankie phoned the Lewis County Sheriff's Office. A deputy came out, took a report and photographed the damage. Shortly after the deputy left, David came back, took all of Frankie's clothing from a closet and dresser drawers, piled them on the bedroom floor and poured bleach over the clothing. Once again he did this without any sign of emotion, and walked out without saying a word to Frankie. Incredible as the circumstances were, Frankie stayed with him. By now, she had no job, nor any means of support on her own. And as Aggie Eldred had noted, many women found one excuse after another why it was preferable to stay with the abuser than to leave. Finances were nearly always near the top of the list.

David's control over Frankie's life was almost complete by that point. He monitored any calls she received and wanted to know who had called her. He became irrationally jealous if she even looked in the direction of another man. And he demanded to know where she was at all times.

Lane asked Frankie if Gerard ever spoke about his childhood. She said that he had, and he'd said that his father left the family when David was young. David also said that his mother was abusive, but this wasn't something that Lane had picked up from the other siblings. According to David, when he was young, his mother had struck him on the side of the head with a frying pan that left a dent in his skull. He also told Frankie that he left home as a teenager and made a living working on a farm as a handyman. Whether these stories were true or not,

Frankie couldn't say for sure. He also told her that he was served drinks at the Red Barn Restaurant when he was only fourteen years old. Both Lane and Frankie wondered if Gerard had lied about this.

David told her very little about the other women he'd known before her. Lane asked Frankie if Gerard had ever mentioned Patty Rodriguez or some woman he had known who had perished in a fire. Lane was surprised to learn that Gerard had indeed told Frankie about Patty Rodriguez and the house fire. But in Gerard's version an uncle of Patty's had set the fire and had gone to prison for it. This, of course, was not true. Patty had no uncle.

Lane asked if David was secretive about his possessions, or if there was anything off-limits to her. Frankie replied that Gerard had told her that she could never look inside his wallet. Lane asked if she ever had, and Frankie replied, "Of course! When he told me I couldn't, then I made sure that I did." Frankie went through the wad of papers that Gerard always had stuffed in his wallet and found the names of lots of women and their phone numbers written down on cocktail coasters. These were not women's names that she knew. Frankie did wonder, however, if these were names of women from David's past, or names that he was still collecting when he went out, while they were together. Even though they were living together, David was often out on his own. He had a life out there that she knew nothing about.

Lane asked if there was anything else that David had that was supposed to be "secret." Frankie responded that he had a metal box in a closet that he told her she should never look inside. That was like waving a red flag at Frankie, and she did peek inside the box when he wasn't home. Frankie indicated to Lane that the box was a little larger than a lunch box. Inside the metal box she discovered more wads of papers, women's addresses and photographs of various women.

Lane later showed Frankie photos of Carol Leighton, Elaine McCollum, Patty Rodriguez and a woman named Connie Rolls. Connie had disappeared from Aberdeen in 1984. Frankie scanned the photos, but she didn't recall seeing any of those women's photographs in the metal box. Lane asked if there had been anything like jewelry in the metal box. Frankie said that she didn't see any, but she admitted that she hadn't pulled everything out of the box, which was mainly stuffed with paper. She felt that if she'd moved the paper around too much, David would know she had rifled through its contents and possibly give her a beating for doing so. And Frankie told Lane she hadn't seen any jewelry in the box at that time. However, she later began to have memories of some jewelry being there. Frankie spoke of it as being cheap costume jewelry. She thought it might be something that a person would pick up at a county fair. Lane wasn't sure if Frankie had actually seen that jewelry, or if his previous question about jewelry had somehow planted a seed in her mind that she had seen some. Her memory was often a jumbled mishmash of places, times and events.

Lane asked Frankie whether Gerard had committed any crimes while the two were living together. To Lane's surprise, Frankie told him about a big heist that Gerard had pulled off. Frankie said that in early 1999, they had been living at the Park Motel in Central Park, just east of Aberdeen. One day they drove to Montesano so that Frankie could buy a birthday cake at the Thriftway store. Frankie walked to the bakery of the Thriftway while David strolled to the back of the store. She saw him heading toward an area that contained an office and a restroom. At the time Frankie assumed David was going to use the restroom.

Frankie continued shopping for a cake, and then she noticed David coming toward her at a very fast pace. She described it to Lane as a "kind of skip." Gerard told her, "Let's go! Let's go!" and indicated that she should follow him right away. She did as instructed, perplexed by what was happening. She even abandoned purchasing the cake she had just selected. They got into his car in the parking lot, and Frankie looked over at him, confused about what was taking place. One thing she did notice was that his pants legs had a large bulge in it, underneath the waistband.

David drove for a short distance, then stopped the car behind an apartment complex. He then reached down into his pants and withdrew a bank bag. David cut the bag open with a knife, since it was zipped and locked on top, and pulled out a large wad of cash and checks. David began counting the money, and Frankie could see that it came to over $5,000. After he counted the money, David stuffed the wad of cash into his pocket and then tossed the bank bag, containing the checks, into a Dumpster. He told Frankie never to tell anyone about what had just occurred, or he would hurt her if she did.

After this revelation Lane contacted MPD lieutenant Jeff Myers and provided him with information about what he'd just learned from Frankie. Lieutenant Myers confirmed that a bank bag containing over $12,000 in cash and checks had been stolen from the Thriftway store in Montesano. Police at the time suspected the theft was an inside job, and they had questioned employees and gave the assistant manager a polygraph test. The assistant manager became the primary suspect of the theft and was later fired by the store for a crime he had not committed.

Interestingly, this was the same Thriftway store where Kurt Cobain first heard the Melvins and fell in love with punk rock.

Lane recalled, "At my request the Montesano PD held off questioning Gerard until the statute of limitations was almost up on the case. While clearing the assistant manager's name, and charging Gerard for the theft, was important, my ultimate goal was to have David Gerard answer for the other crimes he committed. Especially if he had murdered Elaine McCollum and Carol Leighton."

When the statute of limitations on the bank bag theft was almost up, Lieutenant Myers obtained a bank bag similar in appearance to the one that had been stolen. He cut it open in the area of the bag that Frankie had described, placed it into an evidence bag, and sealed it with evidence tape. He also took a blank videotape, put it into an evidence bag and sealed it with evidence tape. Lieutenant Myers attached some official-looking tags on the evidence bag, then drove to the Clallam Bay Corrections Center (CBCC), where David Gerard was housed at the time for his attempted murder of Frankie Cochran. He wanted to give Gerard the impression that the bank bag had been recovered, and the theft had been caught on the store's surveillance system.

Lane was convinced that the ruse would be futile, since David Gerard never confessed to anything. He would make up a story—no matter how outlandish—and then stick with it. But Lieutenant Myers believed it was worth a shot. All it would require was a drive up to Clallam Bay.

Myers recalled about that trip: "I drove up to Clallam Bay with Detective Bob Wilson. We tried every technique in the book on Gerard, but nothing worked. He just had this thousand-yard stare. It was like talking to a block of ice. I likened him to a Ted Bundy, without the personality.

"Usually, criminals want to know what facts you know. So they start talking to see what they can learn. Not Gerard. After a while he lost interest in the whole thing. All he would say was 'I didn't steal the bag.' He finally said, 'Can I go back to my cell?' We let him go. He wouldn't admit to anything."

As things turned out, Lane had been absolutely right about David Gerard. Lane recounted, "Lieutenant Myers later told me that despite the 'evidence,' Gerard would only say that he didn't steal the money, and he didn't know what Lieutenant Myers was talking about. At least the trip to Clallam Bay was a nice drive."

Looking into the aspect of Gerard destroying Frankie's clothing and other items when he became upset at her, Lane requested a copy of that report from Lewis County. Detective Glade Austin, of the LCSO, eventually sent him the report that concerned malicious mischief. Along with the report Lane asked for any photos that Detective Austin had taken at the time. When Lane received the report and photos, he scanned through them and saw from the photos what incredible damage Gerard had done. There were photos of overturned furniture, broken dishes, destroyed photographs and a pile of ruined clothing. He hadn't just thrown the items on the floor, he had demolished them.

One LCSO photo absolutely jumped out at Lane. It was the photo of a folding pocketknife. The blade was open and appeared to be about three inches in length. The handle was of dark brown wood, and there were some brass pieces on the end of the handle. To Lane, it looked exactly like the one described by a friend of Carol

Leighton's named Nadine J., who had spoken about the knife that Carol had carried for protection. Lane always believed that Carol had pulled that knife on Gerard, and he had wrestled it away from her. Once he had it, he slaughtered her with her own knife. Carol's knife had not been found at the crime scene, even though Nadine J. said that Carol always carried it with her. Lane surmised that David Gerard had kept Carol's knife as a souvenier after he had murdered her.

Lane asked Frankie about the knife in the photograph. Frankie said the knife wasn't hers, and she believed at the time that it had belonged to David, although she didn't see him purchase it. One thing was for certain—when David Gerard's car and apartment were searched after his attack on Frankie, no knife of that description was found. He made certain he had gotten rid of that particular knife.

14

INCRIMINATING PATTERNS

Moving in a different direction, Lane Youmans now knew that David Gerard had purchased Les Schwab Classic Premium tires months before Elaine McCollum was murdered. The receipt that Detective Stocks had recovered in 1991 about the transaction listed Gerard's name, post office box, and many other things, including the odometer reading of his vehicle at the time. There was everything in there except the license plate number and Gerard's residence address. While there was a space on the work order for the license plate, the person at Les Schwab hadn't written that down.

Lane contacted Les Kennedy, who was the manager at the Les Schwab store in Aberdeen, and asked if there was any way to get a list of every item that David Gerard had ever purchased from that location. Lane hoped that Gerard was a repeat customer at the Les Schwab store. Kennedy gave Lane a phone number of the Les Schwab headquarters in Prineville, Oregon, and Lane phoned them.

In fact, the headquarters was very helpful and they sent Lane a number of copies of work orders done for David Gerard at the Aberdeen store. Most of those work orders had his license plate numbers on them, and Lane was able to conclude that the vehicle with Classic Premium tires had been Gerard's 1980 Ford Thunderbird. Lane could see from one receipt that in July 1991, Gerard had the steering on his Thunderbird repaired. Lane said later, "I surmised that repeatedly running over a person would be hard on the steering of a vehicle." On further examination of the records, Lane noticed that Gerard had sold the Thunderbird to the Aberdeen Auto Wreckers in 1997. Lane made a phone call to the wrecking yard, hoping against hope that the vehicle was still there. He was not surprised when he learned that it had been scrapped years before.

Another vehicle that Gerard had owned was a black 1980 Jeep J10 pickup truck. That vehicle also could have been used to kill Elaine McCollum. Lane checked with the Department of Licensing and found that the vehicle was still around. It was currently owned by a man named Thomas in Auburn, Washington. Lane drove out to Thomas's residence, but no one was home at the time. But Lane did see a 1980 Jeep J10 pickup parked near the house. The Jeep had been jacked up to accommodate larger tires and it had a brush guard mounted on the front end. Lane didn't want to examine the Jeep without the owner's permission, so he left a business card on Thomas's front door.

Lane received a call from Thomas the next day, and

Lane explained to him that he was investigating an old
hit-and-run accident that had nothing to do with Thomas.
It had occurred before Thomas owned the Jeep. Lane
then identified the previous owner as being David
Gerard, and asked for permission to come out to Auburn
and examine the Jeep. Thomas assented to the request,
and Lane drove out to Auburn the next day.

Lane began photographing the Jeep's exterior from
every angle. He then put on a green cotton jumpsuit and
crawled beneath the Jeep. He lay on his back, a flashlight
in one hand and camera in the other, examining the undercarriage of the Jeep for damage. Amongst all the dirt,
grime and grease on the undercarriage, Lane began finding some hairs and fibers stuck in the grease and on the
metal framework. He carefully collected each hair and
fiber after photographing them.

As he recollected, "I became more and more excited at
these discoveries, and upon finding a small swatch of
fabric snagged on a piece of metal by the gas tank, I sat
up to get a closer look and, *wham,* I struck the trailer
hitch with the top of my head. I had always heard about
people seeing stars at times like that, but I never believed
it until then. I lay there on the ground beneath the Jeep in
a backyard in Auburn, a hundred miles from Montesano,
in a state of semiconsciousness when I realized that no
one from the sheriff's office knew I was there. The only
person who knew I was there was Thomas, and he was at
work somewhere. I lay there for some time, trying to clear
out the cobwebs in my head, before I was able to focus
once again and get on with my work."

Once Lane had regained his composure, he spread out
a large tarp on the ground beneath the truck and spent
the next several hours carefully removing crud and dried
mud from the undercarriage, placing it onto the tarp. He

collected twenty pounds of mud, dirt and oil and placed it into plastic containers. After he had collected all that he thought was feasible, he transported it back to the GHSO office in Montesano.

Lane spread butcher paper out on a large table in his work area and dumped the collected debris onto it. Then with tweezers and a magnifying glass, he slowly picked through the soil, grease and dried mud, plucking out every hair and fiber that he could find. He put the remainder into the evidence room and later submitted the hairs and fibers to the state crime lab, along with Elaine Mc-Collum's clothing and hair samples.

Lane waited awhile, as was usual, and finally received a report from the lab saying that there was no match to the hairs and fibers he'd collected from beneath the Jeep in connection to Elaine McCollum, although the hairs were definitely human. This created a new mystery, and Lane checked with the Highway Interdiction Traffic Safety (HITS) Unit in the Washington State Attorney General's Office for any reports of a homicide where a woman was run over by a vehicle. They came back with no such hits, but Lane still wondered if some woman, such as a prostitute or homeless person, had been hit by the vehicle. She might not have been killed, but rather had decided not to tell the police about it because of the activities she was engaged in. Or had some woman who had gone "missing" been killed by Gerard and then her remains never found? Maybe a woman who didn't live in Grays Harbor County or even Washington State. This discovery of hairs and fibers on the undercarriage of the Jeep opened up many new possibilities.

Lane knew that the vehicle David Gerard was driving by the time of Carol Leighton's murder was a red 1990 Geo Metro. By that point Gerard no longer had the Ford

Thunderbird that may have been used to kill Elaine. Lane discovered citations issued to Gerard, before and after the murder of Carol, stemming from driving infractions. Lane contacted the licensing bureau and requested the owner history of that Geo Metro. When the report came back, it listed Gerard as selling the Geo to a wrecking yard in December 1996, four months after Carol's murder. Lane next found an accident report made out by Gerard, which stated that he had wrecked the Geo when he tried to avoid a deer in the road. The Thunderbird he had owned had supposedly been wrecked after he ran it into a ditch. Lane called the wrecking yard where the Geo Metro had been located, but learned it had been sold for scrap years before, and all evidence it might have contained was long gone. It just seemed suspicious that Gerard's vehicles did not last long after a murder had been committed in the area.

Looking at a different angle, Lane checked the records from Les Schwab and noticed that Gerard drove his vehicles a lot around the area. In fact, during one month, he had put five thousand miles on his car. This confirmed what Frankie had told Lane about Gerard constantly driving around on back roads, no destination in particular. Along with this driving around a lot, and changing vehicles, Lane discovered that Gerard moved from residence to residence a lot as well. Fourteen places in fifteen years. These were mostly located in Grays Harbor County, but also in neighboring counties as well.

As Lane said later, "I compiled a paper trail of law enforcement contacts about Gerard, but I could find no records of his travels. He always paid in cash—no credit card receipts, no gas cards. He was like a ghost. He left no footprint—just the occasional contact with law enforcement and the occasional body."

* * *

Not only did Gerard's vehicles and tires interest Lane Youmans, but an angle about shoes did as well. When Elaine McCollum's body was found, her right shoe was lying a short distance away from her, along with her pants, purse and hat. Lane had originally assumed that her shoe had been knocked off her foot by the impact of the vehicle. Later he began to wonder if Gerard had pulled off her shoes, as well as her pants, when he raped her. Then Elaine had possibly gathered them up as she fled, only managing to get one shoe on, before she was struck and killed. The interesting thing to Lane was that Carol Leighton's left shoe was off her foot and lying a few feet from her body where she had been murdered as well. The shoe, a flip-flop type, was found sitting upright in the road.

Lane began to wonder, did David Gerard have a foot fetish? Was it important to him to remove a woman's shoes before raping her? Was there something about a woman's foot that turned him on?

Then things really got interesting. In February 2003, Frankie Cochran phoned Lane and asked him what had happened to one of her milking boots. She had talked to Eugene Clark at the dairy and he told her that when he found her, she was only wearing one rubber boot. Lane told Frankie that when he arrived at the scene, both milking boots were standing upright near the bottom of the ramp that led into the milking parlor. Lane added that at the time he assumed that the paramedic crew had removed Frankie's boots and placed them there. Now he began to wonder. One crime scene where a woman had a missing shoe was a coincidence; two crime scenes was a matter of interest; three crime scenes was a pattern.

Lane contacted Eugene Clark, who repeated the information that when he first saw Frankie lying on the floor, she was only wearing one milking boot. Clark couldn't remember on which foot. Lane then pulled the milking boots from the evidence box and began to examine them. They were still grungy and covered with dried cow manure. There was some cow manure inside the left boot, as though it had been tossed aside on the floor and some manure had splashed inside it. The boots were calf height and tight-fitting. The boot wouldn't have just come off by itself while Frankie was being attacked. Lane concluded that David Gerard must have pulled the boot off. But why? Did it make him recall the other women he had murdered? Was it part of his sexual/murdering mode? Lane began looking for more clues.

Lane pulled the crime scene photos from the McCollum and Leighton cases and studied them very carefully. Suddenly something hit him. Both of the women were lying on their backs, along the south shoulder of the road, with their heads pointing toward the west. Both women had their heads tilted toward the side, one arm bent at the elbow with a hand toward the head, the other arm straight, with that hand pointing toward their feet. Like the missing shoes, the head and arm positions were exact opposites between the two women.

And then another thing struck Lane. He looked at a photograph of Elaine McCollum and a photograph of Carol Leighton lying in the road, and he noticed they were mirror images of each other. It suddenly occurred to Lane that when Gerard looked in his rearview mirror at

Elaine's body, he saw an exact opposite of how she really was. So when he murdered Carol Leighton, he posed her body in the manner in which he had seen Elaine's body in his rearview mirror. It was posed 180 degrees differently than Elaine's body had been.

The coincidences didn't stop there. Both women were Caucasian, between thirty-four and forty-one years of age, and both frequented taverns in the area. They were about the same build; both had light-colored straight hair; both had worn coats that were open; both wore red shirts; both were smokers; both wore no jewelry or makeup. Both women were last seen at taverns in downtown Aberdeen, right across the street from each other. And both were slightly intoxicated when their bodies were discovered. Lane said, "The final coincidence was that both had sex with David Gerard shortly before they were murdered—Carol possibly willingly, and Elaine most likely unwillingly."

Reexamining eight-by-ten photos of Elaine and Carol's bodies, Lane once again noted the partial bloody handprint on the leg of Carol's jeans. Suddenly the reason why struck him, too. He surmised that as Gerard posed Carol's body, he made it try to look like what he recalled about Elaine's body. Lane began to believe that Gerard had taken hold of Carol's pants with one of his hands and moved her the way he wanted. There were footprint scuffs around Carol's body, but not around Elaine's. Lane conjectured that Gerard had not gotten out of his car in 1991, but merely looked in his rearview mirror for signs of life in Elaine. When he didn't see any, Gerard concluded she was dead, but that image in his rearview mirror really stuck with him. Lane posited that when Gerard murdered Carol five years later, he posed her body in the manner in which he had last seen Elaine's body, lying on the right side of the road. Right down to removing one of Carol's shoes. Not only that, he had repeated the process when he hit Frankie Cochran in the head with the hammer and left her for dead. Gerard must have removed one of her boots and left it on the ground, not knowing that, unlike Elaine and Carol, Frankie would live.

15

OTHER BODIES

Lane Youmans mainly disagreed with the FBI profilers'
assessment that the killer of Elaine McCollum and Carol
Leighton was not one and the same. But one thing he did
agree with them on was that there seemed to be too much
of a time gap between the killings *if* the same individual
had done the murders. Usually those types of killers
would murder with less of a time gap between murders,
mainly because they were in some kind of rage, or they
just plain liked to kill. In that regard, Lane began to
wonder if David Gerard had murdered some other woman
in the area in the time period between Elaine and Carol,
and no one knew about the connections. After all,
Gerard's odometer readings showed that he was traveling
around the region at a prodigious rate, and Frankie confirmed that. And Frankie spoke of Gerard, not just traveling around the Olympic Peninsula, but elsewhere in
Washington State as well.

Lane contacted Bob Gebo, who was with the Washington
State Attorney General's Office HITS Unit, and asked

him for a list of unsolved murders in the counties that
surrounded Grays Harbor County. Lane wanted the list to
go as far back as 1980, when David Gerard was eighteen
years old, involving women whose bodies had been found
outdoors. Gebo came back with a list of nine names, including two in Grays Harbor County.

The earliest case concerned Connie Rolls, a Hoquiam
resident who disappeared in 1984. Connie was twenty
years old that year, and her younger sister, Teri, remembered that Connie was her "cool big sister." Teri said later,
"I didn't spend much time with her until I was fifteen and
she was twenty. She loved to draw and she was very
talented. Amazingly so. She loved music—things by
Rush and early Heart. We used to have a horse and she
spent a lot of time riding.

"At that time Connie was about twelve weeks from
completing beauty school, but she quit. She had some sort
of fight with a classmate and dropped out. Honestly, she
didn't seem that passionate about it. She was just trying to
get some kind of good job for her future. About that
fight—she wouldn't instigate them, but she also wouldn't
let people get the better of her. She was tough and loyal,
to a fault. Mess with a friend or loved one meant messing
with her. She'd have done anything for me."

Teri related, "Very near that last time I saw Connie, she
got into a very serious argument with my mother's new
boyfriend, who later became my mom's husband. It was
an argument with him and his brother. I was the only
person there besides Connie. It nearly came to blows.
Right after that fight Connie packed her things and left."

Connie packed a suitcase and left a note with her
mom that she was going to visit a friend, Melinda, in the

town of Yelm. Yelm was about eighty miles away from Hoquiam, east of Olympia. Connie was probably going to take the bus, although Lane learned that she might have hitchhiked if that was the only alternative. Connie was last seen standing at a bus stop in front of the Montgomery Ward store in Aberdeen. Even though she was last seen there, the bus driver was later interviewed by an Aberdeen police officer, and he said that he had not picked up a young woman matching Connie's description. This left open the possibility that someone had given her a ride in his vehicle.

There was also a strange sideline to all of this. Connie's sister, Teri, related, "A friend of Connie's said that she saw Connie walking through the downtown streets of Aberdeen with a shotgun. It seemed implausible, but then later my mother's boyfriend reported one of his shotguns missing."

If Connie really was carrying a shotgun, then it is improbable she got on a bus. And if someone picked her up, and she was really carrying a shotgun, then it may well have been someone who knew her. It is very unlikely that a stranger would pick up a hitchhiker carrying a shotgun. Whatever happened, Connie went missing on January 25, 1984.

Eventually a missing persons poster was created by the Hoquiam Police Department and Thurston County Sheriff's Office. Thurston county was involved because Yelm is located there. The missing person poster showed a photo of Connie and described her as five feet six inches in height and weighing 135 pounds. She had blond hair, blue eyes, and was last seen wearing a white sweatshirt with a black panther or cat across the top, blue jeans, red leather jacket and suede oxfords. She was carrying a small soft-sided gray or blue suitcase. There was no mention of a shotgun.

A year and a half went by without any trace of Connie Rolls, and then in September 1985, two mushroom hunters, John and Chresensia Buttles, were out in the woods near the town of Shelton in Mason County, about forty miles northeast of Aberdeen. As they searched through the woods, they suddenly came upon a human skull and a few other bone fragments and bits of clothing. Stunned and shaken by what they had found, the Buttleses contacted the Mason County Sheriff's Office (MCSO).

MCSO deputy Rick Thompson went out to the area off South Grapeview Loop Road and determined that the remains were indeed human. Chief Detective Bob Shepperd was called, and he arrived on scene to cordon off the area and take photos. Soon other detectives and techs arrived, and a preliminary estimation put the time of death for the victim at between January and March 1984. Since there were no Mason County residents listed as missing from that time period, other surrounding law enforcement agencies were contacted.

Deputies cordoned off the whole area and a large scale search was conducted for the next two days. Even five members of the Mason County Trackers combed the woods and logged areas, spreading out from the initial site. An Explorer Scout search-and-rescue troop also joined the investigation.

Since this was not far from the Puget Sound area, where numerous young women's bodies had been found over the years, the Green River Task Force (GRTF) was called in to participate in the investigation. The Green River Task Force had been put together as the bodies of women started being found in alarming numbers south of Seattle, in the Green River area. As time went on, the pattern of bodies seemed to spread outward in an increasingly large area. The task force was put together because the bodies were found across jurisdictional lines, but the perpetrator seemed to be one person.

GRTF detective Dave Reinhardt told a reporter that his agency was involved in the Mason County Jane Doe case because of the similarity of terrain where the remains were found to other locations tied to the so-called Green River Killer. Just how common the same type of area was for the GRTF could be determined by a short article in the *Daily World* of Aberdeen. The newspaper noted: *The pattern is sickeningly familiar—the remains of a young woman are found in a wooded area, and the Green River Task Force is called in to investigate.* In this case it was not only for the remains found by the mushroom hunters near Shelton, but also that same weekend the GRTF investigated the body of a young woman discovered just south of Seattle in Lakeview Park. That young woman appeared to have been in her teens and was fully clothed when found. She was about five feet six inches tall, had brown hair, and was wearing jeans and a T-shirt. She had been killed by a gunshot.

As time went on, however, the GRTF backed off from thinking that this Mason County victim was one of theirs. She didn't fall into the profile of so many of the others they had researched. Indications pointed to this having been done by someone other than the Green River Killer. Perhaps a local, or at least someone who lived on the west side of Puget Sound. Someone who knew how to maneuver around the back roads.

Lane later said of the GRTF people who looked at Connie's recovery site, "Somehow the GRTF determined that Connie Rolls wasn't a Green River Killer victim. I could never understand how they could make that determination so quickly, since the Green River Killer eventually admitted that he changed his MO to throw police off. I believe the GRTF was selective so that they didn't end up with hundreds of potential victims. None of the local victims were ever tied to the Green River Killer, but he did move around, and he took some of the skulls of women he killed in King County, down to Oregon. Whether he killed anyone on the Olympic Peninsula, I don't know."

Mark Papworth, deputy coroner for Thurston County, and a forensic specialist at Evergreen State College, worked on trying to determine the sex and age of the deceased Mason County woman that the mushroom hunters had found. He finally assessed that the person had been female, between the ages of eighteen and twenty-five. And this early estimate made detectives wonder if the skull and other remains were those of Connie Rolls, missing since 1984. It also brought up another chilling murder case. These remains had been found not far from a site where the remains of nineteen-year-old Carin Conner, of Tacoma, had been found in 1983. She, too, had been missing for a while, and then her remains were found in the forest off the Grapeview Loop Road. If there was such scant information on Connie, there was even less on Carin—at least information that found its way into public view beyond the police files.

To make all of this even more mysterious, the Mason County Sheriff's Office received a phone call from a woman in California who stated she'd just had a terrible dream. The dreamer was Tina Bittner, of Rancho Cordova, California, who had been raised in Hoquiam, Washington. The dream had been so vivid and terrifying that she phoned the Grays Harbor Sheriff's Office just before the skull and remains had been found in Mason County. Bittner described to a deputy at GHSO that in her dream "either a child or small adult was in trouble, and they were near a log and sobbing." After that, Bittner was sure they had been murdered. Bittner had no knowledge of Connie Rolls being missing, or of anything about her. Bittner said of her dream, or vision as she called it, "It was astonishing! It was scary!"

Detective Mike Bagley took this news seriously and told a reporter, "There is good documented evidence about psychics being right sometimes. Suppose we didn't look and there was a person dying out there."

By September 25, the *Shelton-Mason County Journal* was reporting, *Remains found in woods may be Hoquiam woman's.* What made identifying her so difficult was addressed by Connie's mom, Becky, who said that her daughter's medical records had apparently been lost by the army. By now, Connie's dad was retired from the army and living in Texas.

MCSO undersheriff Bud Hays added, "We are investigating all young ladies of that age missing in that time period, from several different communities. We can't give any family member out there hope that maybe we found their daughter."

Quite a bit of time passed, but finally dental records proved that the remains, in fact, were those of Connie Rolls. But it could not be determined how Connie had been murdered. And another very strange occurrence had happened in connection to her. Lane related that on

July 17, 1984, someone made an anonymous phone call to the Grays Harbor Sheriff's Office. The person said, "While out in the woods I came across a blue suitcase with woman's clothing, off of a side road. Clothes are in good condition and don't look as if someone threw them away. Location, north of Promised Land Park, to the first gravel road on the right. Take the spur off to the left. Suitcase is not far back on that road." This person never identified himself.

Lane recalled, "The area was checked, and no suitcase or clothing was found. I began to wonder if David Gerard had made that phone call. This is the kind of thing he would do. He would give out false information that was one hundred eighty degrees opposite of where a crime scene was. When Frankie was assaulted, he said he was driving the Loop and up at Forks. When Patty Rodriguez and the others perished in the house fire, he said he was drinking in Olympia. He always tried setting up some kind of smoke screen to what really happened."

Looking in a different direction, Lane researched a case from Lewis County that had some similar character- istics to the Connie Rolls case. On May 5, 1985, a woman's corpse was found in a rural area between Inter- state 5 and the town of Winlock. Once again it was a mushroom picker who found the remains. The first arti- cle in the *Lewis County Daily Chronicle* noted that be- cause of decomposition, not even the age or sex of the victim could be determined.

By the next day's article more details were forthcom- ing about the body. It was determined by the Lewis County Sheriff's Office that it was the body of a woman, she had been completely nude, and she had been somewhere between thirty-five and fifty years old. She had been about five feet seven inches tall and weighed around 150 pounds. She'd had brown hair, and the cause of death was determined to be a homicide. An autopsy indicated that the unknown woman had been dead from six to eight weeks. Even though sheriff's deputies, detectives and Washington State Patrol officers scoured the marshy area, none of the woman's clothing or other items were found.

Chehalis dentist John Hendrickson found evidence of extensive dental work, which, he said, would make identifying her much easier than if she'd had no dental work done at all. Hendrickson created a dental chart, and it was compared to missing women from surrounding counties. Fingerprints were taken by LCSO techs and compared with missing women from all over the Northwest.

A week went by and the *Daily Chronicle* reported: *Police still have no ID of corpse.* And it went on to report, *The exact cause of death still has not been released.*

Undersheriff Randy Hamilton said, "We're not sure if we'll be able to release that until we know more about the identity of the body."

That was easier said than done. Another week went by and the *Daily Chronicle* reported, *Police ask for help with ID.* Hamilton told a reporter that because dental records and fingerprints had not been helpful in identifying the woman, he doubted that she had ever been reported missing. Hamilton said, "If she was missing, the description given was not detailed enough." He also noted that she may have been a transient, homeless person or a prostitute.

Hamilton later gave out more information about the

dead woman. He said that she had a narrow pointed nose, was Caucasian, and had a large jaw and an overbite. Hamilton added, "She would be remembered for her bucktooth appearance." Then Hamilton gave a phone number for citizens to call, but no one did so. The dead woman from the marsh remained a Jane Doe.

16

THE LOST GIRLS

That case had barely died down in Lewis County when another young woman went missing in the area, as Connie Rolls had done in 1984. This young woman was eighteen-year-old Roberta "Dee" Strasbaugh, of Grand Mound. And just like Connie, there was a missing persons poster put out on Roberta. She was listed as being five feet four inches tall, 115 pounds, with brown hair and hazel eyes. She had last been seen wearing blue jeans, white sweater, tennis shoes and possibly a bright red ski jacket. She went missing on September 29, 1985, and her vehicle was found on Harrison Street in Lewis County, just south of the Thurston County line. The poster related, *Suspicious circumstances surround Dee's disappearance.* The suspicious circumstances related to the fact that it appeared that the vehicle she was driving had run out of gas, and she probably had gone down the road with a gas can to get some more.

Three weeks went by and then on October 18, a dead body was found in a rural area by a logger working near

Lincoln Creek, about twelve miles northwest of Centralia. LCSO deputies and detectives began treating the scene as a homicide and scoured the area for clues. Once again the body was that of a young woman, and almost immediately they and the local newspaper turned their thoughts to eighteen-year-old Roberta Strasbaugh, who had been missing since September 29.

Back around that time detectives determined from a witness that Strasbaugh had probably accepted a ride from a man who was in his fifties and had a few day's growth of beard. He had driven a four-door full-sized sedan, and he'd been wearing a "Harrison Ford–style hat" made popular in the movie *Raiders of the Lost Ark*. The body was found about eleven miles from where Roberta had last been seen. Whether the gray-bearded man with the Harrison Ford–style hat had anything to do with her death could not yet be determined. He may have given her a ride to a gas station, and as Roberta walked back toward her car, she may have been picked up once again by her abductor and possible killer.

By October 21, the *Daily Chronicle* reported: *Death probe continues—autopsy indicates body found near Lincoln Creek is that of missing Grand Mound teenager.* By "teenager" they meant Roberta Dee Strasbaugh. Once again dentist John Hendrickson was called in to confirm that teeth found in the dead woman's body matched that of Roberta's dental chart.

LCSO detective Glade Austin didn't give out many details, but he did say that the dead young woman appeared to have been killed by blunt-force trauma. And the Lewis County coroner declared that the cause of death was due to "multiple traumatic injuries." He added that he couldn't determine the time of death or whether the body had been moved.

Because the young woman's body had been discovered so close to the Thurston/Lewis County line, both TCSO and LCSO were working on the case. The chief criminal deputy Jerry Palmateer met with all the detectives in his agency, and Thurston County sheriff Dan Montgomery had a meeting with his detectives. Eventually a joint task force of LCSO and TCSO was put together to investigate the murder.

One more detail came out about Roberta and her last journey. Her purse had been found on the seat of her pickup truck, and the pickup's gas tank was found to be empty. And it was added that the sedan in which the fiftysomething-year-old man had been driving was tan. Asked for more details by a reporter, Detective Austin replied, "There were certain things found at the site where Strasbaugh's body was found. We'll be following up on those. I can't be more specific about them."

What really caught Lane Youmans's eye about the Roberta Strasbaugh case was that she had been murdered by blunt-force trauma, much as Gerard had tried killing Frankie Cochran by blunt-force trauma—just as Carol Leighton had been struck in the head, possibly several times, before being killed by a knife slash to her throat. And even more intriguing was the fact that Roberta Strasbaugh was the daughter of the Strasbaughs who owned the Red Barn Restaurant in Grand Mound, the restaurant that David Gerard let his acquaintances know was his favorite. It was the same restaurant where he would start dating Frankie many years after Roberta Strasbaugh's death.

By October 22, the *Daily Chronicle* reported: *Final ID made on body.* It was indeed the body of Roberta Strasbaugh. The ID had been confirmed by John Hendrickson's dental record chart. By now, three detectives from

LCSO and three from TCSO were working on the case. The only new evidence disclosed to the media was that the body had been badly decomposed by the time it was found. Roberta had been lying facedown, and part of her clothing had been removed. It was also noted that the body had been found near Weyerhauser Company land that was currently being logged.

And then, not unlike the Connie Rolls case, Elaine McCollum case and Carol Leighton case, the Roberta Strasbaugh case went cold. But that was far from the end of Lane's investigation into what murders David Gerard might have committed in the area. On October 24, 1988, only days after Roberta Strasbaugh's body was discovered in Lewis County, a man was in the Vance Creek area outside of Elma. He was walking through the woods, looking for elk and chanterelle mushrooms—the mushrooms being worth a lot of money. As he scanned the forest floor, he spotted a jawbone containing four teeth. Not recognizing what kind of animal it came from, he picked it up and examined it more closely. It was then that he noticed a filling in one of the teeth. Obviously, the jawbone was not from an animal.

The man called GHSO and later led detectives to the spot where he had discovered the jawbone. After a thorough search of the area, Lane and the other detectives recovered 90 percent of the remains and some fragments of clothing as well. Along with those things, they also recovered a pearl ring, a blue sapphire earring and a spent large-caliber bullet. The skull had been shattered from the bullet striking it between the eyes. It became apparent that the jaw was broken prior to death.

The remains were found at the end of a spur road, about five miles from the nearest paved road. A forensic pathologist later determined the body was that of a female, possibly

Native American or Asian, about twenty-eight years old,
five feet tall, one hundred pounds, with shoulder-length
dark hair. All attempts to identify the remains failed.
The experts concluded she had been dead from one to
five years.

Lane looked very closely at the Roberta Strasbaugh
and Elma Jane Doe cases, and that of the murder of
Teresa Franich as well. Teresa was last seen in Tacoma
in 1987, and then her body was later found on a logging
road forty miles away. She was lying on the side of the
road, and she had been shot in the head.

There was another case that really attracted Lane
Youmans's attention. It had occurred in Mason County,
not far from where Connie Rolls's remains had been
found, and this time it concerned a Mason County girl
named Tracy West. From the circumstances of the case,
everything pointed to the perp as someone who knew the
area. Especially its back roads.

Tracy was seventeen years old in 1988, and she attended Shelton High School. Tracy was bright, and had a
real knack for languages. She studied French, Spanish
and some German. Tracy was in the foreign languages
club at school, and part of their annual moneymaking
event was called the Foreign Fair. People who attended
the fair turned in their dollars for francs, pesos and
marks; then they could buy ethnic food and items at the
fair. All of this was to raise money for the club's future
events.

Like Frankie Cochran, who was a waitress, or Roberta
Strasbaugh, whose parents owned the Red Barn Restaurant, Tracy had restaurant connections as well. After school
and on weekends she worked at the Taylor Towne Restaurant,

near Shelton. She mainly worked as a busperson and washed dishes, but lately she had also been a cook's helper. To get to the restaurant, which was about two miles from her home, Tracy rode a motorized trail bike along a private road, which was owned by the Simpson Timber Company. The reason she did so was that even though she had a driver's license, this did not include a motorcycle permit, which would have allowed her to ride the trail bike on Highway 101 to the restaurant. The route she took wound through dense forest, then cut across to the highway.

At 4:00 P.M. on October 26, 1988, Tracy left home on her motorbike for work. Schoolchildren, who were getting off a bus, saw Tracy's motorbike in her driveway just before 4:00 P.M., and a little later it was gone. It normally took her ten minutes to ride down the Simpson Logging Road to the Taylor Towne Restaurant, but on October 26, she did not arrive there at 4:30 P.M,. as usual.

Tracy's father, Roy, who was a manager of Hoodsport Seafood, was working on the family's boat that evening, and Tracy's mother, Eunice, was working the swing shift at the Auburn Boeing plant. Shirley Randall, Tracy's aunt, was taking care of Tracy's younger sister, Daisy.

Around 9:30 P.M., one of Tracy's friends called the West home, where Shirley was taking care of Daisy, and wanted to talk to Tracy. Shirley told this friend that Tracy was at work. This friend had actually taken Tracy's shift at the restaurant, and didn't tell Shirley that Tracy had never shown up there. The friend thought that Tracy had a reason for not showing up—one that she might not have told her parents or her aunt. This friend didn't want Tracy to get in trouble. The friend did, however, tell the restaurant manager, Brad Wilson, about her conversation with Shirley Randall.

Wilson was surprised by this turn of events. He would

later tell a reporter, "Tracy was an excellent worker, with a good personality. She had never done anything like this before." Wilson was so concerned about this situation that he phoned Shirley Randall and told her what he had just learned. Hearing this, Shirley became distressed and called her husband, Tom, to come over to the West house immediately.

Not long thereafter, Roy West returned home from working on his boat, and became alarmed as well. He called a friend, Dennis Carlson, who owned a four-wheel-drive vehicle that was capable of negotiating the small, bumpy logging road that Tracy took to work.

The two men set off and searched all up and down the road, but they couldn't find a trace of Tracy in the dark woods. They returned to the West home, where someone—and it's not clear if it was Shirley Randall or Eunice West—had already called the sheriff's office. By 1:30 A.M., there were search-and-rescue personnel in the forest, along with a K-9 team.

Scouring the woods, an officer spotted Tracy's motorbike turned upside down right in the middle of the Simpson Logging Road, near a large tree. Why Roy West and Dennis Carlson didn't go to that section of road is not clear. The motorbike was only a half mile from Tracy's home, and the key was still in the ignition. The glasses that Tracy almost always wore were lying in the road, not far away. Sheriff Bob Holter said later that there was no indication of excessive speed, quick acceleration or braking action. He related, "There was no apparent reason why it should have turned over." And then because of the situation, he added, they were looking at this as if Tracy had either run away from home, or she was the victim of foul play.

The search soon grew to foot searchers, off-road vehicles,

officers with search dogs and even a spotter plane. Other than the overturned motorbike and the pair of glasses, there were no other clues of why and how Tracy West had disappeared. Sheriff Holter told a reporter that there were also no indications that Tracy had been having problems at school or at home.

Tracy's parents addressed this issue with a local newspaper reporter, saying that Tracy wouldn't run away. They gave a long list of reasons why. Tracy was just a few months short of getting her diploma at Shelton High School in January, rather than May, and she was doing well in school. They said she was taking a computer course, and she wanted to work part-time and go to college part-time when she graduated from high school.

They said Tracy was a collector of keepsakes and if she'd run away, she would have taken some of her most prized possessions with her. Tracy's bank account, where she had built up money, saving for a car, was untouched. In fact, she hadn't even taken her wallet when she left home on the motorbike.

Tracy's parents also pointed out that she had a very strong relationship with her seven-year-old sister, Daisy. She wouldn't have just taken off without telling Daisy good-bye. And Tracy had no serious boyfriend with whom she might have run away.

When Roy West saw the area of where Tracy's motorbike had overturned, he told the reporter, "There's nothing along the trail where the motorcycle was found to cause an accident. No rocks, overhanging branches or bends. The bike probably left the trail at no more than fifteen miles per hour. There weren't even any skid marks to indicate she'd slammed on her brakes." Roy gave out a few more details as well about the actual condition of the motorbike when it was found. It was lying upside down, balanced on its seat and handlebars. The ignition was on, and it was in first gear. The clutch and throttle cables on the handlebars were damaged when it tipped over. Something, or someone, must have startled Tracy as she rode down the dark forest road.

The tracking dogs were able to pick up Tracy's scent from the bike overturn site back to the West home. And the dogs had picked up an earlier scent of Tracy from the restaurant's back door. There was no scent of Tracy wandering off into the woods, if she had done so after being hurt from overturning the motorbike.

MCSO picked up a story that in the weeks before her disappearance, some man at the restaurant had made a comment to Tracy about taking her home. A detective checked out that man, and his alibi held up that he had nothing to do with Tracy's disappearance. Brad Wilson said that his waitresses at the restaurant every once in a while got inappropriate comments, like the one Tracy had received, and they learned how to deal with them. Those comments were usually just some guy trying to be macho.

As the days went by, a reward fund was set up for anyone with information about the missing girl. A large jar was set on the counter at the Taylor Towne Restaurant, and customers stuffed it with spare change and dollar bills. Eunice West told a reporter, "We get alarmed every time we hear the phone ring." She never knew if it was going to be good news or bad news.

Then, as had happened in the McCollum, Rolls and Strasbaugh cases, the newspaper a week later stated, *No Clues on Tracy.* The newspaper related that nothing new had come in to help sheriff's detectives in their quest to find out what had happened to Tracy. The only new thing reported was that her motorcycle helmet and gloves had been found near the motorbike. The newspaper also reported that the West family had been impressed by the search efforts that had been made and were heartened by the amount of local support they were getting.

Weeks went by, and then on October 17, 1989, a hunter, Rick Leffler Jr., was walking through the woods and found a human skull on Taylor Ridge, outside the town of Shelton. Leffler alerted the sheriff's office to what he had found, and they had dental records checked. The skull turned out to be that of Tracy West. Surprisingly, her skull was found quite a distance north of where her motorbike had been overturned. That meant that her killer had to have driven her, either alive or dead, back past her own house and up onto Taylor Ridge. A forensic archaeologist aided in determining that the remains were those of Tracy West.

Detectives worked for five days with the forensic archaeologist, and a jacket was found with the logo *Certified Aerospace* upon it. That was the jacket Tracy had been wearing when she disappeared. Other items of clothing were also consistent with the clothing she could have been wearing at the time of her disappearance.

MCSO lieutenant Howard Armfield told a reporter that the detectives and search-and-rescue people scoured a five-acre area around where the skull had been found. They turned up the clothing and "significant bone structure." It was surmised that Tracy might have been buried in a shallow grave, or covered up with tree limbs and needles, but an animal had overturned all of that, exposing the bones. The MCSO sheriff said, "We are pleased with what we were able to find."

MCSO, however, was less pleased from that point forward. It was indeed the remains of Tracy West, but just how and why she had disappeared, and who had killed her, remained a mystery. The efforts by the MCSO came up with a big zero when it came to finding a suspect connected to the murder of Tracy West.

Meanwhile in Grays Harbor County, Lane Youmans turned his search of possible victims connected to David Gerard back to Lewis County. He learned that in 1991 a woman named Minyan (sometimes written as Mignon) Hensley went to a job interview at a strip club outside of Tacoma. Apparently, she didn't get the job, and not long after that she disappeared from the Tacoma area. A few weeks later, Hensley's skeleton was found forty miles away in Lewis County, hidden in a pile of brush near a state highway. No cause of death was ever determined, but all indications pointed to homicide.

Lane later said of the Hensley case, "She was allegedly eight months pregnant when she tried to get the job. She didn't seem like Gerard's type, but then you never knew. He was an opportunist more than anything. He would be driving along, spot a vulnerable woman and take advantage of the situation. He certainly did that with Julie at the bar. And he may have done that with more women. Obviously, Elaine McCollum had needed a ride on the night that she was murdered. Minyan Hensley may have needed a ride somewhere as well."

As Lane noted, "All these cases were different, and then they weren't. I knew that David Gerard liked to travel a lot, and I found that he liked to spend time around the Pacific Highway, in southern Pierce County. Not that Minyan Hensley was a prostitute. She may have just been in the wrong place at the wrong time. This area, however, near Tacoma, was an area that I learned was known for its prostitution activities. It was there, that on

September 27, 1996, Gerard was arrested in a 'john sting,' by the Pierce County Sheriff's Department." This john sting put him right in the area where Minyan Hensley had disappeared.

Lane learned that on that date Gerard had propositioned an undercover woman police deputy, and they agreed to have sex for $40. At the time Gerard was driving his Jeep, and this was only a few weeks after the murder of Carol Leighton. The undercover deputy told Gerard to meet her at a nearby motel room. Gerard did as instructed, and when he entered the motel room, clutching two 20-dollar bills in his hand, he was arrested.

Yet, even caught red-handed, Gerard did as he always did—he made up a lame excuse and stuck with his story. He denied wanting to have sex with anyone, and he said that he always walked around with money in his hand. Even when it was pointed out how ridiculous that sounded, he would not change his story.

What was interesting to Lane now was that this arrest was only weeks after the murder of Carol Leighton, who was known to engage in prostitution activities. During the arrest on September 27, 1996, in Pierce County, Gerard spoke of being stabbed by a prostitute a few weeks earlier. When PCSD officers looked into this, they found that Gerard had filed a report on September 18, 1996, about being robbed by a woman while he was on South Tacoma Way. He said that he'd been on his way home from his warehouse job in Auburn and had stopped at a 7-Eleven store outside of Tacoma, where he'd gone to get something to drink. According to Gerard, a woman was standing outside the store and asked him for a ride. Then he said she asked him if she could borrow $40.

According to Gerard's report, the young woman suddenly grabbed his wallet, which was sitting on the vehicle's console. Gerard said that she quickly removed $110 from the wallet, bolted out the door, fleeing. He denied that it was a "prostitution date" gone bad. During his later interview with Pierce County officers, Gerard mentioned almost as an afterthought that the woman had pulled out a small knife and stabbed him superficially. He also said that he wasn't able to do much at the time to stop her, because his right arm was in a sling.

Lane was intrigued by this remark that Gerard's arm had been in a sling at the time. Lane began to suspect that Gerard's arm had been in a sling because of his repeated and savage stabbing of Carol Leighton, only weeks before. During that attack Gerard's actions might have been so violent as to injure his right arm. Lane requested and got medical records on Gerard from the Community Hospital in Aberdeen for the time in question. Indeed, Gerard had gone to the Community Hospital around that time, complaining of an injured shoulder. Gerard said he'd received the injury from moving heavy furniture. Lane Youmans thought otherwise.

Because David Gerard was constantly driving all over the Puget Sound area and Olympic Peninsula, Lane Youmans began looking at an unsolved case in Pierce County, near Tacoma. It concerned a teenager named Misty Copsey, who went missing in 1992, and in some ways it had similarities to Tracy West's case. Both girls were not prone to running away; both had good grades in school; both were considered to be "good girls" by their friends. Misty was athletic and played on a softball team and volleyball team. She had never been in trouble with the law, and her friends all said that she did not drink or do drugs.

Fourteen-year-old Misty lived in Spanaway, Washington, with her mother, Diana. Misty's parents had separated when she was very young, and Misty and her mom moved from a mobile home park to a duplex in Spanaway in 1992. On September 17 of that year, Misty begged her mom to let her go to the nearby Puyallup Fair with a friend, fifteen-year-old Trina Bevard. After continual pleas, Diana finally let Misty go with Trina to the fair, unescorted by an adult.

When Misty left home, she was wearing a pair of stonewashed jeans with distinctive stitching. The girls had fun at the fair, and everything would have been okay, except that the girls missed the 8:40 P.M. bus from Puyallup to Spanaway. At 8:45 P.M. Misty called her mother, and said, "Mom, I missed the bus!" Misty wanted to get a ride back home with a boy she knew named Rheuban Schmidt, but Diana did not trust Rheuban. He was eighteen years old, whereas Misty was fourteen years old. In the past Diana had thought that Rheuban had paid way too much attention to her young daughter. Diana told Misty that she did not want her riding home with Rheuban.

Trina Bevard got a ride home with a boy she liked, but whom Misty didn't like. Misty did not ride back to Spanaway with them, and the last that Trina saw of Misty, she was walking down a road toward a bus stop. All night long, Diana waited for her daughter to return, but she never did. Eventually, in a panic, Diana called 911. The dispatcher said that nothing could be done at that point because the chances were that Misty was a runaway. Diana adamantly disagreed, saying that everything had been fine between herself and Misty, and that her daughter had not run away.

Eventually some at the Puyallup Police Department

(PPD) began to think that perhaps Diana was right. Captain Gary Smith, who often dealt with runaway teenagers, wrote a note to Sergeant Herm Carver: *This is one of those jus' don't feel right reports. There is nothing here that points to foul play, but it just don't feel right. It has been a week and nobody has heard from the girl. Mom is contacting the media complaining that the cops aren't doing anything.*

Matters weren't helped any for Diana after a student who knew Misty told the police that she'd seen Misty at a rock concert several days after Misty was reported missing. This only added credence to the police theory that Misty was indeed a runaway. Later, however, this student admitted that she wasn't positively sure the girl she had seen had been Misty.

Diana started going to a victims support group, and one of the individuals there was the father of Mignon (Minyan) Hensley, the murder victim whose body had been dumped in Lewis County in 1991. Soon thereafter, Diana was contacted by a local man named Cory Bober, a self-styled sleuth, who was absolutely convinced that a man named Randell Dean Achziger was the Green River Killer. Bober was also convinced that Misty Copsey was one of Achziger's victims.

Bober continually phoned Diana and they began an uneasy alliance. She didn't totally trust Bober, but with almost no help from the police—now that they believed Misty was a runaway and not a murder victim—Diana threw her lot in with Bober. Not unlike Bober, Diana believed that Misty's remains were somewhere in a field or forest outside of Puyallup. Bober was so sure of this, he convinced Minyan Hensley's father to accompany him on scouting trips in Pierce County to look up and down Highway 410 for signs of Misty's dump site. One region

Bober keyed in on was highway marker 30. The bodies of two teenagers, Kim DeLange and Anna Chebetnoy, had been found near there in previous years.

On February 7, 1993, Bober started one more search near the thirty-mile marker on Highway 410, with several volunteers, including Misty's mother, Diana. The volunteers started walking down a Weyco Mainline Road, off Highway 410. One of the volunteers was fourteen-year-old Jeremy Brown, who was a Boy Scout. Brown poked along a roadside ditch with a stick. Suddenly he stopped and pulled out a pair of blue jeans from the ditch with his stick. Then he yelled to the others, "Hey, there's some clothes here!"

Diana rushed over and just stared at the clothing that Jeremy had pulled out of the ditch. Then she began wailing and nearly collapsed. The clothing that Jeremy had pulled from the ditch was a pair of blue jeans with distinctive stitching. Diana knew those were the jeans that Misty had been wearing on September 17, 1992, when she had gone to the fair.

Eventually the searchers also found a pair of Hanes brand panties and a pair of blue socks. Trina Bevard later remembered Misty changing from white socks to blue, because they matched some of her other clothing. The searchers did not find Misty's blouse or shoes.

The lead Green River Killer detective from King County, Jim Doyon, came out to the site and admitted to the press, who'd gotten wind of the discovery of the jeans, that seven women's bodies had been found between Enumclaw and Green River since 1984. In fact, Kim DeLange and Anna Chebetnoy, whose bodies had been discovered not far away from the jeans site, were on Doyon's list of possible Green River victims. And then Doyon added one more thing. He said that there were also dissimilarities to the jeans site from the other Green River body dump sites.

Doyon met Cory Bober, and neither one became a fan of the other. Doyon believed Bober was a megalomaniac in his belief that Achziger was the killer of Misty Copsey and all the other Green River victims. Bober, for his part, was convinced that Doyon was just one more inept law enforcement detective. As time went on, in fact, Doyon and other law enforcement detectives began to wonder if Bober was actually Misty's murderer, who had gone to the Weyco Mainline Road before the searchers found the clothing items and had planted the jeans there. He might have had the jeans because he killed her.

Herm Carver's notes outlined this mistrust of Bober: *Why weren't the clothes strewn about? Taken off pants and placed there? Planted. If still on victim—wouldn't be found like that!*

Carver asked Cory Bober to come in and take a polygraph test to prove his innocence. When Bober heard that, he exploded, but he agreed to do so. Later he canceled this test, and never did take one. And yet, because of the search he organized, this was the first tangible evidence that Misty Copsey was a murder victim and not a runaway.

Bober was correct once again when DNA tests proved that the blue jeans had belonged to Misty Copsey. There was no blood on the jeans or semen. Several foreign hairs were found upon them, however, and three tiny red paint chips. These paint chips were deemed to be transfer chips, and might have come from a vehicle.

Then on November 30, 2001, the Green River Killer was finally arrested—Gary Leon Ridgway. Ridgway was charged with forty-eight murders, although he claimed that he had killed seventy-two women. Wondering if

Misty Copsey was one of his victims, detectives asked Ridgway if he had murdered the girl. Ridgway didn't remember killing her, and said that he hadn't killed any girls down near Puyallup. Then he added, "I will not take credit for killings I did not do."

Detectives later took Ridgway on various roads, where he pointed out where he had dumped bodies. On four different occasions detectives took Ridgway out on Highway 410, right past the area where Misty's jeans had been discovered along the Weyco Mainline Road. Not once did Ridgway indicate that he had murdered anyone there or deposited their clothing there. And he'd already claimed that he'd killed seventy-two women. One more wouldn't have made any difference to him if he had murdered Misty Copsey.

Lane Youmans thought that Gerard was a possible suspect for this murder. Gerard was an opportunist, and a girl walking alone down a road at night might have seemed too good an opportunity for him to pass up.

There was even another case of a fourteen-year-old that got Lane Youmans's attention. He said, "It was kind of early in the chronology of possible cases that might have been connected to David Gerard. It happened back on July 4, 1981, when he would have been nineteen years old. The victim was a girl named Carla Owens. She was a fourteen-year-old who disappeared while babysitting at a residence in Kalaloch, Jefferson County. The baby's mother spent the night at a place called the Horn In Tavern and stopped by the house a few times to check that things were all right. The mom eventually wound up sleeping in her car. When she went home, she found the baby alone and no sign of Carla. There was a note, supposedly from Carla, saying that she was going home, and a smashed wine bottle on the floor with blood on it. Carla seemed to have been assaulted in the residence, so this would have been different for Gerard. Of course, he was just nineteen then, so his MO might have changed over the years from that point forward. He was more of the type to take advantage of a woman who needed a ride somewhere. Carla's remains were never found."

This case in some ways had an aspect like that of Colleen Moran, of Kitsap County. She had left her three-year-old with a babysitter and walked to a cocktail lounge in Port Orchard, in Kitsap County, on August 20, 1985. If there was little information available to Lane on Carla Owens, there was even less on Colleen Moran. She simply disappeared after going to the cocktail lounge and was never seen again.

With a lot of these cases, Lane Youmans had one particular gripe. He said that rotating detectives in and out of investigations meant there was little continuity on a cold case. Lane added, "I always thought it was a shame that a lot of smaller departments rotated detectives through the system. The reasoning was that it gave the officers more experience in the department. But I felt that at least some of the detectives needed to stay within Investigations. If I had not done that, I don't think I ever would have connected the name David Gerard from the milking shed to the house fire to the Weyco Haul Road."

Then Lane added, "Did I think David Gerard was connected to all of these murders? No. But he definitely could have been connected to some of them. Each one had to be studied to see if there was a connection and how he fit into the case."

* * *

As Lane Youmans collected various criminal reports, he decided that he shouldn't just limit his search to murdered women in the area. By now, Lane knew that Gerard's murders stemmed from rage, as much as anything else. When in such a state, he could just as easily have murdered a man as a woman. True, Gerard picked women more often because he viewed them as easier targets, and also because he became angry at them when some "romantic or sexual" situation turned bad. But this didn't exclude men from being targets of his rage.

Lane looked at two cases concerning missing men in Grays Harbor County, and one particulary interested him. Bill Delano had gone deer hunting in the eastern Humptulips area in 1983. He went missing and his vehicle was found where he had left it on a logging road. A massive search in the area turned up nothing. One thing that was known was that Delano had gone hunting with a .270-caliber rifle, but the brand was unknown.

Lane discovered that when David Gerard was arrested in Lewis County for destroying Frankie Cochran's clothing and other items, the deputies there took two of Gerard's rifles. One was a .22-caliber rifle, while the other was a Voere Shikar .270-caliber rifle. Lane learned from people who had known Gerard that he liked to hunt deer, elk and bear around the Humptulips area. Lane was able to prove from a hunting citation that Gerard had been hunting in that area in the early 1980s. In 1984, Gerard had been cited in the Humptulips area for selling bear meat illegally and hunting without a license. And Lane already knew from the report about David attacking his brother Donald that Gerard told an officer he was going bear hunting on that particular day. It also proved that

David could become extremely violent with another male when he was "pissed off."

Try as he might, Lane could not find a serial number connected to Bill Delano's .270-caliber rifle. For whatever reason, the investigating deputy had not obtained that serial number or even the make of the rifle when he wrote the report in 1983. Lane tried contacting the Delano family about the rifle, but by 2003, Bill's father had died, and the rest of the family members couldn't recall any other information about the rifle.

Lane wondered, "Did Bill Delano and David Gerard's paths cross one day in 1983? The rifles were still in the Lewis County Sheriff's Office evidence room. I received permission to check the rifles out of the evidence room. I photographed them, then took them to the WSP Lab in Tacoma, where they were test-fired, and the bullets and casings were entered into the Automated Ballistic Identification System (ABIS) computer system, which can compare the rifling and firing-pin marks. I felt that there might be a bullet or casing in the system that might match Gerard's rifle. But it never went beyond that."

By 2001, Lane Youmans recalled, "I was putting a case together against David Gerard, and I got to the point that I thought about him all the time. I knew eventually that we would have to question him. We had DNA evidence that now tied him to Carol Leighton. Elaine McCollum's panties were sitting on a shelf in the state crime lab evidence refrigerator, waiting to be analyzed. I wanted to be prepared for the interview even though I was pretty sure he would not confess. Gerard never had confessed to anything in his life, and instead he came up with ludicrous stories. Nonetheless, it was worth a try."

Gathering even more information on Gerard's background, before going to talk with him, Lane spoke with one of David's former girlfriends, Tracy Hall. She told Lane that shortly before they broke up, there had been a fight between them, and she went outside one day to find that the tires on her vehicle had been slashed. They were Les Schwab tires that Gerard had bought for her. A witness had spotted Gerard's car in the area, shortly before Tracy's tires had been slashed. At the time Detective Tony Catlow had questioned Gerard about the slashed tires, and Gerard said he hadn't slashed them.

Then quite unexpectedly, Gerard added, "I didn't do it. I hired someone to do it." Just why that would somehow look better in law enforcement's eyes was hard to comprehend. Gerard refused to name the person who had supposedly slashed Tracy's tires. He was charged with malicious mischief and pled guilty. In fact, law enforcement officers believed that Gerard had done the actual tire slashing, and not some unnamed person whom he had hired.

Tracy Hall moved to Springfield, Oregon, and shortly after moving there, her tires were mysteriously slashed again. Once again it brought up the possibility that Gerard had traveled all the way to Springfield, just to slash her tires. Or this time he actually had hired someone to do the dirty work. What was interesting to Lane now was that this was the only time that Gerard even came close to confessing to a crime that he had committed. Of course, Gerard probably knew that for a crime such as slashing tires, there wasn't much of a penalty. It would be something he could live with, if it gave him the satisfaction of wreaking havoc on his ex-girlfriend's car.

17

COVER PLAN

Lane Youmans wanted help in putting together a plan on how to question David Gerard. He once again contacted Bob Gebo, a former Seattle police detective who had been trained at the FBI's Behavioral Science Unit, and now worked for the Washington State Attorney General's Office in the HITS Unit. Gebo put Lane in touch with Special Agent Faye Greenley, who worked in the BSU, and was assigned to Seattle's FBI Field Unit. Greenley and Gebo agreed to meet Lane at the attorney general's office in Seattle and discuss a game plan on how best to approach David Gerard.

On March 30, 2001, Sergeant Dave Pimentel, Detective Tony Catlow and Lane Youmans drove to downtown Seattle and met with Greenley and Gebo. George Fox, who was with HITS, and a few other investigators were also there. Most of these were former Homicide Division detectives, and they had years of experience in the field. Lane unpacked all the case files on Gerard and eight-by-ten crime scene photos, and began describing the various cases possibly connected to Gerard and his background.

After his initial presentation Lane asked the others what would be the best way to approach Gerard, especially on the possible house fire murders of Patricia McDonnell and Patty, Joshua and Matt Rodriguez. He wondered if Gerard should be approached the way Seattle Fire Department (SFD) investigators had done with serial arsonist Paul Kellor. Those investigators had prepared by arranging numerous empty boxes with Kellor's name written on them, lined up in the interview room. There were also photographic blow-ups of Kellor displayed on the walls of the hallway leading into the interview room. All of it was a ruse to make Kellor think they had piles of documents and evidence already collected against him. In the end it worked. Kellor not only confessed to the arsons they suspected him of committing, but many more that they didn't even know about.

The case with Gerard would be somewhat different, however. Lane remarked, "Paul Kellor had a great deal of respect for the fire department, and he had wanted to become a fireman himself. David Gerard, on the other hand, hated the police, and had no use for what they represented. After hearing all this, the group was in agreement that a low-key approach with Gerard was best. They said that I needed to somehow gain his confidence, sympathize with him, suggest that the women who died got what they deserved. Just get him talking."

Lane Youmans was certain of one thing—if David Gerard ever did start talking, he probably wouldn't stop. Lane believed it would all come pouring out like a tidal wave. However, Lane also believed that Gerard would be clever in all of this. He would talk, and talk, and never confess to anything. Lane said, "He would probably make up some lame story and stick with it. That's what he always did when cornered. No matter how outrageous the story, he would stick to it, despite how ludicrous it sounded."

The two-hour meeting did help Lane formulate a plan, where Gerard would be removed from prison and be sent down to the sheriff's office in Montesano. Lane was somewhat concerned that Undersheriff Rick Scott would be the one who would want to question David Gerard. Scott had questioned several homicide suspects in the past. In fact, he had questioned one man who had gone to his estranged wife's home late at night and shot the wife's boyfriend through the bedroom door with a shotgun. The suspect fled in his car down a county road, and his vehicle broke down a quarter mile from the crime scene. The man then hid his shotgun in tall grass near the road, next to his car. He was at a nearby house, trying to get help in fixing his car, when the first deputy arrived. Taken in for questioning, the man broke down and confessed under Rick Scott's technique. Scott's style was to start out quietly, becoming more and more animated and frustrated as time went on, then ended up yelling at the suspect. In this case it had worked, and the killer confessed.

Lane, however, said, "I was sure this technique would not work with David Gerard. He would shut down and not say anything. It was imperative that I convince Scott to avoid that technique at all cost. His aggressive nature would end the interview. Even though we had DNA evidence on the Carol Leighton case, prosecutor Steward Menefee wanted a confession as well. While other departments in other areas got convictions with just physical evidence, our prosecutor always wanted more, so as to have an overwhelming case."

* * *

Lane Youmans once again used a cover plan, saying he was doing research on domestic violence, and wanted David Gerard's take on it. Lane phoned Corydon Whalley, who was an investigator at the Stafford Creek Corrections Center, west of Aberdeen, and told Whalley that he needed to question Gerard at the Clallam Bay state prison. Whalley gave Lane the name of an investigator at Clallam Bay, and a meeting was arranged with Gerard.

On August 9, 2001, Lane drove three hours up to Forks, where he and his band members had played their memorable show so many years before at the Antlers Inn, and then on to the small town of Clallam Bay. When he arrived there, Lane locked all his weapons in his Ford Expedition, then contacted the guards at the main office. He secured his cell phone, pager, belt badge, pocketknife, keys and everything metal in a small locker. He then walked through the metal detector, carrying only his notebook, pen and credentials.

Clallam Bay prison could have hardly been in a more isolated area. On the very northwestern tip of the Olympic Peninsula, Vancouver Island in Canada was right across the straits. The prison was officially known as Clallam Bay Corrections Center and it had opened in 1985. By the time Gerard was housed there, it was a "close-custody" prison. This meant it was a medium-security prison and above by that point.

Escorted to a room in the visiting center, Lane spotted David Gerard sitting on a metal bench down the hall; a quizzical look was on David's face. Gerard was wearing a white jumpsuit and looking much thinner than the last time Lane had seen him. Lane introduced himself and stuck out his hand. Gerard reluctantly took Lane's hand in one of his and shook it weakly.

They went into an interview room and sat down on metal chairs on opposite sides of a long metal table. Lane began by telling Gerard about working on domestic violence cases, and wanting to know why these things occurred. Especially why someone would abuse a person whom, he said, he loved. Gerard rarely made any eye contact with Lane, and mostly stared at the table in front of him. When he did look at Lane, it was as if he were looking right through him. Lane tried being friendly, and spoke in a conversational pleasant manner, seeing if he could gain Gerard's trust.

Lane tried talking to Gerard about the assault on Frankie Cochran. Lane said that he wanted to know what happened, what suddenly made him snap. Lane also said that he wanted to know what Gerard had done with the hammer. Suddenly, and unexpectedly, Gerard perked up and said that he was appealing the sentence on that case. Gerard added that he'd gotten word from another inmate in the prison that he had a good chance of overturning that sentence, because it was too harsh. For that reason Gerard claimed he didn't want to say anything about the Frankie Cochran case.

Lane was surprised by this statement, since Gerard had initially gone so willingly into the plea deal. Moving in a different direction, Lane began talking about Gerard's early years and his family. Gerard, in return, gave mostly one-word answers to questions, and would not elaborate. Gerard did say that he left home as a teenager and took care of himself from that point on. He added that his dad had left their home when David was young, and their relationship was strained. Other than that revelation, Gerard offered very little about his past.

After their meeting was over, Lane recalled, "I did accomplish what I had set out to do. I wanted a glimpse of who I was up against. Gerard struck me as someone who was not very bright, but he was streetwise. He seemed kind of happy to be in prison. His was in a single-person cell, he had a job working in the prison mess hall, and he didn't like to interact with people very much." In fact, it seemed as if David Gerard had found his niche in life. In prison parlance "three hots and a cot" is what he now had. In other words, three hot meals per day and a place to sleep at night. All of it furnished by the state of Washington.

What was interesting to Lane was what he learned from a prison investigator. He discovered that one of the few people Gerard had any contact with was a man named Gary Davis. Davis was a Grays Harbor man who, in 1999, built a bomb for a meth dealer named Steven Pink. Davis then set the bomb in the carport of Pink's parole officer, Tom Perrine. The bomb was sitting on the ground next to Perrine's truck and was covered with trash. When he was on his way to work, Perrine spotted the trash near his vehicle and scooped it up to throw it into a trash can. At that point the bomb detonated, blowing nails and shrapnel into Perrine's legs, and blowing off Perrine's index finger. Perrine nearly bled to death before he was rescued.

Steven Pink, Gary Davis and Davis's girlfriend were later convicted and sent to prison. Lane learned that it was Gary Davis who had convinced Gerard that he could somehow get his sentence overturned. In fact, Davis seemed to be Gerard's only friend at the state prison. Lane also learned that none of Gerard's family had tried visiting him in prison, although his sister, Kathy, had tried, but David had turned down her request.

Lane told Gerard that the sheriff's office still had some of his effects, and that if he wanted, Lane could turn those over to Kathy. Gerard said that it was okay if he did so. This was a good opportunity for Lane to talk to Kathy about David, something he'd been wanting to do for a while.

Lane's last words to Gerard that day were "I'll see you later." Gerard responded, "Okay," without much enthusiasm, and then was led back down the hallway to his cell without another word.

After the interview was over, Lane gathered up his belongings and went and sat in his vehicle. He recalled, "I sat there, staring out the windshield at the surrounding forest. I had tried very hard to maintain my composure while talking to Gerard. I didn't want to betray my true feelings. I knew that Gerard was a murderer, but he had no idea at that point that I knew his secret. All he knew was that I was aware of his assaulting Frankie Cochran, and that's all. Sitting alone in my vehicle, I could now relax. I sat there listening to my breath, my mind racing."

David Gerard's comments that he was going to try and overturn his "harsh sentence" were more than just words. In November 2001, he followed through on his words by writing out in several documents an Affidavit of Defendant in Support of Motion to Vacate Judgment and Sentence. It's possible he had legal help in writing these documents, since the language was very precise and legalistic. In one document Gerard claimed that he was advised by his attorney Brett Ballew to plead guilty to attempted first-degree murder. Gerard stated that he got intense pressure to make the plea. According to David, his lawyer had told him that he could receive the death penalty if he didn't make a plea deal. This section must have concerned Frankie if she died of her injuries at some point.

Gerard went on to write, *I feel that my case was not properly investigated and that my witnesses were not interviewed. I had alibi witnesses and there were no doubt other witnesses who were at the scene of the alleged assault of the victim Ms. Cochran. My attorney failed to interview or consider them as potential witnesses.*

Gerard went on to say that he had not been properly informed what his sentence might be for signing the agreement. And he added that he thought the final sentence was far outside the bounds of being reasonable for the crime.

In a second document Gerard noted that he signed the plea agreement with the understanding that he would receive 249 months in prison, but had instead received the *exceptional sentence of 420 months.* He had appealed this sentence in the Washington State Court of Appeals, Division II, but they had upheld the conviction on May 23, 2000. For that reason he was now withdrawing his guilty plea and wanted the judgment and sentence vacated. Once again in his document Gerard cited, *Ineffective assistance of counsel.* Gerard wrote that he not only got bad advice, but that he was *rushed through the process and pressured to plead guilty.* Gerard cited *State* vs. *Jury* for lack of preparation by counsel, and *State* vs. *Visistacion* in failing to contact witnesses for the defense.

In a third document Gerard stated that since he was incarcerated in Clallam Bay prison, he had restricted use of telephone privileges and could not do investigative work on his own behalf. For that reason he wanted a professional attorney to help him in his motion to overturn his sentence. Gerard also wrote: *This litigant lacks an education to enable him to research and understand rules of the courts, state, federal and common law to the degree and effectiveness that would help him handle this case now at the bar.*

Taking all of this into account, Judge McCauley appointed James Foley, of Olympia, Washington, to be David Gerard's new attorney. Gerard's legal battle in this case would play out over the next few years. Meanwhile, Lane Youmans kept up his efforts to have David Gerard convicted for one or more murders, especially those of Elaine McCollum, Carol Leighton or Patty Rodriguez.

18

SHOWDOWN AT STAFFORD CREEK

Lane Youmans's case files on David Gerard were growing by the day, and his reports now ran into the hundreds of pages. Because so much had been gathered by this point, and there was the DNA evidence connected to Carol Leighton, Lane Youmans and the other detectives had some alternatives now. One was discussed in a formal GHSO meeting to see if David Gerard would confess and make some kind of plea deal, as he had done in the Frankie Cochran case.

By trying to set up some kind of meeting with Gerard, GHSO could either seek a superior court order to have David Gerard transferred to the Stafford Creek Corrections Center, close to Aberdeen, or they could do it where he would have to come to the sheriff's office. Speaking with him at Stafford Creek would take less hurdles through the system, but by going the sheriff's office route, Gerard could stay under sheriff's office control and not state control.

Eventually it was decided to bring Gerard down to Stafford Creek, but Lane didn't like the setup. He would have preferred to have Gerard in the sheriff's lockup, "on their turf. There were just too many variables with having him go to Stafford Creek. It would be the prison system who would set up the conference and how it would go down, not GHSO."

Another thing that bothered Lane was that he was sure by now they had plenty of physical and circumstantial evidence tying David Gerard to the murders of Elaine McCollum and Carol Leighton. But County Prosecutor Steward Menefee still wanted more. Menefee wanted an outright confession from Gerard, and Lane was sure that was going to be a very difficult task, if not impossible. All past indications were that Gerard just clammed up, even when faced with overwhelming evidence against him. Either that or he made up some outrageous alibi and stuck with it—no matter how ludicrous it was.

Undersheriff Rick Scott contacted Corydon Whalley, the investigator at Stafford Creek, and Gerard was transferred to that facility. Eventually Undersheriff Scott, Sergeant Pimentel and Lane Youmans made their way to Stafford Creek to question Gerard. Once again, their guns, keys and all metal objects were taken before entering the interview room. All they carried with them were some notes, photos of Elaine and Carol, along with some photos of local prostitutes.

Lane, Rick Scott and Sergeant Pimentel met Gerard in the Intensive Unit of the facility, because of the seriousness of his crime. The Intensive Unit was the most secure area at Stafford Creek. Like at Clallam Bay, Lane and Scott and Pimentel escorted Gerard into a room that only

had a metal table and metal chairs. Gerard was wearing
white coveralls, ankle cuffs, belly chain and handcuffs.
The guards walked Gerard over to a metal box in the
corner and handcuffed him there, with a chain that ran
down to a secure spot on the floor. The guards left, standing just outside in the hallway. Lane, Scott, Pimentel and
Whalley stayed in the room with Gerard.

Right from the start, Lane Youmans felt that the whole
situation was bad. He wanted another low-key interview
with Gerard, one where Gerard would feel more comfortable and not set upon. Lane wondered, "With this setup,
how could he feel comfortable with us? How could we
read his body language? He was tied up, hand and foot.
It was ridiculous. At least Whalley agreed to have
Gerard's handcuffs removed so that he could hold the
photos we'd brought along. But I was very displeased
with the way things were handled. I think the other detectives from GHSO were too. It was stacking the cards
against us, right off the bat."

Undersheriff Scott conducted the interview, and Sergeant Pimentel assisted. Lane turned away from Gerard
and took notes. He felt that two pairs of eyes staring at
Gerard were more than enough. Gerard did not want to
talk to Pimentel or Lane, but things began to change
when Rick Scott started talking to Gerard. Scott had
grown up on a dairy farm and knew all about the way
they operated. In fact, both Scott and Gerard knew many
of the same dairy farmers in the east county area. Scott
and Gerard got down to mostly small talk about farms
and dairies. While this was going on, Gerard was re-
laxed and seemed to be enjoying the conversation about
places he had worked and areas that he knew. As much as
any law enforcement officer had ever done, Rick Scott
had some rapport with David Gerard.

Then Scott told Gerard why they were there, and Gerard's mood began to change immediately. Scott told Gerard they were looking into some old homicides concerning women who had hung out around downtown Aberdeen. These women had often gone to taverns in downtown Aberdeen and across the river in south Aberdeen as well. In fact, the women's bodies had been found on the other side of the river from downtown Aberdeen.

Scott said to David that they knew that Gerard had frequented those taverns as well, and probably knew many of the same people that these women had known. Scott then showed photos of Elaine McCollum and Carol Leighton, along with prostitutes who worked in the downtown area. Then he asked Gerard if he'd ever seen any of these women before.

Gerard briefly looked at the photos and denied ever having seen Elaine or Carol, but he did say that he thought he had seen one of the other women in Aberdeen. Scott then told Gerard that murders had occurred on the Weyco Haul Road, and he asked if he'd ever been on that road. Gerard replied that he knew where the road was, but claimed that he'd never been on it.

At that point Rick Scott picked up the photos of Elaine and Carol and handed them to David Gerard. He asked once again if Gerard had ever seen these two women. Gerard looked at one photo for several seconds, then at the other. There was no expression on his face. He handed the photos back to Scott and said that he'd never seen either woman. Lane shifted in his seat during this process, to get a better view of Gerard and his reactions. Lane said later, "I saw no reaction in his face. No change. Nothing that would betray his inner thoughts. Just a blank stare, with dead eyes. I knew that he would never confess, but at least we had him in a lie. Or several lies. I could put him on the Weyco Haul Road, and I could put him there with Carol Leighton, shortly before she was murdered because of his DNA."

Not giving anything away, Rick Scott asked Gerard if he'd ever heard any rumors about who had killed these two women on the Weyco Haul Road. Scott knew that many suspects would come up with some name, just to take the scrutiny off themselves. But Gerard said that he hadn't heard any rumors at all concerning the two women. He just sat there like a sphinx.

Lane said later, "In most interviews you'll see the person have flashes of emotion—anger or shame or something. Not with Gerard. He never got angry, even when pressed. The only time he showed a flash of anger was when Rick Scott asked if he had anything to do with the death of his mother. David heatedly said, 'I didn't do it!' And then he shut down again. He wasn't reward driven. He wasn't fear driven. At Clallam Bay prison a lot of prisoners are motivated by drugs or power or sex. Not David. He was a loner who kept to himself most of the time. It was like trying to talk to a brick wall."

Scott asked Gerard if he'd give them some hair samples, because some hair had been found at the murder scenes. This wasn't critical, since law enforcement already had Gerard's DNA. But it could be useful as one more building block in a case. Surprisingly, Gerard agreed that it would be okay, and Lane put on latex gloves, grabbed a pair of tweezers and plucked out several hairs from Gerard's head. Lane then asked Gerard to hold the tweezers and pluck out several of his own pubic hairs, which he did. All the hairs were placed into separate envelopes.

After this was over, Rick Scott asked Gerard if they

could come and talk to him again if they had any more questions. With little enthusiasm Gerard said, "Sure," and the interview was over. The detectives thanked Gerard and left.

Once they were in the parking lot, they discussed what had just occurred and how to proceed from there. They agreed that the next step was to get Gerard into the sheriff's office, away from guards, ankle cuffs and waist chains. What they needed to do was get a court order. Lane had one big concern about this, however. He knew that Gerard liked where he was in prison—with his job and his single cell. He didn't want to "piss" him off. Lane said, "He didn't have much in prison, and actually he didn't need much or want much. Losing those things were important to him, and they might make him unhappy and uncooperative. He would blame us for screwing up his little world. But our County Prosecutor wanted a confession. In most counties, what we had already was more than enough for charges to be filed. But Steward Menefee wanted more."

In the end Lane Youmans was right. David Gerard was "pissed off" that his comfy little world at Clallam Bay had been upset. Gerard was sent to another prison, this time in Arizona, because of overcrowding in the Washington State prisons, and he lost his single cell and all the privileges he had accrued. If Gerard had been uncooperative in the past, he was doubly so now. There would be no confession coming out of David Gerard for the Carol Leighton, Elaine McCollum or any other cases. The detectives were going to have to paint Gerard into a corner where all the evidence pointed to him as the murderer on at least one of these cases. The last thing the detectives wanted was for Gerard to be out walking the streets in case his sentence on Frankie Cochran was ever reduced. And as time went by, Gerard was fighting hard to do just that. He may not have had a whole lot of education in the school system, but he was slowly learning the legal system and becoming a "jailhouse lawyer."

19

WHERE THERE'S SMOKE, THERE'S FIRE

Since he was looking at every angle of David Gerard by now, Lane Youmans decided to reinvestigate the deaths of Patty Rodriguez, Matthew Rodriguez, Joshua Rodriguez and Patricia McDonnell in the house fire of 1995. Lane noted, "Detective Parfitt had examined the scene and shot several rolls of film. And I had attended the autopsies conducted by Dr. Daniel Selove at the Coleman Mortuary in Hoquiam. Dr. Selove said that a blast of superheated air could have ended the lives of Patricia McDonnell and the boys quickly, before any soot would collect in their throats or lungs. Patty Rodriguez, by comparison, had a lot of soot in her throat. Her carbon dioxide level was eighty-nine percent, easily a fatal dose. The problem was, she sustained a concussion on the right side of her skull."

It was that concussion that Lane examined once more, very carefully, keeping in mind the hammer blows Gerard had inflicted to the side of Frankie Cochran's head when he tried killing her with a hammer, and the possible blows to the head of Carol Leighton before she was killed with a knife. It was true that Detective Parfitt and Lane had gone back to the fire scene a few days after interviewing David Gerard in 1995, and had located a two-by-six piece of burned lumber that was about eighteen inches in length, lying near the spot where Patty Rodriguez had died. But with so many factors pointing to an accidental fire, the fracture on the side of Patty Rodriguez's head did not seem that important at the time.

Lane commented in 2001, "We didn't seize that piece of burned wood, and that has always haunted me. I relied upon Gary's expertise, and went along with his assessment. There just did not seem to be signs of foul play at the time. Things seemed to point to an accidental fire."

It was only in retrospect that Lane discovered there had been no photos taken of the deceased Patricia McDonnell or the boys in the interior of the house. And there were no close-up photos taken of the woodstove or stovepipe. In fact, no samples were taken of anything in the burned house. Even after Gerard's strange behavior, upon being questioned about his whereabouts during the time of the fire, the official conclusion had been that all four victims had died because of an accidental fire.

When Lane told Detective Parfitt that he was going to reopen the investigation on the fire, Lane recounted, "He was open to it, but not really enthusiastic." Nonetheless, Parfitt gave Lane everything he had on the case, including documents and photos. Lane started reading all the material connected to the fire, and made his own copies of files and photos. Because of the official cause of death listed as accidental, Lane knew he had many hurdles to overcome in this aspect about Gerard. If things were difficult in bringing David Gerard to trial for the murder of Elaine McCollum or Carol Leighton, they were doubly so for the victims of the fire. Lane knew that a good defense lawyer would cite Grays Harbor County's own reports that the fire was accidental.

Lane Youmans began reinterviewing people who had known the victims and David Gerard. He was able to locate Steve Stoken, who had known David Gerard since high school. Stoken told Lane that he didn't recall any trip with Gerard to the Tyee Lounge in Olympia, or eating with him at the Red Barn Restaurant on the night of the fire. And he certainly didn't know anyone named "Mike," who they had supposedly gone drinking with on the night in question. In fact, Stoken said he wouldn't have gone out drinking without his wife, and he was 100 percent sure the story Gerard was using was not true.

Lane next located Brian McDonnell, Patty's brother. Brian was a volunteer fireman, and when Lane told Brian about the story from Gerard about a stovepipe clogged with soot, Brian laughed out loud. Brian said that when Patty's ex-husband, Sergio Rodriguez, had installed the stovepipe, he had done so incorrectly. Brian went out to the house and discovered that the wood around the stovepipe in the attic was beginning to char. So with Brian's aid, Sergio took that stovepipe out and installed a safer one, to Brian's satisfaction.

Brian said of this new pipe that it was not filled with creosote, as Gerard had indicated, and Brian said that his mother, Patricia, was afraid of fires. Brian added that when she started the woodstove at night, she would open the damper up full. The stove would get so hot, the metal would glow red. Patricia did this to keep the stove free of creosote. Because of Brian's occupation and knowledge about fire safety, Patricia was very cognizant of the dangers in a wood-burning stove.

Brian also said that his mother was very good about the smoke detectors in the house. He knew that they were in good working order, because he had tested them only two weeks before the fatal fire, and the batteries had been in good shape then. Brian doubted Gerard's claim that he had recently bought batteries for the smoke detectors. Gerard also had said he didn't know if Patricia McDonnell had replaced the old ones. In fact, Brian was sure that all the old batteries would not have gone dead at the same time, and he was sure that he had bought batteries for his mother only weeks before the fire. If so, Gerard's story that he had bought batteries for her for the smoke alarms must have been one more of his lies.

Brian told Lane that deep in his heart, and that of his sister, Michelle Traverso, they always felt that David Gerard had somehow been responsible for the deadly fire. Lane Youmans contacted Michelle and asked her about the story he had picked up from Frankie Cochran, in which David told Frankie that Patty Rodriguez's uncle had been convicted for setting the fire. Michelle said that she, Brian and Patty didn't have an uncle, but that they did have a brother who was convicted of murder, and was on death row in Oregon for a 1988 murder. She didn't know how this might have fit into Gerard's story to Frankie. It was obvious that this brother could not have set the fire, however. He was incarcerated at the time that it had occurred. Michelle thought it was quite possible

that Gerard had used this false story to try and throw
Frankie off, as far as the true nature of things concerning the fire.

Lane had Michelle identify a large gold ring that Patty
had owned. Michelle said that it had belonged to their
father and contained a brown stone. Lane told her the ring
was not found on Patty's finger when her body was discovered. Michelle insisted that Patty always wore that
ring, and Lane wondered if Gerard had stolen the ring
after hitting Patty in the head, before starting the fire.
Gerard often seemed to keep one or two items from his
victims. (At least those victims had some things missing
when their bodies were discovered.)

There was also another twist to this story about rings.
David Gerard had said he wanted to go to the burned-
out house several days after the fire to look for an engagement ring that he'd given Patty. Michelle said that
neither she nor Brian knew anything about this alleged
engagement ring. Then Michelle added that after the funeral she had been in Hoquiam at the home of a woman
named Pearl Payne. Pearl was a lifelong friend of Patricia
McDonnell's, and Michelle had known Pearl all her life.
While they were there, David Gerard showed up at Pearl's
house and sat down in a chair in the living room. Then he
just stared at the floor. He sat there for several hours and
didn't say a word. Michelle said she finally got him to
talk. He spoke very little, and just before he left, he told
the two women he was so depressed that he was going to
kill himself. Of course, he did no such thing.

Lane noted later, "Michelle described the same catatonic state I saw when Detective Parfitt and I questioned
Gerard in 1995, and when Undersheriff Rick Scott tried
to grill him at the Stafford Creek facility. When dealing

with something he was accused of doing, or might be accused of doing, he just shut down."

After Michelle Traverso, Lane Youmans interviewed Margaret Jimenez, who was a good friend of Patty Rodriguez, and who had been with her on the last evening of her life. Jimenez had known Patty for four years, and their husbands were good friends. Margaret described Patty as being a very independent woman. She did not want to be tied down to being a housewife without any means of support—especially with a guy like David Gerard, who never held a steady, good-paying job.

Margaret said, "At first, Patty thought that David was okay. She said, 'He's a nice guy, but I can't stand him. He helps my mom out, but he's not for me.'"

Margaret told Lane, "Patty hated anyone who tried to control her. I didn't believe David Gerard had a steady job, and I knew that Patty would never marry him because of that reason. David was very possessive, and Patty hated that kind of thing. When Patty used to bring the kids over to visit, David would never come along with her."

Margaret added that Patty worked for a weather station up at Quinault. Quinault was a small town north of Aberdeen, on Highway 101, situated on the edge of Olympic National Park. Patty worked four days on, and three days off. Patty had trained for this job in Oregon. According to Margaret, Gerard had gone up to the weather station at Quinault after Patty's death and got some of Patty's things, which he never gave back to her siblings. (Just what items he might have collected is not known.)

On the evening before she died, Margaret said, Patty had taken her kids to Godfather's Pizza in Aberdeen, and

hen she and Patty joined Nora Huffman, another friend,
for some drinks at Muddy Waters in south Aberdeen.

Margaret added that Patty was "trying to get her life
back together, when Gerard came along. Within a short
amount of time, David wanted them to get married." He
even would say later that he and Patty had been engaged,
but Margaret stressed that she and Patty were good
friends, and Patty would have mentioned something like
that *if* it was true. The last thing Patty wanted was to be
married to a guy like Gerard.

At Muddy Waters that evening Patty expressly told the
others that she did not want to marry David Gerard. She
even said, "I just got rid of one bum, and don't want to
marry another one." Patty spoke of how Gerard had no
steady job, and it didn't look like he ever would. He
wanted her kids to call him "Uncle David," which she
didn't much like, and he had already moved some of his
clothing into the house that she and the boys shared with
her mom.

While Patty, Margaret and Nora were at Muddy Waters,
Gerard came in and sat down at their table. At least that
is what happened according to Jimenez. (Nora's story
would differ in some details.) According to Margaret,
David and Patty began to argue, and they soon took their
argument outside. Apparently, Margaret either went outside, or was close enough to hear what was being said.
She told Lane that she heard Patty tell Gerard that they
were through and that he had to take his stuff out of her
mom's house. David, according to Jimenez, was very
upset about this. He especially didn't like being told off
by a woman in front of others. David left, and Patty drove
over to Margaret's house, with Margaret as a passenger.
Patty was clearly upset and said very little on the drive.

Patty let Margaret off, and that was the last time Margaret saw her alive.

Margaret added that Patty's mom, Patricia McDonnell, was very concerned about a fire in the house, and she always kept her fire alarms up to code. In fact, Margaret said Patty had told her not long before the fatal fire that they had just bought some new batteries for the smoke alarms. These appeared to be a different set of batteries than the ones Gerard had spoken of. In this scenario Patty had bought the batteries, and not Gerard, as he had indicated.

And Margaret wondered why the dogs in the house would not have barked and awakened the people inside about a fire. Margaret told Lane, "Patty had a large black-and-white husky, and Mrs. McDonnell had a little dog. Both dogs would bark whenever anybody would approach the house. They wouldn't bark if Gerard came around because they knew him."

Margaret added that she was pretty sure that David Gerard had gone out to Patricia McDonnell's house sometime on the afternoon before the house fire. He supposedly had gone out there to pick up some fencing material.

Margaret also related that in 1999, when she read in the newspaper about David Gerard assaulting Frankie Cochran, she began to wonder if he had killed Patty and the rest of the people inside the McDonnell home, then set the fire. Margaret began to question why Patty's mom could get out of a chair and move twenty feet toward the door, but Patty never made it out of her bed. Margaret began to believe that David had killed Patty in her bed, then caught Patricia McDonnell near the door and murdered her. In Margaret's mind he had probably killed the dogs first, and then the boys as they slept on the floor.

* * *

Lane Youmans contacted Nora Huffman, who had known the Gerard family for many years. In fact, this was the same Nora Huffman who had heard stories about David raping a three-year-old girl in the projects when he was only thirteen. Speaking about some of David's girlfriends before Patty Rodriguez, Nora recounted one as being Donna Torres. Huffman said that when Torres broke up with David, he had stalked her and smashed the windows of her vehicle.

Another girlfriend of Gerard's after that, according to Nora, had been a young woman named Tracy. Huffman said that Tracy had been five months pregnant when David got mad at her one day. They were driving along to a farm in Oakville, and David got so mad at her, he pushed her out of the car while it was still moving, and she lost the baby.

Right from the start, Huffman said, she'd told Patty Rodriguez that David Gerard was "bad news." According to Huffman, just before Christmas, 1994, Patty found out that she was pregnant by Gerard and decided to have an abortion at a location in Olympia. Huffman said that Gerard later found out about the abortion, and this is what led up to the confrontation at Muddy Waters. Huffman was the only person to come up with this pregnancy story, however.

Huffman recalled a somewhat different set of incidents at Muddy Waters than Margaret Jimenez's recollection. Nora remembered Patty phoning the place where Gerard worked in Westport at a restaurant and telling him to come and get his clothes. In essence, she was telling him that they were through. A while later, while Nora, Patty and Margaret were at Muddy Waters, Gerard came into the tavern in a very angry mood. He and Patty argued, and then, according to Huffman, David slammed his fist down on the table and shouted at Patty, "You killed my baby!"

Gerard and Patty went outside and continued yelling at each other, until Patty stalked off to her Chevy Blazer. Patty pulled items of David's clothing out of the Blazer and threw them at him, saying that they were finished. Huffman recalled that both she and Jimenez were outside and witnessed this. Huffman also recalled David telling Patty, "This isn't over yet!"

After Gerard left, Patty gave Nora a hug and said that she had to go, because she had to work at the weather station the following day. Margaret Jimenez climbed into the vehicle and Patty drove her home. After they were gone, Nora went to the Smoke Shop Restaurant and suddenly had an urge to phone Patty later that night. She did so, and got no answer. Whether Patty and the others were already dead at that point was hard to determine. It wasn't until the next morning that Margaret Jimenez phoned Nora and informed her about the fatal fire.

Huffman told Lane that she had worked at many taverns around Aberdeen over the years, and she knew David Gerard very well. She said she never liked him and that he was a blowhard and a braggart. Lane learned that Nora Huffman had worked at the Smoke Shop Restaurant at one time, and he showed her photos of Elaine McCollum and Carol Leighton. Lane's ears really perked up when Nora told him that she knew Elaine, and that she had seen Elaine and Gerard together at various times. Huffman also said, "That other woman, (Carol), she sometimes worked as a prostitute in downtown Aberdeen."

Nora added that a few months after the fire in 1995, she and a friend were eating at the Red Barn Restaurant when David Gerard and a young woman walked into the place. David introduced the young woman as his girl-friend. Approximately five months later, Huffman said, she saw this same woman in the Aberdeen area, and the woman had a black eye. Asked what had happened, the woman said, "I ran into David's fist when I broke up with him." Just who this young woman was, Nora didn't know.

Nora told Lane, "He's always been immature and couldn't handle rejection. He's also very jealous and tried to control the women in his life. And he was a racist. There was one time that Patty and I met a black man at the Smoke Shop. The man was working for an oil com-pany in the area, and he was a nice guy. We all became friends. We also became friends with the man's wife. When he finished his job here and was moving back to the East Coast, Patty and I exchanged phone numbers with him. Patty and I were at her place on East Hoquiam Road one night when the man called, wishing us a happy holiday. David was present at the time. As soon as he re-alized who we were talking to, he started yelling at us, 'Nigger lovers!' Patty's mom was so angry at this, she told him to get his coat and get out. David then called Patty's mom a 'fucking bitch' and left."

Nora related one last curious incident. Several months after the fire, Gerard contacted her and asked if she wanted to go out to the burned remains of the McDonnell house and pick some flowers with him. She refused. She said he gave her the creeps.

Lane Youmans contacted Dr. Selove, and despite having done hundreds of autopsies by that time, Selove was still bothered by the injury to Patty Rodriguez's head. There was just something about it that didn't seem right.

Dr. Selove told Lane that he could not say with a degree of scientific certainty whether Patty had received the injury to her head by a falling timber or from a blow to the head by a blunt object.

After the visit to Dr. Selove, Lane Youmans contacted a man he knew and respected for his forensic anthropological work, Dr. John Lundy. Dr. Lundy taught at Clark College in Vancouver, Washington, and also worked with the Oregon State Medical Examiner's Office. Lane sent Dr. Lundy close-up photos of Patty Rodriguez's skull injury and photos of the piece of fallen burned wood from the attic. Dr. Lundy looked these over and later contacted Lane, saying that there was no way the fallen piece of wood caused the fracture. The fact that Patty had been lying on a mattress, and the fact that it was only six feet from the ceiling to the mattress, made it impossible for a piece of wood that size to strike with enough force to cause the ring fracture on Patty's skull. Dr. Lundy went on to say that the fracture was more consistent with a blow from a wrench or hammer, and that he would be willing to testify to that at a trial.

Lane Youmans next contacted Ernie Shumate, who had lived next door to the McDonnell residence that burned. Shumate had told Detective Parfitt in 1995 that he had been awakened by the sounds of gunshots in the early-morning hours of February 15, 1995, and saw that the McDonnell house was on fire. The man who had fired the gun turned out to be an individual who had been driving on East Hoquiam Road that morning and had fired his pistol as an alarm when he saw the McDonnell house ablaze.

As Lane Youmans began interviewing Ernie Shumate,

Ernie said, "I'm glad you're investigating this case. This is something I've never told anyone else. I went to bed that night and I was awakened by a woman's scream. It was a single scream and it stopped by the time I was fully awake. I lay there, wondering if I had really heard it or was only dreaming. After a few minutes I drifted back to sleep."

It was only after this "scream," and his drifting back to sleep, that Ernie heard the gunshots. Because of his drifting into sleep, he couldn't say how much time had elapsed between the woman's scream and the gunshots. All he knew was that after he heard the gunshots, he fully awoke to see the next-door house on fire. Ernie quickly jumped out of bed and raced to see flames coming from the living room and front porch of the McDonnell home.

Ernie once again told of flames being everywhere in the living room. Ernie ran around to the side of the house to a sliding door that opened to the dining room. He slid the door open and stepped inside. The room was full of smoke, clear down to within a foot of the floor. Ernie yelled to the people inside the home, but there was no response. The only sound was the crackling fire. Because of the intense smoke and heat, Ernie did not go into the house beyond that point.

Lane asked Ernie if he had heard any smoke detectors going off. Ernie responded there were no sounds like that. He also never heard any dogs barking. This was strange to him, because when he was first awakened by the gunshots, there were only flames in the front part of the house, away from where the dogs' bodies were found. Other parts of the house had not been greatly affected by the fire at that point.

A thought suddenly came to Lane. "Who the hell knows where smoke detector alarms are in someone else's home? Why would Gerard know those locations when he marked them on Detective Parfitt's diagram in 1995, unless he had looked for them to disable them? Gerard hadn't lived in that house on a steady basis. He had only been there a short period of time. He might have been aware of the location of one smoke alarm. But not all of them," he recounted.

Lane also shared how he thought, "If the fire created a blast of superheated air, then how was Patricia McDonnell able to get out of her recliner and hobble twenty feet before collapsing in the dining room? How did Ernie Shumate open the sliding door and not be engulfed by flames when the fire received fresh air from the open door? How were the dogs able to make it from the living room to the laundry room, near the back door? The sound of the smoke detector near Patty's room should have still been sounding when Ernie Shumate opened the sliding door. If it was a slow accumulation of smoke, why, then, didn't the dogs alert everyone in the house? There were just too many questions for this to have been an accidental fire."

Lane e-mailed fire investigator Richard Carman and told him that even though Detective Parfitt and the local fire chief had ruled it an accidental fire, he still had problems believing that was the case. Carman agreed to meet Lane and discuss the situation. Carman usually charged thousands of dollars for his work, but there was something about the deaths of those four people that bothered him as well. He told Lane that he would look at these disturbing matters for free.

Lane and Deputy Steve Smith, who became the GHSO fire investigator after Detective Parfitt retired, drove to Carman's home about an hour and a half away from Aberdeen. They all sat down at Carman's dining-room table, and Lane laid out his documents and photos concerning the McDonnell house fire. Lane told Carman about the heated argument between Patty Rodriguez and David Gerard, just hours before the fatal fire.

Lane emphasized how after the fire the boys and Patricia McDonnell had been found with no soot in their lungs. Lane also told about Patty Rodriguez with the ring fracture to her skull and having a level of 89 percent carbon monoxide in her blood. Lane recounted, "As I described things, I could see wrinkles forming on Carman's forehead, and he started asking me questions about the boyfriend. Like, did he have trouble with the law before? Then he asked questions about the house. As I told him more details, he said the conclusion about the fire originating from the stove was wrong.

"After I laid out the whole story, Carman said, 'I can't believe a man would kill four people and start a fire, just because his girlfriend broke up with him.' At that point I jumped in and said, 'Let me tell you about David Gerard!'"

For the next hour Lane told Carman about Elaine Mc-Collum, Carol Leighton and Frankie Cochran. Lane also noticed that the wrinkles on Carman's forehead started disappearing bit by bit. At the end of Lane's tale about David Gerard, Carman said, "Well, there you go. Now it makes sense."

Carman added that he would look into the matter unofficially, and then decide if he should do so officially at some later point. Carman also wanted to talk to a colleague about this, and Patty Rodriguez's brother as well, since Brian McDonnell was a volunteer firefighter and knew about the McDonnell residence.

Lane realized there would be fallout from this trip to see Carman. There would be some in the GHSO who would not look kindly if the official conclusion of death in 1995 for four people had to be changed from "accidental" to at least "undetermined," which could set the stage for "murder" later on. Lane said, "The fact that we would probably end up looking bad for not getting it right in 1995 was something I could live with. If you mess up one time, or miss something, then you learn from your mistakes. You get it right the next time."

Fallout or not, Lane Youmans went ahead with a disposition report to GHSO entitled "Officer's Opinion and Recommendation." It was to be sent not only upward in GHSO, but to County Prosecutor Steward Menefee. The report started out by stating, *The case against David Gerard for the deaths of Patricia McDonnell, Patricia Rodriguez, Matthew Rodriguez and Joshua Rodriguez is largely circumstantial. There is no fingerprint or DNA evidence. But given the circumstances, one could conclude that Gerard was responsible for the deaths of the four individuals.*

The report then went on to list Gerard's supposed alibi for the night in question. Gerard had, of course, said that he went barhopping with Steve Stoken and some individual named Mike. They supposedly went to the Pioneer in Montesano, the Tyee in Olympia and the Red Barn in Grand Mound. Lane wrote, *Steve Stoken told me he has never been to the Pioneer in Montesano. He knew Gerard, but he did not recall this incident. I traveled the route as Gerard described. Allowing one hour for breakfast, he would have returned home at 4 AM. This still left 45 minutes for him to travel the eight miles to the*

Rodriguez residence. In his alibi, he described making a loop, just like his alibi for the Frankie Cochran assault. And, of course, everyone knew that David Gerard had been lying about driving the Loop on the Cochran case.

As far as motive went, Lane wrote in part: *Gerard stated that his last contact with Patty Rodriguez resulted in a "little spat." Two witnesses at that meeting at Muddy Waters told me that Patty Rodriguez told Gerard to get his belongings out of her residence.*

Gerard wanted to marry Patty Rodriguez, but she told friends that she wanted nothing more to do with him. He went to the location after the fire to search for the remains of a ring he had given her. Patty had told friends that Gerard tried to give her a ring, but she refused. This type of rejection set him off before when Frankie Cochran broke up with him.

As to the cause of the fire, Lane wrote: *It was concluded early on in the investigation that the fire was caused by the wood stove and that the fire was accidental. I believe this conclusion was reached too quickly and that the scene should have been more thoroughly investigated, although we had nothing pointing to foul play. No samples were taken, as well as an insufficient number of photographs to thoroughly document the scene.*

Sergio Rodriguez initially installed the wood stove with an improper stovepipe that caused the wood in the ceiling to char. He replaced the pipe with an insulated type pipe around 1993. Brian McDonnell, who was a firefighter, told me that his mother was very concerned about the wood stove and would get the fire roaring every night in order to burn out any creosote buildup. This is inconsistent with Gerard's statement to us in 1995 in which he stated you could hit the stovepipe and cause the creosote to fall.

The first person to spot the fire saw that it was coming from the living room, as well as a firebox on the front porch. The door between these two locations was a solid core wood door with a small window. I do not believe that the fire could have gotten to the wood box in the early stages of the fire.

This left the implication that David Gerard had set fire to these two locations in order to make the house burn down more quickly and cover up his murders.

Lane also addressed the issue of smoke detectors: *Brian McDonnell told me that he had changed the batteries in the smoke detectors in the week or so before the fire. He also tested the detectors to assure that they were working properly. David Gerard knew the location of the smoke detectors and pointed them out to Detective Parfitt. I find it very interesting that Gerard would notice the location of the smoke detectors in a house he did not own.*

Ernie Shumate was able to gain entry into the residence through the sliding glass door in the dining room area. The residence was full of smoke but the flames had not reached that point. Shumate did not hear a smoke detector going off, even though one of the smoke detectors was at the far end of the house next to Patty's room.

Detective Parfitt describes in his report that, "the battery and an exterior metal part of a smoke detector was located on the floor in the hallway adjacent to Patricia Rodriguez's bedroom." No photographs were taken of the smoke detector and it was not seized.

What Lane was getting at here was that he believed that Gerard had removed the batteries from both smoke detectors before starting the blaze.

* * *

In the next section, detailing sequence of events, Lane Youmans wrote of Ernie Shumate's home being only thirty feet from the McDonnell residence. It was close enough that he heard the door in the McDonnell home shut sometime around one o'clock on the night of the fire. Shumate spoke of a single female's scream sometime in the early-morning hours. Shumate later told Lane that he could not remember if the scream was minutes or hours before he heard the gunshot and saw the McDonnell house on fire. He had drifted back to sleep, not knowing if the scream was real or only in a dream. Lane, of course, believed it was Patty Rodriguez screaming just before David Gerard hit her in the head with a hard object, possibly a hammer.

Lane noted that if the fire had originated in the stove, the house would have filled up with toxic smoke. However, it was Patty Rodriguez in the back bedroom whose lungs had filled up with smoke, not Patricia McDonnell or the boys. Lane noted: *Patty Rodriguez had abundant soot in her airways and a pink change to the blood and muscle tissue, which is consistent with the inhalation of combustible products. No soot was observed in the airways of Joshua Rodriguez, Matthew Rodriguez and Patricia McDonnell. Dr. Selove summarized in his report that the boys were either dead before the fire began or that they inhaled super-heated air, which caused their deaths without leaving any soot. Dr. Selove summarized in his report that Patricia McDonnell had died at the early stages of the fire due to her heart condition, and that she died as a result of thermal burns. This does not explain how she was able to get out of a recliner and travel a distance of approximately twenty feet without inhaling any soot. The skulls of all three victims sustained extreme fire damage and it could not be determined if they had sustained any injuries prior to the fire.*

Lane also noted that as the smoke built up in the room, the first person to be affected should have been Patricia McDonnell, and the second would have been the dogs. Yet, Mrs. McDonnell and the dogs were able to travel some distance before collapsing. Lane wrote, *This is inconsistent with being exposed to super-heated gases.*

Lane also noted the *post fire behavior of David Gerard,* and wrote that Gerard later told Frankie Cochran that it was Patty Rodriguez's uncle who had set the fire and gone to prison for it. But Patty did not have an uncle. Lane also spoke of Gerard's bizarre behavior at Pearl Payne's house after the fire and his going back to the McDonnell residence to search for the ring that he had bought for Patty. It was also noted that Patty always wore a brown onyx ring. This was missing when her body was found. Lane conjectured that Gerard had taken the ring off Patty's finger after he had killed her, and before he started the fire. Items were also missing from the bodies and crime scenes of Elaine McCollum and Carol Leighton.

Finally, in conclusion, Lane wrote, *I believe that Patty Rodriguez told Gerard to get things out of her house and left him at 10:30 PM. He went out drinking like he told us, and arrived back in Aberdeen at 4 AM, drunk and angry. I do not believe his friends drove his rig back to Hoquiam because he's admitted to us that he always drives drunk.*

I believe he drove to Patty's house and went in through a back door. Everyone would have been asleep and the dogs wouldn't bark because they knew him. I believe Gerard went to Patty's bedroom and confronted her. She started to get up and he struck her with an object, fracturing her skull. Her mother must have heard the commotion and got up from the recliner to investigate. Gerard confronted her in the dining room. I believe it was Patricia McDonnell who screamed and Gerard struck her in the head. If the boys woke up, they were probably too scared to move. Gerard probably struck them as they lay on the floor.

He knew he had to cover up the crime, so he decided to burn down the house. He was aware of the previous problems they had with the stove pipe. He dismantled the smoke detectors so the next-door neighbors would not be alerted. He may have merely set fire to the paper and wood that was probably sitting next to the stove, and then returned to his home. Instead of going to the house the next morning to get his belongings as Patty told him to do, he drove to a friend's house in Montesano and they told him about the fire.

David Gerard gets revenge when he believes he has been wronged by a woman. His revenge involves violence against the woman. Patricia McDonnell, Matthew Rodriguez and Joshua Rodriguez were witnesses to his violence against Patty, and they were in the wrong place at the wrong time. Gerard must be made to answer for these four deaths.

Then Lane signed the document, *Respectfully, Detective Lane Youmans.*

It wasn't long before Aberdeen's *Daily World* got wind of this, and they began backing up Lane Youmans's contentions. In the article DEADLY FIRE MAY HAVE BEEN MURDER, the newspaper reiterated many of the points Lane had made against David Gerard. They also sent a reporter to interview Pearl Payne and Brian McDonnell. Pearl told the reporter, "I feel more strongly every day that he (David Gerard) is guilty. I didn't like him. He was very aloof and wouldn't look you in the eye."

Brian McDonnell spoke of being a firefighter and about the situation as well. He said, "The story Gerard told the investigators about the creosote was an outright lie. Sometimes the stove would burn so hot, it glowed red, burning out the creosote. And the batteries in the smoke detector? I had just tested them. That's what's always bugged me. Why didn't they wake up?"

Even Lane Youmans was quoted in the newspaper. He told the reporter, "I kept my thoughts to myself for a while about all of this. I didn't even tell my wife. I could have been wrong, so I wanted to see if I could exclude David Gerard as a suspect. For several months I kept my suspicions bottled up and used my spare time reviewing this case. It's very improbable that Patty Rodriguez was killed by a falling beam. But I don't have someone who will say definitively it was caused by one thing or another."

The newspaper also spoke with two friends of David Gerard's, who had stuck by him through thick and thin. These were Paul and Paula Dean, of Hoquiam, who knew Gerard since he was a boy. They said he was a nice boy, but somewhat slow. The Deans spoke of themselves as Christians, and said that they still wrote to Gerard in prison, despite the fact that he had admitted to attempted murder on Frankie Cochran and was suspected of actual murders against other women.

Paul Dean told the reporter, "We've never mistrusted him. He's always been good to us and we never had a reason to be afraid of David. I feel sorry for the people he caused harm to. But I hold no ill feelings toward David.

We're Christians, and we believe in forgiving one another. We've never asked David if he's done any of those things. That's between him and God."

Ironically, Paul Dean was an assistant fire chief in Hoquiam.

Then the reporter spoke with the one person who mattered most in all of this—County Prosecutor Steward Menefee. Menefee said, "He (Gerard) is not like the Green River Killer Gary Ridgway or the BTK Killer. They both stood in court and gave detailed descriptions of what happened. What we get from Mr. Gerard is that you can have him nailed nine ways to Sunday with the facts of a case and he just sits there and says, 'It wasn't me. It wasn't me.' He's like a serial suspect. Is Gerard responsible for every unsolved crime he's a suspect in? Probably not. But I can't put it past him. So we wait and hope something breaks."

Lane was sure that there was enough circumstantial evidence already on David Gerard for the murders of Patricia McDonnell, Patty Rodriguez, Matthew Rodriguez and Joshua Rodriguez. But he wasn't the one who could bring them to trial. Only the county prosecutor could do that.

After speaking with the reporter for the *Aberdeen Daily News,* Lane Youmans went back and looked at a photo they had run in the newspaper right after the fire in 1995. He said later, "It hit me like a brick! In the photo I could plainly see where tires on Patty's vehicle were flat. These were tires farthest away from the fire. The tires of her vehicle closer to the house were not flat. I began to believe that Gerard had gone there in the early-morning hours, after a night of drinking, and flattened Patty's tires by slashing them. Just as he had done on two occasions with another ex-girlfriend when he was pissed off at her. After slashing Patty's tires, Gerard must have decided to up the ante by going into the house and confronting Patty. In Brian McDonnell's theory of what happened, Brian suspected that David went into the house and woke Patty up and they had an argument. Gerard became so incensed, that he struck Patty in the head with some hard object. Maybe a hammer. Mrs. McDonnell heard the ruckus, went to investigate, and then tried to flee. McDonnell believed that Gerard caught her before she got to the door, and it was Mrs. McDonnell's scream that Ernie Shumate heard. David killed Mrs. McDonnell right in front of the boys. They were too afraid to even move at that point, and David killed them, too."

Theories and speculations were all well and good, but they were not making County Prosecutor Menefee move any closer to bringing David Gerard to trial for the murders of those four people. And yet, all of this wasn't for nothing. In the end the official ruling on the house fire was moved from "accidental" to "cause unknown." And as far as Lane Youmans was concerned, that was one step closer to murder charges. One thing Lane had was lots and lots of patience, and a bulldog tenacity at unearthing more facts. And as time went on, he devoted all his spare time to nailing David Gerard for the one murder that had more facts than any other, as far as his participation: the Carol Leighton murder.

20

PAINTED INTO A CORNER

Lane Youmans was right about one thing—it was going to be a long, tiring process to get the McDonnell house fire charged as an act of murder against David Allen Gerard. And it was going to be an uphill battle on the Elaine McCollum case as well. The best possibility of getting David Gerard charged with murder was with the Carol Leighton case. There was plenty of physical evidence that tied him to Leighton, unlike some of the other cases. And there was plenty of circumstantial evidence as well.

Up until 2003, the things Lane Youmans and other detectives had done were not revealed to the general public as far as the Leighton case was concerned. But in that year things began to change. GHSO started letting reporters at the *Daily World* have more information about the Elaine McCollum and Carol Leighton cases, and exactly who they thought was responsible. Journalist Lisa

Curdy reported that *DNA hits have warmed up two cold homicides in Grays Harbor, including one that dates back twelve years. DNA samples from several men were recovered from the bodies of Elaine "Brooke" McCollum and Carol Leighton. But only one person's DNA, David Allen Gerard, was found on both of them.*

GHSO told Curdy that Gerard knew both women, and that he was now the prime suspect in both cases. Curdy began researching how the long DNA trail had eventually led to only one suspect in the two murders. She discovered that in the 1970s, the array of various crime labs in Washington State were organized under the umbrella of the state patrol to insure uniform standards of testing. By the 1990s, there were seven Washington State Patrol Labs, the nearest one to GHSO being in Olympia. Even then, it could take up to twelve months for DNA testing to be completed on any particular case.

Curdy learned that detectives had picked up hair strands, blood and other DNA-laden material from the McCollum and Leighton crime scenes and sent them to the lab. And over the years the testing techniques had become better and better. The first DNA testing at Olympia was restriction fragment length polymorphism (RFLP), and it could determine that one in 2 million people could have been the contributor. As George Johnson, of the Olympia Crime Lab, explained, "RFLP testing was very good. But the problem with RFLP was that it required large samples. Something between the size of a nickel and a quarter."

The next generation of DNA testing was known as polymerase chain reaction (PCR). PCR could use much smaller samples, down to the size of a pencil point. The drawback was, it could only say that the sample came from one person in twenty thousand.

Then in 1999, short tandem repeats (STR) made a great leap forward in DNA testing. It could isolate the DNA from a subject to one in 1 quadrillion. There weren't that many people on planet Earth. The DNA used in STR testing linked back to one person, and one person alone. And STR did not need as large samples as RFLP had. STR DNA testing became a very useful tool for law enforcement around the nation after 1999.

By the year 2000, all felons in Washington State had to have their DNA put into a database. In Washington State, that added up to 35,000 people. And one of those individuals was David Allen Gerard because of his attack upon Frankie Cochran.

Over the years Lane and the other detectives had taken some evidence out of storage on the McCollum and Leighton cases and sent that evidence to the WSP Crime Lab to be tested. But it wasn't until Gerard assaulted Frankie Cochran, was arrested and convicted as a felon, that his DNA went into the state's database. And by then, the very sensitive and specific STR testing was in use.

There was only one fly in the ointment to all of this. Both Elaine and Carol had other men's DNA on and in their bodies: Elaine because of her boyfriend, David Simmons, and Carol because of her prostitution activities with some unknown john besides David Gerard. No matter how sure that Lane and the other detectives were that Gerard was their man in the McCollum and Leighton murders, everything had to run through one person before it ever went to trail—County Prosecutor Steward Menefee.

Menefee spoke with Lisa Curdy on this very matter, and he told her, "DNA places someone at the crime scene, but it doesn't tell you that someone did something. That person's DNA could have been there for hours, days or even weeks. Before deciding what to do with the case, we need someone to come forward with information that links Gerard to the women before they were killed."

And there was the crunch. People could put David Gerard around these women weeks or even days before they were murdered, but no one could place him with them on the nights they actually were murdered. Karen Luther never saw what vehicle Elaine McCollum had climbed into at the Smoke Shop on February 5, 1991. And no one saw Carol Leighton with David Gerard on August 2, 1996.

Lane Youmans and the other detectives were frustrated. They were sure they had plenty of circumstantial evidence to tie David Gerard to the murders of Elaine and Carol. The odds that his semen should have been connected to Elaine and Carol when their bodies were found on the Weyco Haul Road, years apart, seemed just too big a coincidence to explain away by mere happenstance. But County Prosecutor Menefee stood by his guns. He didn't have to convince the detectives that David Gerard was the killer, he had to convince a jury beyond a reasonable doubt.

In August 2004, that bridge was finally crossed. Undersheriff Rick Scott told journalist David Wilkins, of the *Daily World,* "After we got the DNA hit to Gerard, we met with the prosecutor's office and began to reevaluate the investigation and what we needed to do to tie up the loose ends. It wasn't really anything new. We went over the witness statements, police reports and timelines. We saw some places where people needed to be reinterviewed, and issues addressed that could be a cause for concern when charges were filed, in order to make for a more tightly woven case."

Undersheriff Scott went on to say that they knew Gerard had a history of violence with women. Frankie Cochran was living proof of that. Scott also touched upon the rape of Julie in 1997, by David Gerard, without mentioning Julie's full name. Then Scott added that at present the county prosecutor's office would only be going after Gerard for the murder of Carol Leighton. Rick Scott related about Elaine's case, "There are some obstacles there that are more difficult to address." Undersheriff Scott did not amplify what the obstacles were.

Steward Menefee was a county prosecutor who liked to have as much concrete evidence as possible before taking a case to trial, and by August 2004, he had plenty in the case against David Gerard concerning Carol Leighton. In a motion and declaration to the court, Menefee particularly stressed the DNA connection between David Gerard and Carol Leighton. Menefee wrote that semen had been found in Carol's vaginal and anal areas during the autopsy. Semen was also found in a condom located a short distance down the road from where her body was discovered. Menefee stated that DNA from these sources was collected and put into a data bank, but no hits came back as to their donor before Gerard's attack on Frankie Cochran.

Then after May 1999, when David Gerard was convicted and sentenced for the attempted murder of Frankie Cochran, his DNA data was placed in the Washington State DNA data bank. A hit came back from the condom to Gerard, and further testing got a hit to Gerard from the vaginal and anal swabs connected to Carol. Menefee went on to say that advances in DNA technology had allowed a swab from Carol's mouth to be analyzed. And Gerard's DNA was consistent with a swab of Carol's mouth.

Menefee cited the Pierce County sting operation when Gerard had been busted for soliciting prostitution. And by his own admission, Gerard had spoken of another incident in Pierce County where a prostitute had supposedly stolen his wallet and stabbed him with a small knife. Menefee noted that Carol's body had been on the Weyco Haul Road for four to six hours before being discovered. This was consistent with the amount of time the used condom had been on that same road, only two-tenths of a mile from her body. And in that condom was semen from David Gerard.

Because of all this information, Menefee wrote, *There is probable cause to believe the defendant intentionally killed Carol Leighton by stabbing and cutting her numerous times.* A judge agreed that there was enough evidence for the case to proceed toward trial, and a charge of first-degree murder was made against David Gerard.

Reporter Wilkins spoke with County Prosecutor Menefee again, and Menefee told him that under the circumstances he filed charges against Gerard because the "case is as tight as it can possibly be. We have run down all of the available leads, given the time factors involved. We have checked and rechecked the physical evidence to the extent that we can, and that meant we had to make a decision on the case. Based on the facts, we felt we had enough evidence to file charges against Mr. Gerard."

Menefee went on to say that if convicted, Gerard might spend the rest of his life in prison. But even with Washington's three strikes law, he probably wouldn't qualify for an automatic life term. And Menefee agreed with Rick Scott that additional barriers in the McCollum case made it more difficult to prosecute, if Gerard was ever brought up on charges in that murder.

Meanwhile, Lane Youmans told Wilkins he had a sense of relief when he knew that charges had finally been brought against David Gerard for the murder of Carol Leighton. Lane had been gathering evidence against Gerard on this case for five years, ever since he had the epiphany after Gerard's attack upon Frankie Cochran at the milking shed. Lane added, "I haven't told the families yet. At least there's some light at the end of the tunnel, although this is just the beginning, and there's a long way to go."

A court appearance was the first step in the long journey, and it occurred on August 19, 2004, at the courthouse in Montesano. Wearing an orange prison jumpsuit, a belly chain, leg irons and handcuffs, Gerard was led into the courtroom to face superior court judge Mark McCauley. County Prosecutor Menefee filed second-degree murder charges against Gerard, and Judge McCauley asked Gerard if he understood the charges. Gerard gave a slight shrug and answered, "Oh, I guess so."

Judge McCauley assigned David Hatch as Gerard's defense attorney. When he was out of the courtroom, reporter David Wilkins asked County Prosecutor Menefee if he was also going to press charges against Gerard for the murder of Elaine McCollum. Menefee answered, "That case is still open and under review. Just like in the Leighton case, we got a hit on the DNA, but that was just the beginning. The DNA gave us a direction. We've been running down witnesses from ten years or more ago and getting their recollections. That being said, we still have to meet certain standards for filing a case."

On August 30, 2004, David Gerard pled not guilty in a brief court appearance at superior court. His attorney, David Hatch, then moved that the matter should move forward for trial, and the judge agreed.

In the following months, both the defense and prosecution were hunting down various witnesses and getting their case in order. In fact, all through October and into November, Hatch was following different avenues in gathering information. On October 7, Hatch spent seven and a half hours in a conference with Gerard. The next day Hatch spent eight hours reviewing discovery documents and researching case law on DNA evidence. By the next week, Hatch was reviewing more discovery documents and photos as well. On October 22, Hatch drove out to the Weyco Haul Road and took notes and photos of the condom drop area and the spot where Carol's body had been found. By the third week of November, Hatch had spent fifty hours reviewing different aspects of David Gerard's case.

Hatch wasn't the only one compiling information on the case. Various detectives were reviewing and compiling evidence and sending it on to Steward Menefee. The trial was originally set to commence on January 11, 2005, but it was rescheduled for March 1, 2005. On January 25, Menefee wrote the presiding judge and said that the date would have to be moved forward once again. The reason was, as Menefee noted, "Detective Lane Youmans and Gary Parfitt, along with their family members, have made arrangements for an extended cruise and have purchased nonrefundable tickets for the cruise. These two officers are necessary to establish both condition of the crime scene, the location of the items seized at the crime scene and to establish chain of evidence from which DNA evidence was later extracted." Menefee noted that this DNA and fingerprint evidence was the very heart of the case, and he asked for a postponement of trial until March 15, 2005. This extension of time was granted.

All during January 2005, David Hatch was busy. He set forth a motion for an additional counsel to help him prepare for trial, and once again he reviewed crime scene photographs and videotape. He also had a conference with Lane Youmans, and on January 7, he met with Lane at the sheriff's office to look at actual crime scene items, such as Carol's clothing and other evidence. Then Hatch had a phone conference with Dr. William Brady concerning autopsy and pathology evidence. If Menefee was working hard on the case from his frame of reference on the prosecution angle, Hatch was working just as hard from the defense side.

On January 11, Hatch had a phone conference with Dr. Brady concerning the DNA expert material, and the next day Hatch reviewed evidence on the Elaine McCollum and Patty Rodriguez cases, just in case those became an issue at trial. The prosecution, of course, wanted that material to be heard by a jury, while Hatch did not. And then by January 14, Hatch wrote, *Review proposed offer.* That was it as far as the notations went. Hatch did not reveal what the offer was, but obviously there was one now being put forward by the county prosecutor's office.

Offer or not, Hatch kept on gathering material and files, and wrote on January 17, *Prepare for trial. Review autopsy reports.* For the following week, in his tally of time spent working on the Gerard case that would be charged to the county, he amassed seventeen hours preparing for trial.

Then, once again, on January 25, Hatch was reviewing a plea offer. He had a phone conference with Steward Menefee and one with Tom Keehan, who was David Hatch's co-counsel. By the next day Hatch and Keehan were in the county jail, discussing the plea offer with David Gerard. This went back and forth into early February as well. Hatch shuttled between talking to Gerard and then talking to Steward Menefee. There was even a phone conference with Gerard's siblings, whom Hatch did not name in his file on the matter. By February 8, Hatch wrote, *Phone conference with client. Conference with client at county jail. Conference with Menefee.*

Things were getting very close to a plea deal once again, just as David Gerard had done in Frankie Cochran's case. And then on February 9, 2005, David Hatch had an Alford plea in hand for David Gerard to review. An Alford plea, in essence, stated that a suspect said he was not guilty of the charges, but that a jury might find him guilty, anyway. Instead of going to trial, he would plead to agreed-upon charges and be sentenced. Often the person who took the plea deal got some kind of compensation in way of less time. Sometimes those who were facing the death penalty took an Alford plea in exchange for life without parole.

Both David Hatch and David Gerard went over the plea, line by line, in the county jail. Hatch explained to Gerard that by signing the plea, he would be giving up certain rights. These included the right to a speedy public trial before a jury of his peers, as well as the right to remain silent on the charges against him. These also included the right to hear and question witnesses, the right to be presumed innocent until found guilty and the right to appeal a determination of guilt after a trial. This was important. Gerard could never come back later and try to appeal the guilty plea.

On this present case, which concerned Carol Leighton, if he signed the form, Gerard would be admitting to murder in the second degree. The elements were *in Grays Harbor County, Washington, he'd had the intent to cause the death of another person but without premeditation, causing the death of another person.*

Gerard understood that the standard range of confinement would be anywhere from 154 months in prison to 254 months in prison. The maximum term could be life in prison. But by this being a second-degree murder, he would not be facing the death penalty. It was noted that by signing the agreement, Gerard agreed that the prosecutor's statement of the case was correct and complete. And if he was convicted of additional crimes before the time he was sentenced, he had to tell the judge about those convictions. Under the circumstances this was very unlikely to occur. In addition to a sentence, Gerard was going to have to pay, if he could, $500 to a victim's compensation fund.

Line H was particulary important, in light of what had happened in sentencing after Gerard was convicted in the Frankie Cochran case. Line H in this agreement stated that the judge in the present plea did not have to follow anyone's recommendations as to the length of the sentence. Line H did add that if the judge did rule beyond the standard range, Gerard could appeal this decision.

Gerard also was told that this plea was considered to be a "strike" against him. He already had one strike for the attempted murder of Frankie Cochran. If he got one more

strike, either in state or federal court, it carried a mandatory
life imprisonment sentence.

Finally on line 11 was a section where Gerard had to
make a brief statement in his own words of what he had
done to be guilty of the crime. Gerard wrote, *I make this
plea of guilty in the form of an Alford Plea to take advantage of the plea agreement. I acknowledge that facts and
evidence exists upon which a jury would convict me, on a
more probable than not basis.*

Once again Gerard did not actually say that he had
murdered Carol Leighton. Instead, he related that a jury
would probably look at the facts and find him guilty of
murdering her.

David Gerard put his signature to the document and so
did David Hatch. In short order Steward Menefee signed
it, as did Judge Gordon Godfrey. Within a space of six
years, David Gerard had made plea deals for the attempted murder of Frankie Cochran and murder in the
second degree of Carol Leighton.

About the plea, County Prosecutor Steward Menefee
told journalists, "I think this is a fair outcome. The reason
we made the deal was because of the age of the case, the
nature of the evidence and the fact he's currently serving
a thirty-seven-year sentence."

Gerard might have been serving that thirty-seven-year
sentence for the assault on Frankie Cochran, but that was
not the end of that matter. In fact, there was trouble brew-
ing, and Menefee addressed that very matter. Menefee
said, "That is another good reason for this conviction. By
making this plea agreement, we are insured that he will
serve most of his original sentence."

What Menefee was talking about was a matter in

the United States Supreme Court where that court had recently ruled that "exceptional" sentences handed down by judges were unconstitutional. The U.S. Supreme Court said that only juries could hand down exceptional sentences that were longer than the standard range. And everyone in law enforcement and the judicial community had been surprised when Judge McCauley gave Gerard a thirty-seven-year sentence for the assault and attempted murder of Frankie Cochran. Most in the GHSO at the time thought Gerard was going to be given fifteen to twenty years.

Menefee related, "That Supreme Court decision could end up affecting Gerard's sentence (in the Cochran case) if it's applied retroactively."

So now it was very important that Judge Gordon Godfrey hand down a stiff sentence to David Gerard for the murder of Carol Leighton. Before pronouncing sentence, Godfrey asked Gerard, "Out of blank curiosity, why did you kill her?"

And staying true to form, Gerard replied, "I didn't."

In the end Judge Godfrey gave Gerard a seventeen-year sentence for her murder. That was at the top range of sentences that could be handed down for that degree of murder, according to 1996 guidelines, when Carol had been murdered.

After the proceedings were over, David Hatch told reporters that David Gerard had huge chunks of his memory missing. "There were periods of time when he would arrive home and couldn't remember what happened. Years of drug and alcohol abuse might be a contributing factor. He can't read or write well and is described by those who have known him for years as being slow."

In fact, there were two people at court who came to support David Gerard. They were Paul and Paula Dean, of Montesano, who had also stood up for David after the Frankie Cochran case ended in a plea bargain. The Deans had known Gerard for years and considered him to be a friend. The Deans were devout Christians and constantly prayed for Gerard. Over the years they had gone and visited him in jail, when no one else would. Paula Dean told a reporter, "He was always helpful to my mom and stepdad. They were good to him, too, and he would go to their house and eat dinner and help out in the yard and with their dogs." Paul Dean added that he had known David Gerard since David was a boy, and he had never seen the dark and violent side of him. When he and his wife went to visit with David, they never talked about his guilt or innocence. They only went there to visit him and pray for him.

By contrast, there were no family members or friends at the hearings to remember Carol Leighton. No one except Detective Ed McGowan, who was there on behalf of the other detectives who had never given up on the case. It was McGowan, along with Lane Youmans and Matt Organ, who had worked so hard over the years.

County Prosecutor Menefee said later of Detective McGowan, the other detectives and Carol Leighton, "Heroin ruined Carol Leighton's life long before David Gerard took it. She was forced into prostitution to support her habit. It ruined her marriage. Her husband still cared for her, but he couldn't tolerate her habit. It inhibited her from forming friendships. She was one of those invisible people in Aberdeen, someone who lives in the background. And she died that way, too. All alone and forgotten by most. It was law enforcement who stood up for Carol Leighton. Because they wouldn't stop until they found the person who killed her and made sure he was held responsible."

Lane Youmans wasn't at the court for one very good reason, he was on the Caribbean cruise with his wife, and Detective Parfitt and his wife. Lane later recalled, "I wanted to be at Gerard's sentencing, but it wasn't to be. I had arranged for a trip through the Panama Canal on the *Regal Princess* with my wife, Terri, as a thirtieth-anniversary present to her. The cruise ship was heading to Ocho Rios, Jamaica, and I knew that Gerard was going to be sentenced at six-thirty P.M. Eastern Daylight Time.

"At that moment of six-thirty P.M. EST, the four of us were sitting at table number seventy-six in the Palm Court dining room, enjoying lobster thermidor and chocolate soufflé. I glanced at my watch and told Gary, 'It's over.' We shook hands and continued eating dinner. I felt as though a weight had been lifted off of my shoulders.

"After dinner, I walked out on the aft deck, alone. No one was around. The sun was setting and the sky was getting dark. The ocean was an incredible shade of blue, and the sky was clear. There was a warm breeze adding to the pleasant moment. I pulled out a fine cigar, lit it and stared down at the ocean."

Lane savored the moment while he could. He only learned later that Gerard, in essence, hadn't received any more prison time for the murder of Carol Leighton. Lane said of this, "Gerard received seventeen years for a brutal murder. But it was time he was already serving for his crime against Frankie. The judge said his hands were tied as far as a harsher sentence went. It had been five years of my work and time, struggling with a prosecutor that was reluctant to prosecute, and all of the roadblocks and obstacles I had endured. The amazing thing was, I didn't care about all I had gone through. I felt I had done my best to get justice for Carol Leighton and all who loved her. The other murders could be prosecuted someday, and Gerard made to answer for his crimes, when circumstances changed."

As time passed, the image of Carol's face disappeared from Lane's mirror as he shaved himself in the morning. As he had said, he'd done all he could for her. If it hadn't added up to more prison time for Gerard, it had accomplished two things. It had added a second strike to Gerard. And if a case for the murder of Elaine McCollum ever went forward, it was a conviction that would be on David Gerard's record. Then he would have three strikes and never get out of prison.

In some ways, Lane Youmans, Matt Organ, Ed McGowan, Rick Scott and the other detectives at GHSO sticking up for Carol Leighton was law enforcement at its best. It was proof that justice was for everyone, not just for a senator's daughter or a pastor's daughter. It was for someone's daughter who had fallen to the lowest rung of society, ensnared in drug addiction and prostitution. It was justice for an individual who had few good breaks in life. It was justice for all.

21

AFTERMATH

David Gerard kept hoping that his documents to the Court of Appeals of the State of Washington would sway them in rescinding what he deemed to be excessive sentencing for the attempted murder of Frankie Cochran. He tried every avenue he could, including the following: *Prior to my acceptance of the plea, I was pressured by assigned counsel. That is, my trial counsel continuously threatened me with the possibility of me receiving the death penalty and the plea was the best defense he could offer.*

Gerard also stated that he didn't think his case had been properly investigated from a defense standpoint. In one odd reference he said that other witnesses were around to see an attack on Frankie Cochran, and they had never been questioned. Just who they were or what they saw, he didn't specify.

And Gerard wrote that even though he was told that the conviction would be a strike against him, he was never told the ramifications of the strike. Once again he wrote: *For those reasons, I would request that my plea be withdrawn and that the judgment and sentence be vacated.*

When the court of appeals finally got around to this matter, they looked at the various issues that David Gerard had brought up. The court said that the facts were not in dispute, and it was only the "excessive nature" of sentencing that was going to be addressed. It spoke of the attack and then noted: *As a result of the attack, Frankie Cochran endures severe pain and suffering, partial and possibly permanent paralysis, and probable long-term disability.*

The court of appeals noted that the County Prosecutor's office asked for 273 months of sentencing, and the judge actually handed down 444 months instead. It was also noted that the judge in the case spoke of the attack as being "deliberately cruel and savage." The appeals court even stressed that Gerard admitted that his actions had been "*brutal, unthinkable and horrific.*" Nonetheless, he now claims that his actions were not deliberately cruel because his acts did not exhibit gratuitous violence. Gerard claimed that his actions were in line with attempted first-degree murder, something he pled guilty to in the case. Gerard even stated that the number of hammer blows on Frankie's head was in line with what it would take to kill someone. In essence, Gerard was saying he used as much force as he thought would kill her. When he thought she was dead, or soon would be, he quit hitting her with the hammer.

The court of appeals wasn't buying this. It said that Gerard had also stabbed Frankie in the neck. And he was not taking into account that the Grays Harbor Superior Court was not only looking at the number of hammer blows inflicted, but the extensive physical and emotional trauma that Frankie had suffered after the attack.

The court of appeals also found that Gerard's *acts exceeded the degree of violence needed to commit attempted murder, even with the use of a hammer.* The court said that a person could attempt murder with a lot less violence and physical injury to a victim. It cited hitting Frankie with the hammer after the defensive wound to her hand, that she was beaten about the face and head and stabbed in the neck to try and make sure she was dead. Then the court stated: *Cases cited by Gerard relate acts of greater torture than those committed by him, but do not diminish the cruelty of his actions.*

Finally, and most important, the court of appeals ruled that the sentence handed down by Judge McCauley was not excessive in a case such as this: *The sentence of 444 months is only 1 and a half times the standard range and less than the statutory maximum for attempted murder. The duration imposed does not shock the consciousness of this court. It is not excessive.*

So, like it or not, David Gerard was not going to serve any less time for the attempted murder of Frankie Cochran. That suited Lane Youmans just fine. He was still angry about the sentencing on Carol Leighton's case however, which was running concurrently with the Cochran sentencing. Lane said, "Gerard didn't get one more day of prison time for that. I thought that was wrong."

Even after David Gerard made his Alford plea for the murder of Carol Leighton, Lane Youmans did not stop investigating Gerard for other murders in the area, mainly the Elaine McCollum and Patty Rodriguez cases, but others as well. Lane spoke with *Seattle Times* reporter Christine Clarridge, who eventually wrote the article ONE MAN TASK FORCE KEEPS COLD CASES ON THE FRONT BURNER.

Clarridge reported that Lane had never so much as accepted a free cup of coffee during his whole stint in law enforcement and often gathered cold-case information on his own time. With that topic in mind, Lane told Clarridge, "I guess I just think like a lot of cops do, that we speak for the victims and they deserve justice. Somebody needs to find out who is responsible and hold them accountable. Somebody needs to find the truth."

Lane told Clarridge about his take on all the similarities between the Carol Leighton case and Elaine McCollum case: the main one being two murdered women only a mile apart on the same isolated logging road. The article went on to recount the story of Frankie Cochran and the relationship that had grown up over the years between her and Lane Youmans. And Frankie was emphatic about what had kept her going: *"I couldn't let that SOB serial killer win!"*

Lane spoke of tracking down every lead he could on Gerard and even at one point putting a homemade sign on his desk at work, GERARD TASK FORCE. In a way it was a joke—Lane was the task force of one. A fellow detective at GHSO told Clarridge, "Lane endured good-natured animosity from colleagues who had to pick up the slack left by his hunt, but he persisted."

Undersheriff Rick Scott said that Lane never wanted to be promoted upward out of the Detective Division, because he was so intent on the Gerard cases. And Lane talked to Clarridge about this aspect. Lane said that so often a detective would work a cold murder case over the years, but when he left the Detective Division, a new detective had to get up to speed on that case. It was always a matter of trying to play catch-up. By staying in the Detective Division for so many years, Lane was able to remember key dates, key places and key names on unsolved cases. It was one great reason he'd had his "epiphany" in the milking shed where Frankie was found half-beaten to death. The name David Gerard rang a bell with Lane about the house fire years before at Patricia McDonnell's house, and the four people who had perished there. It was Gerard's unusual behavior that had stayed with Lane all those intervening years.

Lane may have been sure that David Gerard was "good" for the murder of Elaine McCollum, and other GHSO detectives were as well, but it was still a hard sell to get the county prosecutor to take action on that case. County Prosecutor Steward Menefee told Clarridge that he didn't believe there was enough evidence to convince a jury that Gerard had killed Elaine McCollum. Menefee said that was why the county prosecutor's office hadn't filed charges in that case or the house fire case. Menefee related to Clarridge, "I've had cops look at a guy on a street corner and say to me, 'I know he's got coke (cocaine) on him.' And I'll say, 'I believe you, but that doesn't mean I can get a search warrant.'"

Menefee added that in McCollum's case, Gerard was not the only donor of sperm in connection to Elaine, since she'd had a boyfriend at the time of her death and apparently had sex with him not long before she was murdered. Menefee told Clarridge that a good defense attorney could argue that a sperm donor other than Gerard was her killer.

Lane, on the other hand, didn't buy this logic. He reiterated that Gerard had already been convicted for a murder less than a mile away from where McCollum's body had been found. And in both cases the murders had been vicious and bloody. Although Elaine's boyfriend at the time, David Simmons, didn't have an airtight alibi, all indications were that he was indeed at home trying to kick heroin. And besides that, Simmons had never been arrested for a violent crime, while Gerard was already convicted for the murder of Carol Leighton and attempted murder of Frankie Cochran.

In his pursuit of justice for Elaine McCollum, Lane Youmans sought out independent opinions from two well-respected King County prosecuting attorneys. These attorneys agreed that with all the evidence gathered against Gerard on the Elaine McCollum case, they would have gone forward to trial in their county. King County prosecutor Steve Fogg told Clarridge, "We would have charged that case in a minute. In fact, we even offered to try it for them (the Grays Harbor County Prosecutor's Office), but they didn't want any part of it."

In the article, as well, was a section about how Frankie Cochran felt about Lane Youmans and the support he had given her over the years. It quoted Frankie saying, *"There's nobody better than him. There's nobody who ever could have cared that much about me."* In fact, Frankie related that she planned to get married to her caretaker, Steve Jones, and when she did, she wanted Lane to walk her down the aisle. Frankie's father had died by then, and in Frankie's mind, Lane was almost like a father to her now. As for Lane, who had two children, Frankie had become like a daughter to him. Lane said later, "It's incredible the amount of pain she fought through just to keep going. It was her iron will that got her to where she is today."

Lane related, "Steve was a friendly guy. A very caring person. I felt that Frankie's luck with men had finally turned around. They seemed very happy together. Steve may have been small in stature, but he was very strong. He used to ride a bicycle almost thirty miles every day."

And yet, with all things related to these cases, there was always the bitter with the sweet. In an amazing reversal of roles, it was Frankie who became Steve Jones's caretaker. Steve got cancer, and though Frankie was still in a lot of pain, she began taking care of Steve during his treatments. Steve lost a lot of weight and had a hard time just keeping his food down. What he had done for Frankie, she now did for him.

Lane noted, "Frankie was going with him when he went for cancer treatment, preparing his meals, and giving him his meds. She tried to make him as comfortable as possible."

In the end there was no walking down the aisle for Frankie and Steve. After about a year from the time he was diagnosed, Steve Jones died from his bout with cancer. Lane said of Steve, "He was a good guy. He cared a lot about Frankie and helped her overcome so much. It was a real tragedy that he died from cancer, just when they were about to start a new life together."

When Steve died, Frankie cried and cried for days. It was as if life, which had been so rough on her, had taken one more hard shot. And yet, with a will that had seen her through so much, Frankie eventually recovered her composure and carried on with life. She went to live in an assisted-living center in Aberdeen, which Lane had helped her move into. Frankie still had to walk with a cane a lot of the time, and had a hard time using her left arm. However, she became a fixture at the center, telling everyone her incredible story. In essence, Frankie became a local celebrity there. One woman, who had suffered abuse from a boyfriend, said, "Frankie is my hero. If she could make it through that situation, then I could make it through mine. I had to have my eyes opened up by her. I admire Frankie so much for all she had to endure."

22

PUZZLE PIECES

Lane Youmans finally did end his career as a detective at GHSO in 2006. However, he was not through with his stint in law enforcement forensics. He became a part-time coroner for Grays Harbor County. He also started working with a group to restore the 7th Street Theatre in his hometown of Hoquiam. The theater was an art deco treasure dating from 1928, but by 2006, it was in great need of repairs. Lane and other volunteers put in new seating, created a new sound system and replaced the old rigging and curtains. One of the most beautiful aspects of the new theater was its lighting system. When the lights went down, it created an atmosphere of sunset in a Spanish garden. Lane said, "It was designed to look like an open courtyard at dusk with the stars coming out."

Despite all his time spent on the theater project, it was still with forensics and cold cases where Lane's passion lay. It was a line of work he never grew out of. The list of John and Jane Does was a long one for Lane concerning people buried in the county's cemeteries who had no identities. Some were murder victims and one was a suicide. One such case concerned a mystery man buried in Block 43, Space 32, in the Fern Hill Cemetery. In an article for the *Daily World,* Lane told reporter Lisa Patterson, "He needs a name. He needs more than John Doe."

A few graves away from this John Doe was one more unknown individual. This person's body had washed ashore onto Grayland Beach in 1997. The man's clothing and identification had been stripped from his body by the powerful surf before his body was discovered. He may have been in the water for three months before coming ashore. All of the ridges on his fingerprints had been battered away.

Because of some suspicious circumstances Lane got a court order and had the body exhumed. The ground over the coffin was dug up and Lane put on a white jumpsuit, white gloves and climbed down into the grave. He opened the coffin lid and the body bag. What he found surprised him. There were millions of tiny insects living in the coffin and on the body. Lane described them as looking like tiny dark mustard seeds. Lane said, "I didn't know what kind of bugs they were, so I scooped some up, packaged them and sent them off to the lab for identification." It was a scene right out of the popular television show *CSI.*

The suicide John Doe was just as curious and baffling in his own way. A young man had checked into an Amanda Park motel near Olympic National Park on September 15, 2001. He wrote his address as being from Meridian, Idaho, but that probably was not his real address. He also wrote his name down on the motel paperwork as Lyle Stevik. This was clearly a reference that he had borrowed from a Joyce Carol Oates fictional novel,

You Must Remember This. In that book the main character was a young person named Lyle Stevick. It was a book about a young man who eventually committed suicide.

The Amanda Park motel John Doe moved from one room to another after he complained of noise in the first room. On September 17, a maid entered this young man's room and found that he had hanged himself on a coatrack. He had closed the blinds so that no one would see him. He had put pillows around his body so that no one would hear him thrashing around in his death throes. He had even left money on a nightstand with a note that it was for his last night's motel payment.

Lane said of this John Doe, "He was polite and thoughtful until the end. He paid for his room as one of the last acts of his life. He had traveled about as far west as you can in America to end his life. Maybe no one still cares about him, but until I find out differently, I'll keep trying to learn who he was."

Lane's constant looking at old cold cases had one unforeseen benefit, especially for the sister of Connie Rolls. Ever since Connie had a big argument with her mother's boyfriend just before she disappeared, her sister, Teri, had been afraid that the mother's boyfriend might have had something to do with Connie's disappearance. Teri related that she had worried all her life that her mom's boyfriend might have killed Connie. The boyfriend had hurled terrible insults at Connie back then, and, according to Teri, even her mom had said that Connie had obtained the boyfriend's shotgun. Teri's mom related that the boyfriend had been questioned by authorities about this, although he would later deny that he had, but he did report the gun as missing. In one e-mail to Lane Teri wrote, *Help me put my fears to rest!*

Finally, in 2009, her fears were put to rest. Not because the killer of Connie Rolls was arrested, but because the facts were laid out by Lane pointing to David Gerard as a credible suspect in the murder of her sister. Teri related that she barely knew where to begin in expressing her gratitude. She said a weight had been lifted from her life. She added that David Gerard did sound like a viable suspect for Connie's murder. And if Connie had actually been carrying a gun on the streets of Aberdeen, it must have been someone like Gerard, who knew her and would give her a ride. Teri even posited that Connie could have met Gerard at a party or a tavern.

Teri wrote about the main fact that Lane offered to explain why her mom's boyfriend had not killed Connie. It was the phone call that had come in by an anonymous phone caller about Connie's suitcases. Teri said that her mom's boyfriend would have never made that call. She said if he had killed Connie, it would have been in anger, and he wouldn't have toyed with the police by making a phone call to them about the suitcases. Then Teri said, "The blue suit case was described exactly. Gerard makes sense!"

As to why the Connie Rolls case hadn't gone any further than it did, in light of the other dead women's remains found up in Mason County, near to those where Connie had been found, Lane had one salient idea. He said, "The case was a prime example of agencies not working together. Connie was a Hoquiam girl, last seen alive in Aberdeen, and her skull was found a year later in Mason County. The agencies may have done their individual part, but they should have been working together. GHSO wasn't brought in to assist. The Green River Task

Force was brought in for a short while but determined it wasn't one of their cases. So that was the end of that."

Lane also had some very interesting things to say about David Gerard in connection to many other cases. "I believe Gerard is unusual in the fact that he didn't have a set area or crime signature that we know of. It's not as if he went out and sought victims. He went through life—fat, dumb and happy—until a woman pissed him off, and he would react with a primal response. Connie, Roberta, Elaine and perhaps others were all in need of something. In their cases it was a ride, and Gerard was in the right place at the right time. For them, he was in the wrong place, at the wrong time. I can see him picking them up, driving them to a remote area, and taking what he wanted. The rape victim who survived, Julie, was highly intoxicated and was unable to put up a fight."

Of this last victim mentioned, Julie, Lane Youmans was about to get a big surprise in the year 2009. Hearing of that story, another woman contacted Lane and told of her own run-in with David Gerard. It made Lane look at Julie's rape in a whole new light.

This new contact, Sandra, told Lane that she had been at a cocktail lounge in 1994 and had three drinks. Lane related, "For some reason she got very drunk, very quickly. Sitting near her at the bar was David Gerard. Sandra told him she didn't feel well and needed to go to Elma. Gerard offered her a ride. She got into his car, and before long, she blacked out. She remembered, later, David's car being stopped at the Montesano off-ramp, and a police officer asking if she was all right. She blacked out again and woke up the next morning. Her shoes were missing and everything that was in her wallet was missing. A few days later, she said, David gave her parents her shoes and a bottle of Tylenol that had been in her purse. He told her parents that he found the items in his car.

"She didn't know why her shoes were off, and she wondered if she had been raped. I have no doubt she was raped, and survived, just like Julie, because she offered Gerard no resistance. It made me rethink Julie's case. It's very possible that Gerard slipped the date rape drug, Rohypnol, into their drinks. I can see Gerard hanging out at taverns, providing him access to women, and slipping the date rape drugs into their drinks. It makes me wonder how often this occurred. Frankie Cochran spoke of David's wallet and 'secret box' being filled with cocktail coasters with women's names penned on them."

Sandra's response to all of this was, "Julie's story sends chills up my spine. It really does sound similar to my story. I guess I really am lucky that nothing happened to me that night. Or if it did, I don't remember it. I'm better off not knowing. I hope Julie is okay and didn't have lasting problems from her experience."

Of all the John and Jane Doe cases in Grays Harbor County, the one that bugged Lane Youmans the most concerned the woman whose remains were discovered by mushroom hunters near Elma in 1988. He and the other detectives had been able to determine that the woman was about five feet tall and weighed about one hundred pounds. She had dark brown hair and was possibly Native American or Asian. Several items of clothing found at the scene revealed that she had been wearing a blue Loren Scott shirt, a floral print shirt and black pants. She also had worn navy blue slip-on shoes, which were new. She'd had a pearl and silver Avon ring and gold earrings with five blue sapphires.

The forensic clay reconstruction of this Jane Doe's head had never produced any viable clues as to who she was or how she died. She had definitely been murdered. Lane began working with a forensic sketch artist to make a better rendering of what the "Elma Jane Doe" might have looked like in life. Lane wondered if a boyfriend or a husband had killed this Jane Doe. And he also wondered if David Gerard had. The body had been found on isolated Weyco property. It was in an area where Gerard had often gone hunting. The bullet that had killed her came from a gun that matched the type of weaponry that Gerard had once used.

Lane later said, "The woman victim was wearing clothing similar to what Grays Harbor prostitutes like Carol Leighton would wear. Nothing fancy. It didn't mean she was a prostitute, but her clothing was not outside the realm of her having been one. Back in the early 1980s, there was a nuclear plant going up at Satsop, so there was an influx of construction workers living and drinking in Elma. I'd be naive to think there weren't hookers working in Elma. Whether David Gerard ever picked up any there, I don't know. He certainly went as far as Tacoma to do that. This was proven by him being busted in a john sting there in 1996. And Tacoma is farther away from Aberdeen than Elma is by many miles. I also knew that Gerard liked hunting in that area around Elma and knew its back roads very well."

The section of timberland where the Elma Jane Doe's remains were found was supposed to have been logged in 1989. Lane related, "Over the next ten years I searched that site sixty-plus times. The guards there were ex-cops, and they helped me as far as Weyerhauser was concerned in keeping new logging operations out of there. The last remains I recovered were in 1994. After 1999, I just couldn't justify not letting Weyerhauser log on that land. It was released as a crime scene and they began logging the area."

Just as in the cases of Connie Rolls and Roberta Strasbaugh, Lane said, "I don't give up hope on her that someone may know something more about the case, one little bit of information that will be the key. I even put a story and a picture in a large Cambodian magazine about the Elma Jane Doe. No responses ever came back."

In going outside the usual channels on this case, Lane Youmans even went on the Internet. He contacted Websleuths. Many detectives roll their eyes when Websleuths is mentioned, because they are a group of amateur unlicensed Internet "detectives." Lane, on the other hand, was willing to see them as a tool that just might come up with a key bit of information.

Lane said of the Websleuths, "The people on the cold-case forums spend many hours going through all of the missing and unidentified persons reports. They do help exclude possible matches. And they dwell on very minor details."

In fact, a few Websleuths on the Elma Jane Doe forum had some very cogent comments and questions, and Lane addressed these on the forum. One person asked Lane if he saw any connection between David Gerard and the Elma Jane Doe murder. This person noted that Gerard's murders had been known for their degree of violence, but that the MOs always seemed to change. In one murder there had been a fire; in another, a vehicle had been used; in yet another, the woman had been stabbed to death. This person had read somewhere about a bone being broken on the Elma Jane Doe and he asked if this had been an accident or done by the perpetrator.

Lane replied: Gerard hasn't been excluded as a suspect. Her jaw was broken peri mortem (at the time of her death). She was shot in the head. Animals scattered the body, and half her skull was never recovered. Her eyes sat close together on the clay sculpture, but it was a guess based on the remaining skull. A forensic anthropologist said she could either be Native American or South East Asian based upon the skull.

Flyers were sent to every Indian tribe in the US and the Royal Canadian Mounted Police. The remains had been found in a wooded area known for chanterelle mushrooms, and we have many Asians pick those mushrooms. She was 200 feet from the end of a logging spur, five miles back into the woods from the nearest paved road.

Another person on Websleuths had picked up about the Elma Jane Doe wearing nice shoes and clothing while out in the woods. This person was someone who picked chanterelle mushrooms as well. She told Lane that it would be extremely unexpected for a mushroom hunter to be out in the woods wearing nice clothing and jewelry as well. She mused that the Elma Jane Doe had not expected to be brought to that location, since she was wearing such inappropriate clothing for the occasion.

Lane replied: The clothing and jewelry didn't fit a mushroom picker, but you never know.

This same Websleuth wrote back that her first thought had been that the Elma Jane Doe was Vietnamese. She conjectured that the person who took Jane Doe out to the isolated spot must have been there before. She noted that the killer hadn't even hidden the body very well, since it was off the beaten track and not likely to be discovered for a while.

In yet another e-mail to Lane, the person who had previously asked about a possible connection between David Gerard and the Elma Jane Doe killing said he was just musing out loud, but the Elma Jane Doe killing sounded more cold-blooded and planned to him than most of Gerard's murders. It seemed to this person that Gerard would generally burst into a rage and then murder. Then he asked if any more details could be given about Jane Doe's clothing.

Lane wrote back: A woman's long sleeve shirt was found, inside out, hanging on a branch about twenty feet from the body. She died with the rest of her clothing on. The top was a floral print shirt, black jeans that were still zipped up. The clothing was casual. Nothing fancy. The shoes are sold at K-Mart stores. A forensic podiatrist estimated that she had only worn them a short time. The whole area is frequented by mushroom, deer and elk hunters. There is an extensive logging road system, and one would need to know where they were going.

The body was 200 feet from the end of the spur road, down a hill. She either crawled under some bushes and logs to try and hide, or she was murdered and logs were stacked over her. She wasn't dumped there. It's too far to carry a body through difficult terrain, and evidence tells me she was murdered where she was found.

Once again the person who knew something about chanterelle mushroom hunting posted a note. She told Lane that there was a very specific season for them, and the land did have to have a certain slope. She asked if he knew if this was a perfect site to find chanterelles. And she also asked how from the evidence at hand, he saw the murder going down.

Lane posted back: The whole area is hilly, and there are a lot of slopes there where chanterelles grow. The woman was killed in either spring, summer or early fall. There was no coat found. Some serial killers will change methods of killing. Their MO will evolve. There is, however, one signature that will not change. The ritual they follow. It could be a physical act or something else. There are some details I cannot discuss. But I firmly believe that if we identify her, we will find who murdered her.

This last item was important. If the Elma Jane Doe had been a prostitute in an area that David Gerard was known to frequent, it put him one step closer to a probability as her killer. The new shoes, and expensive-for-their-era earrings, also pointed toward a non–mushroom picker. Why go out there and ruin new shoes, and possibly lose expensive earrings, when the woman could ill-afford to do so? If she had gone out to that area before, as Carol Leighton had to the Weyco Haul Road, to do a trick, then the Elma Jane Doe might not have been ill at ease as she rode as a passenger out to that remote location. A location where David Gerard had hunted in the past. A location he might have known well from his frequent wanderings all over the area. As Frankie Cochran had said, "He was always driving out on country and logging roads. He knew the area very well."

As far as David Gerard's life went after the conviction for the murder of Carol Leighton, he fell into a pattern that he hated. Gerard was routinely transferred from one prison to another around the United States. Mainly, this was due to overcrowding in some of the Washington State prisons. By 2008, Gerard was in the North Fork Correctional Facility in Sayre, Oklahoma. Sayre was in a locale about as different from Clallam Bay, Washington, as could be found. Situated on the windswept plains of western

Oklahoma, it was closer to the Texas Panhandle than to Oklahoma City.

The North Fork Correctional Facility was one of a new breed of correctional facilities in the United States. It wasn't run by the federal or state government. Instead, it was privately owned. North Fork was part of a chain of correctional facilities run by Corrections Corporation of America (CCA). And just as the name implied, the entity was a business and its stock even traded on the New York Stock Exchange.

One thing about CCA—it had a good reputation in the correctional field. The guards, known as correctional officers (COs), were taught to interact with inmates to ease tensions before they started. And since there wasn't overcrowding, there tended to be less stressful situations than in government-run prisons. One of CCA's statements read, *Correctional officers listen to needs and follow up on concerns to quell disputes and incidents before they arise.*

By 2008, CCA had 75,000 offenders in sixty facilities nationwide. In the North Fork facility David Gerard shared the space with 1,400 other inmates and 245 staff personnel. If he'd wanted to, he could have accessed educational programs at North Fork. These included academic education, vocational training and life skills education. Yet, as Lane remarked, "I doubted that Gerard was into these sorts of things. He was never very interested in any sort of formal education." It's more likely that he took part in the recreational facility that offered card games and board games.

On May 26, 2008, Gerard wrote a letter to the Grays Harbor Superior Court. Once again he was seeking transcripts and the sentence report on Frankie Cochran's case. He just wouldn't let it go. He also seemed to be in a peevish mood. He wrote, *I have previously written you three times seeking same, but obviously those letters must have gone astray.*

Whatever the outcome of this matter, David Gerard soon found himself on the move once again. Never one for enjoying change, he must have been less than happy to find himself going from one prison facility to another on such a regular basis. This time it was a move clear back to Washington State. But the area he ended up at was more like Sayre, Oklahoma, than Clallam Bay. It was near the town of Connell, Washington, in the eastern part of the state. Gerard was once again housed in a facility on a wide, open prairie. Another relatively new facility, it was run by the state of Washington, and not a private entity. And just as at North Fork, Gerard was offered educational courses. These included stress and anger management and something called "Getting It Right."

Yet, as usual, Gerard preferred to be by himself and work on the one thing that consumed so much of his time and energy: overturning the thirty-seven-year sentencing for the attempted murder of Frankie Cochran.

Frankie Cochran enjoyed living in the assisted-living center in Aberdeen. But she always loved the country filled with farms and forests more. And Frankie liked surrounding herself with animals. The assisted-living center only allowed Frankie to have one cat.

In 2009, Frankie moved to a small town north of Aberdeen, where she continued to get on with her life. And as always, Frankie became a bit of a local celebrity—the woman who had cheated death on a milking shed floor. It wasn't long before everyone in the area knew the woman who hobbled around, unsteadily at times, but kept going. Her body still ached, and she got around with a cane a lot of the time, but she got around without the aid of a wheelchair—something many in the medical field originally thought she would be confined to for the rest of her life. Frankie had promised herself not to be bound by one, and she'd kept good on her promise, despite a great deal of pain and struggle.

A reporter went to see Frankie ten years after the attack that had nearly ended her life. She spoke to him about all the particulars of the assault and then had him feel the lump on her head where a four-inch piece of skull had been "superglued" back into place. As he did so, Frankie laughed and said, "I told you I was hardheaded."

And Frankie, being Frankie, was as feisty as ever. She had pulled herself up from the abyss by her incredible will and determination. Frankie Cochran told the reporter, "I kept going because I didn't want that SOB, David Gerard, to win."